Hans Christian Andersen

Pictures of travel in Sweden, among the Hartz Mountains, and in Switzerland

With a Visit at Charles Dicken's House

Hans Christian Andersen

Pictures of travel in Sweden, among the Hartz Mountains, and in Switzerland
With a Visit at Charles Dicken's House

ISBN/EAN: 9783743333987

Manufactured in Europe, USA, Canada, Australia, Japa

Cover: Foto ©Andreas Hilbeck / pixelio.de

Manufactured and distributed by brebook publishing software (www.brebook.com)

Hans Christian Andersen

Pictures of travel in Sweden, among the Hartz Mountains, and in Switzerland

IN SWEDEN, AMONG THE HARTZ MOUNTAINS,
AND IN SWITZERLAND, WITH A VISIT AT
CHARLES DICKENS'S HOUSE.

BY

HANS CHRISTIAN ANDERSEN,

AUTHOR OF "THE IMPROVISATORE," "A POET'S BAZAAR," ETC.

𝔄𝔲𝔱𝔥𝔬𝔯'𝔰 𝔈𝔡𝔦𝔱𝔦𝔬𝔫.

Entered according to Act of Congress, in the year 1871, by
HURD AND HOUGHTON,
in the Office of the Librarian of Congress, at Washington.

CONTENTS.

RAMBLES IN THE HARTZ MOUNTAINS.

CHAPTER I.

PAGE

THE SETTING OUT. — THE SEA. — THE RIVER TRAVE. — LUBECK. — ST. MARY'S CHURCH. — "THE DANCE OF DEATH." — WANDSBECK 1

CHAPTER II.

HAMBURG. — A SIMPLE STORY. — THE THEATRE. — A VISIT OUT OF TOWN. — THE DREAM, AN IDYL. — THE TWO CHARACTERS . . 9

CHAPTER III.

VIERLANDE. — THE TRAVELLER AND THE DWELLER ON THE HEATH. — THE SCHOOL-MISTRESS. — LYNEBORG. — THE ELVES ON THE HEATH 17

CHAPTER IV.

BRUNSWICK. — "THREE DAYS IN THE LIFE OF A GAMESTER." — A CONTINUATION OF THE SAME. — THE MOTHER AND SON. — WANDERING IN THE TOWN. — DEPARTURE. — THE OLD SCHOOL-MASTER 25

CHAPTER V.

GOSLAR. — THE MINES. — THE SPIDER. — BEAUTIFUL MATILDA, A LEGEND. — ILSE. — THE BROCKEN 34

CHAPTER VI.

MORNING. — BAUMANN'S CAVE. — THE ANTIQUARY. — BLANKENBURG 47

CHAPTER VII.

THE RUINS OF REGENSTEIN. — THE TAILOR'S WIFE. — ROSZTRAPPE. — A TOUR TO ALEXIS BATHS 53

CHAPTER VIII.

PICTURES ON WANDERING TO EISLEBEN. — MARTIN LUTHER . . 63

CHAPTER IX.

A JOURNEY THROUGH HALLE AND MERSEBURG TO LEIPSIC. — THE BLIND MOTHER. — ST. NICHOLAS CHURCH. — GELLERT'S GRAVE. — AUERBACH CELLAR 68

CHAPTER X.

THE DEPARTURE. — MEISSEN. — THE FIRST DAY IN DRESDEN. — DAHL AND TIECK 73

CHAPTER XI.

THE PICTURE-GALLERY. — "DAS GRÜNE GEWÖLBE." — THE ARMORY. — A TOUR TO SAXON SWITZERLAND. — PILLNITZ. — LOHMEN. — OTTOWALDER GRUND. — BASTEI. — WOLF'S GORGE. — HOHENSTEIN. — KUHSTALL 78

CHAPTER XII.

A TOUR INTO BOHEMIA. — THE RETURN BY WAY OF PIRNA. — SONNENSTEIN. — MY LAST DAYS IN DRESDEN 90

CHAPTER XIII.

ADALBERT VON CHAMISSO. — THE THEATRES IN BERLIN. — THE THIERGARTEN. — THE PICTURE-GALLERY. — SPANDAU. — AN ADVENTURE. — THE BIRD. — THE JOURNEY'S END 101

PICTURES OF SWEDEN.

I.

WE TRAVEL 111

II.

TROLLHÄTTA 113

III.

THE BIRD PHŒNIX 121

IV.

KINNAKULLA 123

V.
GRANDMOTHER 127

VI.
THE PRISON-CELLS 129

VII.
BEGGAR BOYS 131

VIII.
WADSTENA 133

IX.
THE PUPPET SHOWMAN 149

X.
THE SKJÄRGAARDS 154

XI.
STOCKHOLM 159

XII.
DIURGÄRDEN 165

XIII.
A STORY 168

XIV.
UPSALA 173

XV.
SALA 184

XVI.
THE MUTE BOOK 187

XVII.
THE SÄTHER DALE 189

XVIII.
THE MIDSUMMER FESTIVAL IN LEKSAND 193

XIX.
AT THE LAKE OF SILJAN 198

XX.
FAITH AND KNOWLEDGE 209

XXI.
IN THE FOREST 213

XXII.
FAHLUN 217

XXIII.
WHAT THE STRAWS SAID 222

XXIV.
THE POET'S SYMBOL 224

XXV.
THE DAL-ELV 227

XXVI.
PICTURES AD INFINITUM 232

XXVII.
DANNEMORA 235

XXVIII.
THE SWINE 239

XXIX.
POETRY'S CALIFORNIA 242

IN SWITZERLAND.

I.
RAGATZ 251

II.
THE LION AT LUCERNE 257

III.
THE CELEBRATION AT OBERAMMERGAU 260

A VISIT AT CHARLES DICKENS'S HOUSE . 267

RAMBLES

IN

THE HARTZ MOUNTAINS.

RAMBLES

IN

THE HARTZ MOUNTAINS.

CHAPTER I.

THE SETTING OUT. — THE SEA. — THE RIVER TRAVE. — LU-
BECK. — ST. MARY'S CHURCH. — "THE DANCE OF DEATH."
WANDSBECK.

"Wenn jemand eine Reise thut,
So kann er was verzählen,"[1]

SAYS Claudius; but whether any one will listen to the narrative, is another affair. We live in an age when great historical events succeed each other without intermission — when in one twelvemonth more is developed than in any ten years formerly; meteor follows meteor in the political firmament; how, then shall one have time to notice the individual, aspiring spirit? The world now acts; it works for the coming poet-race, who shall make our time immortal. But if the wings grow the bird will also flutter; and if there be war or peace, marriage or burial, the bird will sing its song until its poetical heart break. There is always one or other kindred soul to be found, in the midst of this great world's bustle, that is refreshed by its tones; and more than this the little citizen of the sky cannot demand. But if now he be a vain bird — and such are for the most part young poets, — so will it attract listeners, be original, and then often twitter and chirp with quite another bill than that our Lord and Master gave him. This really answers sometimes! — aye, the more absurd the poetical screech becomes, so much the more is it remarked; it

[1] When we travel we can tell something.

gathers a party amongst the public; and now the one shows itself more original than the other, for who will not be heard when he first enters the lists as a singer?

If I must be sincere, it was just in this way that it happened to me when I thought of describing this journey of mine. I determined that my recital should be in an original manner, and I had also arranged the whole before I travelled; got my fair readers and those of the other sex seated, and would now give them the whole journey dramatically; this, thought I, will be a new mode of treating a narrative of travels. Thus, it was to be a travelling drama, with overture, prologue, and interludes. In the interludes the public were to be satirical, but in the prologue I would myself be so. The overture must be performed by a full orchestra; the assembled throng by the Custom-house which I would employ as Turkish music; the waves should play a roaring *crescendo*, and the birds and young ladies on "*the long line*,"[1] give forth a soft *adagio*. On the steam-vessel, I should certainly find passengers that I could in haste form into instruments, and my own heart should have permission to play a short solo on the harp. Thus, I thought that in this overture from Copenhagen to Lubeck there would be changes enough. At Travemünde, the prologue should begin, and at Lubeck the piece itself; when adventure on adventure, scene after scene, should link themselves to each other. I had not as yet seen any travels described in this manner: thus mine should be — and I travelled.

Strange places with strange persons succeeded each other; a new world opened itself to me between the mountains; God's glorious nature surrounded me; there was no assumed originality, and yet it looked quite original, it being itself alone. After all, thinks I to myself, is this novel plan of mine a right one? and, before I was fully aware of it, all the self-formed original ideas had evaporated — and I thought. I will give my thoughts as I received them; if they are not original, the

---

[1] "*The long line*," or, as it is called in Danish, "*Lange-linie*," is a fine promenade along the sea-shore, commencing at the Custom-house, and extending beyond the Citadel, toward the Sound. It affords a fine prospect of the sea, the shipping, the holm, or dock-yard, and the Swedish coast. — *Translator.*

reason is, because I myself am a copy: and yet that is not probable; for if the one leaf on a tree be not a copy of the other, how can the man in his whole natural state be so?

The overture, prologue, and interludes accordingly are lost, but nevertheless we may as well remain seated: I will open my heart, and show there the varied row of pictures the journey conjured forth. We will not spread out a sheet upon the wall — it causes too much trouble; we have the white leaves of the book — here now stand the pictures; only slightly sketched, it is true, yet we must remember that they are but dissolving views, or the shadowy pictures of reality. We have plains and mountains, towns and fantastic places — some few parts even are drawn in haste with pen and ink. The poet is not second to the painter!

> A foreground with a little lawn,
> A tree — be sure 'tis lightly drawn!
> A cloud — quick-coursing through the sky,
> A picture these at once supply!
> But for a poem — ere 'tis gone,
> Confess the scene before you one.

But now the steamer is off to Lubeck. The coast is in motion already! will it take the start of us, that we may not run away from it? No, it is we! the black column of smoke rises from the chimney, the wheels cleave the watery mirror, and there stretches a long furrow behind us in the sea.

"O travelling! travelling!" — it is the happiest lot, and therefore we all travel; everything in the whole universe travels; even the poorest man possesses Thought's winged horse, and if he become weak and old, Death takes him with him on the journey — the great journey we must all make. The waves roll from coast to coast, the clouds sail along the wide heavens, and the birds fly over field and meadow. We all travel; even the dead in their silent graves course with the earth around the sun. Yes, — "To travel!" — it is a strange fancy with the whole universe; but we are children; we will also play at "travelling" in the midst of our own and the great natural journey of things.

The sea lay before me like a mirror; not a wave rippled the broad surface. It is delightful to sail between sea and sky, whilst the heart sings its yearning sense of pleasure, and the spirit sees the significant, changing, resonant figures that arise from these tuneful waves.

The heart and the sea are, however, strangely allied. The sea is the world's great heart: therefore it roars so deeply in the stormy night; therefore it fills our breast with sadness or enthusiasm, when the clear starry firmament — that great image of eternity — shows itself on its quiet surface. Heaven and earth are reflected in the sea as in our hearts; but the heart of man never becomes as quiet as the ocean, after life's storm has shaken it to the centre. Yet our life-time here, how insignificant compared with the duration of that great world's bodies! In a moment we forget our pain, even the deepest; in a moment the great sea also forgets its storms, for to a world's body weeks and days are but moments.

But I am growing quite loquacious. It was even thus that I told many stories to a little child as it sat on my lap — stories that I myself thought pretty, very pretty. The child looked me in the face with its large eyes: I really thought that my tales made it happy, for I began to feel amused by relating them to the little attentive thing. In the most interesting part I interrupted myself, and said, "What do you think of it?" and the child answered, "You chatter so much!" Perhaps you are of the same opinion, dear reader? But, then, only think we have in the mean time sailed over the whole Baltic, passed Stævus cliff, with its wandering church,[1] Möen's white chalk cliffs, where the woods already began to be green, and Laaland itself, where the red beacon burnt in the dusky night. The sun has again risen, and it is beautiful to see, but most of the passengers are asleep, certainly thinking like Arv: "The morning is very fine, only it would be as well if it did not come so early in the day."

At length they came forth from the nether world, the one after the other. The deck was the free saloon for conversation, where one might come and go as one listed; our thoughts

---

[1] A story current in Zealand tells us that the church on Stævus cliff recedes a cock-stride every year from the sea; and that although the waves of the Baltic continually wash away some part of the coast here, yet the church remains the same distance inland. — *Translator.*

did the same, and the heart said one thing here and another thing there; but I heard all.

The heart dreams of its love on the sea's glassy surface. There is nothing in the whole of nature that shows a bodily image of this life's holy mysteries more than the great, the glorious sea, which, like the sky, encompasses the whole earth, and shows its infinity on its tranquil surface. Love is also a depth like the sea, on whose foundation life and death build, whilst Hope lets her richly laden barks sail from coast to coast.

I looked on the wide sea, and felt myself happy. There stood a Berliner by my side and made jests: he also felt happy. The steamer sped on, we approached land, and then — then the other passengers were also happy!

We had nearly missed the entrance to the Trave, for a thick fog extended itself over the whole coast; but fortune favored us; we hit the right point, came in, and now the whole of the fog-covered land lay behind us.

It was as if a curtain rolled up. In the foreground stood the beautiful bathing-house and the high light-house, — round about were green fields and woods, and the warm summer air streamed toward us.

To the left lay the little peninsula, Priwall, where the cattle ventured half out in the water, and presented to us a living picture, such as Paul Potter delighted in, with its large, airy background, and the charming groups of animals. To the right lay Travemünde, with its red roofs; round about one could see the heads of men and girls peeping out of the windows: they looked pretty in the distance. O yes! — "distance:" it is, however, life's magical fairy-land — that spiritual Fata Morgana which continually eludes us as we come nearer to it. In the distance lie childhood's dreams, and life's hopes and expectations; in the distance, the wrinkles are smoothed on the furrowed brow, and the gray-haired grandmother stands like a hale, blooming girl. Perhaps it was the case here with the beauties of Travemünde.

The Trave now became smaller; the steamer seemed as if it would take its whole breadth. We soon saw Lubeck, with its seven towers, peeping forth between wood and meadow;

but it played strangely at "bo-peep;" sometimes it was here, sometimes there. It lay under the green table which nature has here spread out with woods and luxuriant pastures. The many windings of the river make it appear as if one did not rightly know whether one sails to or from the town. Thus it is that we sail on life's great stream, where often we are so childish as to weep, nay, even to doubt the steersman's guidance, because the aim of our wishes, like Lubeck, plays at "bo-peep" with us; yet it is the right way we go, but we know not the course of the stream, as we only once in life sail up it.

What a changing picture! what a living idyl is the whole of this country! Here the river forms a little bay; here is a fishing village, where the nets hang in the sun, stretched out between the trees yonder; on the hill rises a village with its church, and in the river itself is a steamer foaming between the green rushes.

We now entered through an old arched gateway, with thick walls on either side, the free Hanse Town,

LUBECK.

Here, what with the old houses, with their pointed gables, narrow side-streets, and our memory which casts an historical drapery over the whole, we fancy ourselves carried a century back: these angular buildings, these stone heroes on the senate-house, and the stained-glass windows of the old church we came past looked thus when George Wollenweber[1] spake a powerful word in the senate. The churches here being open, also lead us to think of Catholicism; and many an image here, although it be not a work of art, impresses us by its poetical conception or its antiquity.

In St. Mary's Church I saw the famed astronomical clockwork, and the still more famous cycle of paintings, called "The Dance of Death." Every rank, every age, from the Pope to the child in the cradle, is here invited to take a part in Death's cotillon, and all in the costume of the time in

---

[1] George Wollenweber took an active part in the so-called Lubeck feud, during the exile of Christian II. of Denmark, and whilst Christian III. was king, when the Lubeckers obtained great commercial privileges. — *Translator*.

which they were painted, which is said to have been in the year 1463. Under each figure stands a verse in Low German — a dialogue between the dancers : these verses, however, are not the original old rhymes, but a later poetical attempt made about 1701. It appeared to me as if the painter had placed an ironical smile in the dancing skeltons' faces, that seemed as if it would say to me and the whole company of spectators who were here, and made their remarks on it, "You imagine, now, that you are standing still, or at most walking about in St. Mary's Church, and looking at the old pictures. Death has not yet got you with him in the dance; and yet you already dance with me; aye altogether! The great dance begins from the cradle. Life is like the lamp, which begins to burn out as soon as it is lighted. As old as each of you are, so many years have I already danced with you; every one has his different turn, and the one holds out in the dance longer than the other; but toward the morning hour the lights burn out, and then — tired, fatigued — you all sink down in my arms, and — that is called death!"

Round about in the walls stood epitaphs, and in the aisles lay tombstones, with illegible inscriptions and half-obliterated knights and dames. I saw a large stone, with a stalwart knight carved on it : he held his long battle-sword in his hand, and yet permitted the new generation to tread on his nose, so that his features and the long beard were almost effaced. He and all these quiet neighbors, whose names have now disappeared like the inscriptions, once rioted merrily in the old city, promenaded many a time on the green ramparts, heard the birds sing, and thought of immortality. The old senate-house still stands, with its small towers, and the great Hanse-hall : the market-place, where the new throng of people busy themselves, lies between it and the church.

From St. Mary's Church I went out into God's great church, which is of far greater magnitude : that is an arch! it preaches when all else is still. The houses on both sides of the street appeared to me to be rows of pews, like bought or rented family pews, where even the domestics had their places. A thunder-cloud, which had drawn up over us, began its sermon in the mean time; it was short, yet there was much in that speech.

I left the old city of Lubeck in the evening; the sun went down so beautifully, and the green woods sent forth such fragrance, that it gave me a delight not to be expressed. How much poesy is there not in such a still evening! The highroad — yes, that was also poetical in its way: it appeared to me to be the way to Parnassus — rugged and uneven.

We all arrived, however, early in the morning, with whole limbs, at Wandsbeck. Here Claudius lived and wrote. I thought of Andreas and Anselmus: the sun shone in my face, so that it brought the water into my eyes. I had nearly driven past the building where the lottery is drawn, without noticing it, but there are thoughts enough here, nevertheless, which, like unhappy spirits, hover about this place, and howl over the unloosened mammon. Claudius and the lottery! — they are two remarkable things in this little town, though, God knows, they by no means resemble each other. But I will not speak disrespectfully of the lottery: life itself is a grand lottery which has again many subordinate divisions, and some of them are quite poetical. . . . .

We now saw the towers of Hamburg; they rose aloft in the air, as if to see whether we were not coming soon; and the sun shone on them and on us with as much splendor as though its purpose had been to give lustre to an imperial pageant.

CHAPTER II.

HAMBURG. — A SIMPLE STORY. — THE THEATRE. — A VISIT OUT OF TOWN. — THE DREAM, AN IDYL. — THE TWO CHARACTERS.

I FELT a sincere and deep respect for the old city, which the narrow streets and thronging masses of people helped to sustain. I really believe our coachman drove us up one street and down another in order to show us the imposing greatness of the town, for it seemed almost an eternity before we came to the "Hôtel de Bavière," in "Neue Jungfernstieg," where we descended. Here within the city itself it looks well, as the Alster, which is broad and large, separates, as it were, the old town from the new. The high towers are reflected in the water, where the swans glide along, and the boats rock with their loads of well dressed persons. The "Jungfernstieg" is crowded with promenaders; and along here, where one hotel lies by the side of the other, the doorways are thronged with waiters, upper-waiters, upper-waiters' upper-waiters.

We will, however, not tarry here, but reserve our visit until the evening, when all is lighted up, although it can well bear being seen by daylight. We will venture into the crowd, amongst hackney coaches, shouting retailers of all kinds, flower girls from Vierlande, and busy moneyed men from 'Change. It looks as if it were but one single shop — so thickly do they press on each other. The streets cross one another, and down toward the Elbe we find some to which the entrance is through a lobby, and where scarcely any one can live that exceeds a certain circumference, unless he live in them continually. I stuck my head into some of them, but durst not go further, for they reminded me of a dream I once had: how the houses in Ostergade (East Street), Copenhagen, where I was walking, also began to walk, but with their fronts toward each other, so that the streets had the appearance of these Hamburg streets; and as they made another step, I sat squeezed in between the walls, and could neither get forward nor backward — which was rather unpleasant.

Yet a swarm of children played about in them, quite pleased and satisfied in that half obscure Hamburger-world.

A poor man was to be buried: four men bore the coffin, and the wife followed; they had some difficulty in passing through the narrow lane; the way was strait; not a sunbeam found its way down here, — it was only when they had emerged into the broader streets that the sunlight fell on the humble coffin. I heard a story about this funeral, which is as poetically touching as it is true.

Within this narrow street, high up in an equally narrow chamber, lay the poor corpse; the wife sat and wept over it; she knew of no expedient to get it buried — she had no means. The window stood open, when a canary-bird flew into the room and settled by the head of the corpse, where it began to sing: it made a strange impression on the woman; she could weep no longer, for she imagined it must have come down to her from the Lord. The bird was tame; it allowed itself to be caught directly; and as she related the circumstance to a neighbor, and showed her the bird, the woman remembered that she had shortly before read an advertisement in the newspaper about a canary-bird that had flown away from its home.

It was the same bird, and the woman, on restoring it to its owners, found there humane hearts, who rendered her such assistance as enabled her to bury the dead.

The city is cut through with canals; I saw some here in this quarter that appeared to me like veritable sewers. High houses on both sides, but no street, only the narrow canal as far as one could see on account of the projecting balconies. On these there hung and lay all sorts of things, whilst far below the dirty water ran, or rather crept. One of these balconies or sheds in this chaos was painted green, and there sat a stout dame before the tea-table, enjoying the beautiful scene.

If in the summer we would avoid the throng of people we meet with almost everywhere here — if we wish to separate ourselves from the world — then we must go to the theatre:

here we shall not be incumbered; the pale hermits sit wide apart from each other in the large boxes.

The house is large and elegant — four tiers of boxes, and pit; the passage behind the benches is so broad that one might very well dance a gallopade. The whole of the interior is painted white, gilded, and lighted by a brilliant chandelier.

They performed "Der Freischutz:" the decorations were excellent, particularly "the wolf's glen." It was a deep rocky gulf, where the moon shone down, and the red will-o'-the-wisps hopped about in their magic circle-dance. The flames shot up from the earth, and the Wild Huntsman — an airy transparency, a group of clouds that formed themselves into these wild forms — darted over the scene.. At the end of the act the living *Zamiel* did not ascend from the bottomless pit, but a frightful gigantic figure, that filled the whole stage, seized *Max* and *Caspar* with his enormous hand as they lay lifeless on the ground, whilst the whole stage was lighted up by a strong red fire, which gave it a grand effect. In other respects *Zamiel's* costume was not good — he looked like a red hussar. A Demoiselle Gned performed the part of *Agathe*. She sang prettily and correctly, but made a fool of herself every time they applauded her: she then quite forgot her part, and made a deep courtesy, which, of course, at once destroyed the illusion. After this grand aria with her handkerchief, which was waved with much studied grace, and as she was about to throw herself into the arms of *Max*, the audience applauded, upon which she made a movement forward, courtesied, and then threw herself into the arms of the poor lover, who had a whole public between him and his beloved one's feelings.

Art is the opposite of nature; but art is not therefore unnatural; it is rather the ideal image of nature: one must forget that it is art; but how can one do so when the artist degrades him or herself by forgetting the natural in art for the sake of a miserable clapping of hands.

The next time I was in the theatre I was entertained with a melodrama from the French, "Cardillac oder das Stadtviertel des Arsenals;" it is constructed after Hoffman's well-known tale, "Fraulein Scudery;" but it was a miserable play. *Oliver's* part was performed by a Mr. Jacobi, who, they say, has his boots and shoes gratis from the shoemakers' corporation in Hamburg, because he played *Hans Sachs*. Why he got them I know not; but it was, perhaps, with the respectable shoemakers' corporation as with an old citizen I once knew, who, when he saw his daughter play at a private theatre, clasped his hands and said, "The Lord only knows where she got all she is now saying!" They also, without doubt, thought that Jacobi himself invented all the fine things he said; and as they were all shoemakers, like Hans Sachs, and as, perhaps, there were poets among them (not like Hans Sachs,) they thought, "Heute dir, morgen mir!" (To-day you, to-morrow me.) "Who knows what Jacobi may put into our mouths if we should happen to come on the stage?"

From the theatre we will go to the Botanical Garden, though I saw the former in the evening and the latter in the morning; but the large hot-houses appear to me be a suitable chain of transition to the free contemplation of nature.

The site is charming; we imagine ourselves far away from Hamburg, and yet there is only the old ditch surrounding the ramparts, and the level walls, with their flower parterres and trees between. The strawberries were already in full flower, and the little birds twittered in the hedges, saying to me, "Do you already perceive that you are travelling southward?"

From the Botanical Garden I wandered out to Altona, where I enjoyed the first fine prospect over the Elbe, and thus came to Ottensen. The well-known tree in the church-yard caught my eye directly: I stood by Klopstock's grave.

I once read of an English traveller who, when he witnessed a Catholic procession for the first time, and saw the whole assembled multitude kneel, also bent his knee involuntarily, though he knew not if it were a god, a saint, or something merely human, that he knelt to; it was almost the same with me here. I know but little of Klopstock; for his "Messiah" — yes, I will honestly confess it — I have never read. Such a great heroic poem has something in it of a deterring nature to me: it was, in fact, more Klopstock's name than his works that awakened my deep, serious feelings by his grave. It was that immortal name which caused my heart's pulse to beat quicker.

I passed on; Nature beckoned me to view her charms. Neat and beautiful green gardens lay along the shores of the Elbe; the steamers glided proudly on the river, and the black smoke rolled along over its surface. It is delightful here: yet thousands have said so before me. Who has not been in Rainville's garden at Blankenese, seen "Das schöne Marianchen," etc. etc.? yes, all who have no idea of Saxon Switzerland say that this place resembles it much. The Elbe is, at least, the same, and here even broader.

The birds sang and the flowers nodded, and in such numbers that when, in the twilight, I got back to Hamburg, I fancied that on the whole of the "Jungfrauenstieg" there were nothing but merry birds and nodding flowers moving there.

I dreamed I was a little bird
   That flew o'er the land and the main;
What the heart felt, what the eye saw,
   I know not well how to restrain.

I sang each thought that was deep in my breast,
   I sang of my pleasures, and then
I took a flight over the foaming sea,
   And saw foreign cities and men.

One morn I sat on the old tree's bough,
   And warbled my gladsome song;
The flowers peeped forth from the emerald sward
   They were many, and lovely, and young.

But one in its scent and its color eclipsed
   The rest of the greensward train;
And on her I looked, and for her I sang,
   And forgot foreign lands and the main.

Here I'll build my nest and with her I'll dwell,
   From her I will never depart;
To her I'll warble the choicest songs
   That gush from the depths of my heart.

Modestly to the wind she bent,
   And I touched her light robe of blue:
Her perfume revealed her thought to me,
   And the sun her warm blushes' hue.

> Bashful she bowed her fair head down —
>   How well I remember the hour!
> I thought I read requited love
>   In the glance of that lovely flower.
>
> There came a sportsman comely and young,
>   His gun o'er his shoulder was cast;
> And stooping, he stretched forth his ruthless hand —
>   And my flower his bosom graced.
>
> A dew-drop fell from the flow'ret's leaf,
>   And methought it was a tear:
> O! that his gun were leveled now,
>   For death have I ceased to fear.
>
> In mem'ry my flower is sweet as ere
>   Its home was the sportsman's breast;
> And I fly over country, and city, and town,
>   Yet my heart finds nor solace nor rest.
>
> Though I mourn, yet my song is ringing still
>   Every time o'er the meadow I fly:
> It may lure the sportsman, for what is life
>   Or song when we wish to die?

It was on the fourth day after my arrival that I left Hamburg for Brunswick by the "postkutsche." There were about twenty passengers, who all stood in a group, with cloaks, boxes, and other travelling attributes, by the "Hohen Brücke," where we were to enter the conveyance.

The street here was narrow and dark, with a great crowd, noise, and shouting; yet in the midst of all its prose lay a little pastoral scene.

The side houses had many outbuildings and bow windows: between two of these was a little wooden shed stuck up; it was so low that no one could stand upright in it, and so small that there was only space for one chair, and no more. Herein sat an old married couple — a shoemaker and his wife. The work-tools lay in the window, and the husband took up the whole space between it and the back wall; the old woman sat close beside him with her knitting, and then came the door: she must, of course, come out of the house first to make way for him.

They really sat there like dolls in a glass case, and looked very glad and happy, chattering and laughing as they looked at us, whilst we were put, one at a time, into the great "post-kutsche."

I got a place in one of the branch-carriages, where I had an Englishman and two Hamburgers for companions; one of them was a Jew.

"Now we shall be interesting!" was the first thing he said, almost before he had taken his seat in the carriage, and looked at us all with a pleased and satisfied mien.

"Our Hamburg is a fine city, a rich city!" and then he began to sing in falsetto:

> "Stadt Hamburg in der Elbe-Auen,
> Wie bist du statlich anzuschauen!"

I was also quite pleased, for I thought, like the devil when things go wrong, "There, I shall have one soul; him I can certainly make use of." I prayed that this young man's originality might put its Sunday's dress on, and in that hope I too hummed:

> "Heil über dir Hammonia!"

Thus we rolled out of the old city of Hamburg.

I mentioned the poet Heine. "Heine!" said he: "yes, Heine is a great man in poetry, and his brother a great man on 'Change. But I don't like his verses — they are so short. You get a rap on the nose, and then that poem is done!"

"Yes," said the other Hamburger, "he is always so ready to give one a rap on the nose! Now, he has written that the Romans and Italians are so handsome, and their features so regular, and that we Germans have 'Kartoffel-Gesichter'" (potato-faces). "Have we potato-faces?" asked he, as he turned his visage toward me, which, if I must speak conscientiously, was not unlike that vegetable product.

"I would not," he continued, "for anything in the world, travel with such a man; for before one knew a word about it, there might be a whole book written about one!"

"Number two!" thought I; "here I have the second soul! What characters for my travels! They will develop themselves by degrees, and make effect in the third chapter."

We had meanwhile come to the end of the first stage; but there they both took leave — both the souls!

It is really annoying for an author to lose his first two characters in this way, without having as yet made use of them; but we will not allow ourselves to be annoyed: we will travel farther.

CHAPTER III.

VIERLANDE. — THE TRAVELLER AND THE DWELLER ON THE HEATH. — THE SCHOOL-MISTRESS. — LYNEBORG. — THE ELVES ON THE HEATH.

WE were now in Vierlande. Small canals crossed each other; everything was luxuriantly green; the cherry-trees had changed their blossoms for fruit, though it was only the twenty-first of May. The whole appearance was of a large kitchen-garden; and it is so to Hamburg and the whole neighborhood.

Neat houses stood close by the way-side, and some of them had panes of stained glass in the windows. Children, boys and girls, ran alongside the carriage to sell us flowers; for a trifle we got both nosegays and wreaths.

A journey through Vierlande to the Hartz is, however, a right living picture of human life. That luxuriant green nature here, where the inhabitants sleep quietly within the dikes, without dreaming of the turbulent stream which in a moment might break in and overwhelm them, appeared to me as the happy green-life's childhood-world, where also grow cherries, plums, pease, and variegated flowers everywhere. But we have scarcely passed out of this happy land, over Reality's Elbe-stream, than Life's great Lyneborg-heath lies before us, which, however, is not so bad as it is given out to be. Here also are woods; and though they are but of fir and pine, yet they afford shade. We also find *men* here; and the birds warble sweetly in the green meadows. Behind all that extent of heath rise the Hartz Mountains, where even the sunlit clouds lie like mists far below us.

At Zollenspicker, which lies on an island between the Elbe and Elmenau, we all got into a large ferry-boat, and sailed over the river Elbe, which ran at a rapid rate toward Hamburg, just as if it had a thousand pieces of news from the Bohemian mountains, which it must have inserted in the "Borsenhalle."

We now landed, and stood in the kingdom of Hanover. The country, as far as Winsen, a Hanoverian hamlet situated by a small river, was tolerably pretty. On the first street-corner here a painter had written the name of the place in large white letters, "Winsen," and by the side of it placed an immense comma, as if to signify that something more than the mere name could be said about this place.

The inhabitants sat on the steps and drank their tea: we kissed our hands to the ladies, and they nodded back, as familiarly as if we were well acquainted. The sun went down behind the old church-tower, and gave us all red cheeks, as we rolled away to the great heath.

It was not uninteresting on the side from which we approached Lyneborg. The young pine-trees stood with their fresh pale-green shoots — the whole forest looked like a mass of Christmas-trees with their small candles, only the presents were wanting.

We rolled onward between sand and pines.

THE TRAVELLER.

Nor mountain, nor sea,
Heaven gave to thee,
But the ling-covered land,
The pine-tree, and sand :
Only these can I see around,
Within the vast horizon's bound.

THE DWELLER ON THE HEATH.

Mountain and ocean God gave to me.
The sky is the boundless sea ;
What sea so great as is this main ?
See, it overhangs the plain ;
Look down : lo ! deeply in the lake,
The stars, like lilies fresh, awake !

Mountains ! Are there no mountains here ?
Do these bright clouds in vain appear ?
They lift themselves with pride and power.
Behold ! one seems a rocky tower
And now down heaven's sea they sail :
Say, wherein do these mountains fail ?

From twenty passengers who left Hamburg together, we had dwindled down to six, and now sat, heart by heart, in the great "postkutsche:" we formed, in a manner, the six of hearts, as there were three on each side.

The one heart — that is to say, with bodily case and appurtenances — was a young student from Hamburg, full of humor and ideas: he found that we just formed a little family circle, and that we ought to know each other intimately. Our names were not asked, but our country; every one got a name after some remarkable man or woman there, and thus we formed a circle of celebrated personages. I, as a Dane, was called Thorwaldsen; my neighbor, a young Englishman, Shakespeare. The student himself could not be less than Claudius; but with our three opposite neighbors he was somewhat perplexed. One was a young girl, about eighteen years of age, who accompanied her uncle, an old apothecary, from Brunswick: he was at last obliged to call her Miss Mumme, and the uncle Henry Love. But the last of the passengers was quite anonymous, as we could not find any famous characters in that otherwise famous salt town, Lyneborg, whence she came. She was, therefore, a step-child; and it appeared as if she had often been treated as such, for she smiled with a strange sadness, when we could not find a name for her in the society. This circumstance caused me to regard her more particularly. She was about fifty years of age, had a brown skin, and some traces of the small-pox; but there was something interesting in her dark eye — something deeply sad, even when she smiled. We heard that she kept a school for young girls in Lyneborg, lived quietly there in a small house, and had now, for the first time, but only for a few days, been in Hamburg. I scarcely heard her speak a word the whole way; but she smiled kindly at our jests, and looked good-naturedly happy at the young girl every time she laughed heartily at what was said.

In the midst of us chatterers she was the most interesting to me, on account of her silence. As we rolled into Lyneborg's narrow streets, where the houses stood in the moonlight, very old, and, with pointed gables, so cloister-like, I heard her speak for the first time: —

"Now I am at home!" said she.

We alighted; the old apothecary offered her his arm to conduct her to her house,—it was close by,—and the rest accompanied her. It was about eleven o'clock: everything was still in this strange old town; its houses, with pointed gables, bow windows, and outbuildings round about, looked singular in the bright moonlight. The watchman had a large rattle, which he made pretty free use of—sang his verse—and rattled again. "Welcome home, Miss!" said he, in the midst of his song; she nodded, and mentioned his name as she went up the high stone steps: here she lived. I saw her nod her farewell, and disappear behind the door.

When the postilion afterward blew his horn for us to enter the diligence, I saw a light in her chamber; a shadow passed over the curtain, it was she, who was looking after us through the window.

That journey was now passed with her, which she, perhaps, had rejoiced in the thought of for several years before: probably it stands as one of the clearest points in her monotonous life, and has since enjoyed it many times in recollection. There is something really touching in such an old maid's still cloister-life. Who knows what worm gnaws at that heart?—there are thoughts and feelings we often cannot confide to our dearest friends. On the morrow she would, perhaps, recommence her occupation in the school, and hear the children in *les verbes réguliers*,—"Aimer, aimant, aimé." How many remembrances lie in such a regular verb!

We left Lyneborg without having seen any of its curiosities—without even a glimpse of the celebrated swine that discovered the salt-springs, above eight hundred years ago.

We however saw the salt-works and the lime-pits, as we left the town; though it was, sure enough, in the same way as Bürger's Leonore, who saw towns and fields fly past in the moonlight.

We were again six in the diligence: the vacant place had been taken by a merchant who was going to Dresden; thus we still formed a six of hearts as we again found ourselves on the heath.

The monotonous grinding of the wheels in the sand, the piping of the wind through the branches of the trees, and the postilion's music, blended together into a sleep-bringing lullaby: one passenger after the other nodded his head. Even our nosegays, which were stuck in the pockets of the diligence, imitated the same motion every time the vehicle gave a jolt. I closed my eyes and opened them again, in a half doze, and certainly dreamt. My eye fell in particular on one of the large carnations in the bouquet I had got in Vierlande: all the flowers had a powerful scent, but I thought that mine surpassed all the others, both in scent and color; and, what was most curious, in the centre of the flower there sat a little airy being, not bigger than one of its leaves, and as transparent as glass; it was its genius, for in every flower there dwells such a little spirit, which lives and dies with it. His wings were of the same color as the leaves of the carnation, but they were so fine that they looked as if the hue were but the red tint that fell from the flower in the moonlight: golden locks, finer than the seed-dust, glided down over his shoulders and waved in the wind.

As I looked more closely at the other flowers, I observed that he was not the only one: such a little being rocked in every flower — its wings and airy dress were as a tinge of the flower in which it lived. They each rocked on the light leaf, in fragrance and moonlight; each sang and laughed; but it was as when the wind passes gently over the attuned Æolian harp.

There soon came hundreds and hundreds of elves, in quite different habits and forms, through the open window of the diligence; they came from the dark pine-trees and heath-blossoms. What a chattering there was, and such rocking and dancing! They often sprang right over my nose, and were not ashamed to perform a circular dance on my brow. These pine-elves looked like real wild men, with lance and spear, and yet they were as airy as the fine mist which, in the morning sun, exhales its fragrance from the bedewed rose. They arranged themselves in different parties, and played whole comedies, which my fellow-travellers imagined they dreamt: every one had his piece.

For the merry, lively student from Hamburg, the scene was in Berlin. A whole flock of elves disguised themselves as

German students; and some were true Philistines, with long pipes in their mouths, and sticks like clubs by their sides: they stood in long rows — it was a college. One of the pine-elves mounted the rostrum, and spoke so learnedly and intricately that I could not possibly follow the thread of his discourse.

Another party played on our Englishman's lips, danced, and kissed each other; and it was to him as if he kissed his heart's beloved, felt her cheek lean on his, and looked into her wise, affectionate eyes.

For the young girl from Brunswick they, on the contrary, played a serious scene of her own life: the tears trickled down her cheeks, and the little elves smiled, and each saw himself reflected in a tear; so that every tear that fell in her dreams showed an innocent smile.

They were the hardest on the old apothecary, because he had trodden one of the flowers in pieces that had fallen down in the diligence, and thereby killed one of the little elves. They fixed themselves on his leg, and then, in his dream, it was to him as if he had no leg, but he hopped about on the stump through the streets of Brunswick, where all the neighbors and strangers stood and looked at him. This, however, grieved the little beings; so they let him have his leg again, and a pair of great wings into the bargain, so that he could fly high above Henry Löve's copper lion, and the high church-tower of St. Blasius; and this pleased the old apothecary right well, for he laughed aloud in his sleep.

For the merchant from Dresden they had formed the whole exchange at Hamburg, with Jews and Christians; and set the rate of exchange so high that it had never yet been the like nor ever will be, for it was only such as airy sprites can bring about in dreams. Me they seemed not to take any notice of until long afterward; when one of them said, "This tall man is a poet; shall he not see anything?"

"He sees us; does he not? that surely is enough for him!"

"Shall we not also let him see what we see? — then he will sing so prettily about it to the others when he awakes."

They held a very long council respecting it — whether I was worthy to be received into their society or not; but as they had at the time no better poet with them, I got a card of admission. The little elves kissed me on the eyes and ears, and it seemed to me that I suddenly became a new and better man.

I looked out on the great Lyneborg heath, which is said to be so ugly. Good Heavens! how people talk! — yes, they talk as they see and hear. Every grain of sand was a glittering rock: the long grass-straw, full of dust, that hung out on the broad high-road, was the prettiest macadamized way one can imagine for the little elves; such a little smiling face peeped forth from every leaf! The pines looked like completed towers of Babel, with myriads of elves from the lowest broad branch to the very top. The whole air was filled with the strangest figures, and all clear and quick as light. Four or five flower-genii rode on a white butterfly they had driven out of its sleep; whilst others built palaces of the strong fragrance and the fine moonbeams. The whole of that great heath was an enchanted world, full of miracles. With what art was not every flower's leaf woven! What a mass of life lay in the green pine-shoot! Every grain of sand had its different color and peculiar combination; and what infinity in the expansive firmament above!

The legend says, that the mermaid alone can receive an immortal soul from man's true love and Christian baptism. The little flower-elves do not demand so much: a tear from a repentant or compassionate human heart is that baptism which gives them immortality, and therefore the elves seek willingly the society of man; and when the pious resigned sigh ascends from our breast, they rise on it to God; thus they also are admitted into the great resplendent heaven, and grow up angels under the powerful sunlight of Eternity.

The dew began to fall: I saw the air-light genii sporting about on the large dew-drops. Many poets say that the elves bathe themselves in dew; but how can that light being which dances on the thistle-down without moving it, cleave its way through the solid mass of water? No; they stood upon the round drop, and when it rolled under their feet, and the light drapery fluttered in the air, they looked like the most charming miniature pictures of Fortune on her rolling ball.

Suddenly I felt a trembling movement in the air. I started up, and the whole had vanished; but the flowers shed a strong perfume, and through the window I saw some fresh green birch branches hanging down. The postilion had decked out the whole diligence with green boughs, because it was Whitsunday. The old apothecary stretched himself in the carriage and said, "One can, after all, dream here!" but neither he nor the other passengers thought that I was cognizant of their dreams.

The sun rose; we all sat quiet — I believe we prayed in silence, whilst the birds sang hymns for Whitsuntide, and the heart itself preached its best sermon.

People were going to church in Uelzen when we got there. The sun burnt like fire; we were almost half dead when we reached Gifhorn, and were still four German miles from Brunswick. I felt so tired that I scarcely cared to look out of the diligence, even when we could see the Hartz Mountains and the Brocken. At length we reached our journey's end, and I found rest and refreshment in the Hôtel d'Angleterre.

CHAPTER IV.

BRUNSWICK. — "THREE DAYS IN THE LIFE OF A GAMESTER." — A CONTINUATION OF THE SAME. — THE MOTHER AND SON. — WANDERING IN THE TOWN — DEPARTURE. — THE OLD SCHOOL-MASTER.

"WHAT do they perform at the theatre this evening?" I asked. "O, ein wunderschönes Stück!" said the waiter. "Drei Tage aus dem Leben eines Spielers."

I knew that it was a piece with much dramatic effect; it had caused a great sensation throughout Germany, but I thought it could not be more effective than "Cardillac."

The piece was not divided into acts, but into days, between each of which there was a period of fifteen years. I bore the infliction of two days, but then I could bear it no longer; the audience were kept on the rack of suspense; but only think of me, poor man, almost jolted to death from the journey!

The first day ended with the gamester taking the life of his old father; the second day he shot a person who was innocent. I felt my blood boil, and fully expected that the third day would be devoted to the murder of the spectators also.

I was in a terrible humor. I went home, but I saw everywhere outcasts of humanity, broken-hearted mothers, and desperate gamblers. I felt such a disgust for cards, that I immediately burnt a pack of innocent visiting cards, merely because they bore the name of cards. My mind was in a state of uproar. I tried to calm it by singing lullabies — nay, I even sat down at last to tell myself a child's story, which you, dear reader, must also hear.

"While the Copenhageners are still quite little urchins, and have not been farther out into the world than to the deer park[1] and Fredericksberg,[2] and their grandmothers or nurses tell them about enchanted princes and princesses, golden mountains and talking birds, — then the little head dreams about the beautiful visionary land, and looks over the sea that joins the sky between the Danish and the Swedish coast. It must lie out there, they think, and paint this new world to themselves in such brilliant colors! but they become older, go to school, and get hold of their geography, which at once breaks up the whole of their land of dreams, though it is in that that *we* must remain.

"Here lived, many, many years ago, — long before any one dreamt of my authorship, and 'Drei Tage aus dem Leben eines Spielers,' — an old silver-haired king, who had such confidence in the world that he could not imagine that any one could tell a lie; nay, a lie was to him such a visionary picture, that he promised one day in council to give his daughter and half the kingdom to him who could tell him something which he must be sensible was a lie.

"All his subjects began to study the art of lying, but the good king took all they said for truth. At last he became

---

[1] "Dyrehaven," The Deer Park, about six English miles from Copenhagen, is, during the months of June, July, and August, a favorite resort of the inhabitants of Copenhagen, of all ages and ranks, from the king to the peasant, the grandfather to the child. It is a pleasant beech wood park, in which are a royal hunting lodge and several springs of fine water. A pleasure fair is held there during six weeks, commencing on the twenty-first of June, and continuing until the first of August, every year. It is situated near the sea, and the drive to it is delightful, being along the beach, and commanding a fine prospect of the Swedish coast, and the roadstead of Copenhagen, with the shipping, etc. Along the road are a number of elegant villas, inhabited chiefly by the gentry and merchants of the capital. Several steamers ply daily between the city and the park during the summer months, when vehicles of every description are also in requisition; so that the road to "Dyrehaven" presents, on a fine Sunday, a sight similar to the Epsom road on the Derby day, though on a less pretending scale. — *Translator.*

[2] Fredericksberg is a royal palace, at present inhabited by the Dowager Queen of Denmark, situated on a lofty hill, about an English mile from Copenhagen, and affording a fine prospect over the city, the island of Amack, the adjacent country, and part of the Baltic. Here are some extensive grounds, laid out in the English style of gardening: it is much frequented. — *Translator.*

quite melancholy, wept, and dried his eyes on his royal mantle, as he sighed, 'Shall I never be able to say, It is a lie?'

"Thus the days glided on, when one morning there came a fine well-grown prince, who loved the princess and was beloved again: he had studied lying for nine years, and now hoped to win her and the kingdom. He told the king that he wished to have a situation as gardener, and the king said, 'Very well, my son!' and led him into the garden.

"Here the cabbages, in particular, were of a fine growth; but the young prince turned up his nose, and said, '*Was ist das?*'

"'They are cabbages, my son!' said the king.

"'Cabbages! in my mother's kitchen-garden they are so large that a regiment of soldiers can stand under every leaf.'

"'It is very possible,' said the king. 'Nature's powers are great, and there is an immense difference in the growth of plants.'

"'Then I will not be a gardener,' said the prince; 'let me rather be your land-steward.'

"'See, here is my barn; have you ever seen a larger or finer?'

"'Larger? yes! If you could but see my mother's! Only think: when they built it, and the carpenter sat at the top of the roof cutting away with his axe, the head flew out of the shaft, and before it reached the ground a swallow had built its nest in the hole, laid eggs, and hatched young ones. That you surely must believe to be a lie, sir king?'

"'No, indeed I do not! human art goes far; why should your mother not have such a barn?'

"Thus it went on and on, but the prince got neither the kingdom nor the beautiful princess; so they both pined away with grief and suspense, for the king had sworn, 'No one shall have my daughter unless he can tell me a lie!'

"His good heart could never believe in such a thing; nay, even when he died — which he did at last — and was placed in the large marble coffin, he got no peace; and they say that he still wanders about the earth as an unblessed spirit, because he never had his desire appeased."

I had got thus far with my story — that is, to the end —

when there was a knocking at my door. I cried out, "Come in!" and imagine my surprise!—there stood the old king before me, with his crown on his head, and his sceptre in his hand.

"I heard you relate my life's history," said he, "and that has brought me to you. Perhaps you know a lie that can procure me peace in the grave?"

I endeavored to recover myself, told him how it was that I had come to relate to myself his life and acts, and then mentioned "Drei Tage aus dem Leben eines Spielers."

"Tell it to me!" said he; "I am very fond of the terrible. I am myself a spirit, as you see, terrible in my old age!"

I began to relate the whole to him, went through scene by scene, and showed him that picture of human life: his features cleared up, he seized my hand, and said with enthusiasm, "It is a lie, my son! it is not so in the world: but now I am released! Thanks be to you, who told me this; thanks be to Louis Angely, who brought it out on the stage; but blessed be Victor Ducange, who wrote it. Now I shall have peace in the grave!"—and then he vanished.

When I awoke next morning, the whole of this story appeared to me as a dream.

I now began my rambles in the city, which appeared to be a very still and peaceful one.

Here all the windows inclined inward, and the flower-pots outward. The servant girls fluttered through the streets in variegated calico dresses, and the children cried, "Her' Jös'!" (Lord Jesus) to every other word they said. The ramparts are leveled; one walks in long avenues, and finds many flower parterres, which one may look at, but not touch.

I went to the "Falleberthor," a historical place in the fifteenth century, for then all the princes and powerful lords in the land assembled there every seventh year, and took part with the people in dancing and revelry. At that period, they threw dice there for everything, even to get a wife; and he who threw the highest was obliged to marry. Round about in parti-colored tents, sat the noble dames in all their state, and looked at the merry multitude without. Everything was now changed; a long avenue, with country-houses, villas, etc., lay before me on both sides. Some of the honest burghers walked about here, enjoying the morning hour, without ever thinking that perhaps their great-great-grandmother had been set up as a prize to be thrown for, in her flourishing youth, as they now put up a child's cloak or a workbox.

It was Whit-Monday: the bells rang, and the people streamed to the cathedral church of St. Blasius; I followed the stream. The organ pealed through the lofty arches, the congregation sang, and the old dukes of Brunswick lay in dust and ashes, down in their copper and marble coffins. This is all that I can tell about my first visit there — but it is truth.

After church-service, there was a marriage. They were a handsome couple, but what struck me particularly was, the singular expression of joy and sorrow depicted in the bride's eyes: she appeared to be looking for some one as she went up to the altar.

"He is certainly in the church," whispered two women who stood by my side.

"Poor Edward! yes, that he certainly is."

A light broke in upon me; but I was certain he was not there. Had it been a novel of Johanne Schoppenhauer's, he would assuredly have stayed, deathly pale, behind a pillar, and witnessed the marriage ceremony: here, on the contrary, it was reality; he was not there, but where? —

THE MOTHER.

Why comest thou from the church, my son?
The nuptial mirth is not begun.
A bride to-day will Margaret be.
But thou art pale! — O woe is me!
And yet, what cause have I of woe?
Thou look'st to-day exactly so,
As when — O God! now I must weep! —
A child, thou in the grass didst sleep;
Thy foot a venomous snake had bit,
And in thy face death seemed to sit:
I doubly suffered then with thee;
But the good God was kind to me.
Thy foot I placed deep in the ground,
Which sucked the poison from the wound.

THE SON.

Yes, mother, earth can ease afford
To poisoned wounds; then pity, Lord!
The venom now is in my heart,
Let earth relieve the poisoned part.
O, bury deep this tortured breast —
Earth, earth alone can give me rest!

"Es ist eine alte Geschichte, doch bleibt sie immer neu,"[1] says Heine.

On coming out of the old church, I looked at the knightly epitaphs in the walls and the ancient buildings that lay round about in the streets. The old senate-house was transformed into a wine-cellar, though it still stood in all its Gothic reverence, with the large stone balcony; and between every pillar was a princely knight, with his consort, carved in stone, of life size.

In a remote corner of the city, near one of the gates, there is a large and beautiful garden belonging to a merchant. It is open to the public; and on the façade of the house stands, "Salve Hospes!" Here was a forest of exotic flowers and fruit-trees, which, planted in large tubs, stood round about the house. All was flower and fragrance. From a place in the garden, which led to an arm of the river Ocker, we had one of the sweetest landscapes imaginable. It was a bleaching ground — a large meadow, full of yellow flowers. At some distance lay several villas, between the beeches and tall poplars; and, in the distant horizon, the Hartz with the Brocken, which, like a gray storm-cloud, rose up between the other sunlit mountains: it was a finished picture! In the mountains themselves we have background without foreground; and in the plains it is the contrary — foreground enough, but no background; here were both, and as finely distributed as one could wish. I saw a young painter sketching the clouds and airy part of the picture. People walked past without noticing him. And so near the city! He should have been at Copenhagen. I remember one of our most famous landscape-painters once told me that he one evening took a walk

---

[1] It is an old story, yet it will be always new.

along the banks of the Pebling Lake,[1] in order to study the appearance of the sky. Delighted with its beautiful reflection on the surface of the water, he stood and looked into it; when a crowd soon collected about him, and all asked, "Is any one drowned?"

I walked past Heinrich Löve's old castle, by moonlight: the large copper lion stood quietly on its pedestal, and looked into the castle on the new generation which, in soldiers' uniforms, peeped out of all the windows.

On the third day after my arrival, I left Brunswick, by the "Schnellpost," and fell into company with two young lieutenants, who travelled incognito, as majors; they directly made me a professor, and, as it costs nothing by way of tax for the title,[2] I submitted to it with Christian patience. We had, besides, a servant-maid of about forty years of age, who was to meet the family at Goslar; and an old original school-master, with whom we must try to be better acquainted. The woman was of a character between the melancholy and the sanguine; she was in tears every moment, because just on that day the great annual target-shooting was to take place in Brunswick, which she had so great a desire to be present at; but now it was the third year she had been obliged to travel on this same day.

I parted company with all my fellow-travellers, except the school-master, at the first station: we were now placed in a small carriage, where there was only room for four persons; the hearts thus came corporeally nearer, and I had now but one figure to occupy myself with. He was a man of about sixty years of age; a little slender being, with lively eyes, and a black velvet skull-cap on his head. He was the express image of Jean Paul's *schulmeisterlein*, Wuz, from Auenthal. My school-master was from a little Hanoverian town; and was going to visit an old friend in Goslar, with whom he would, like myself, ascend the mountains for the first time. He was one of those happy beings whose contentment allies itself with

[1] One of the three lakes that supply Copenhagen with water.—*Translator*.

[2] In Germany and Denmark every person having a title pays a tax, according to rank, from the page to the prince. — *Translator*.

fancy, and twines flowers around every stump; for whom the narrow room extends itself to a fairy palace, and which can suck honey from the least promising flower. With almost childish pride he told me about his little town, which to him was the world's centre; it had also increased in cultivation in latter times, and had a private theatre.

"Yes," said he, "you shall see it! There is no one would ever think of its having been a stable before! The stalls are painted with violins and flutes, by our old painter; and the music itself — yes, i' faith, it is really good, for such a small town! — two violins, a clarionet, and a great drum; they play very nicely! I know not really how it can be, but music goes strangely into the heart, and I can well imagine how it must be with the little angels in heaven. But with us, now, we don't pretend to those hocus-pocuses and tra-la-las which they have in Brunswick and Berlin. No, our old sexton, who is the leader, gives us a good honest Polish tune, and a Molinasky between the acts; our women hum it with him, and we old fellows beat time on the floor with our sticks; it is a real pleasure!"

"And how of the acting?" I asked.

"Charming! for, you must know, in order that those who perform may have courage to appear before us, they are gradually accustomed to it at the rehearsals; and at the general rehearsal every house must send two servants, that the benches may be filled, and that they who perform may have courage."

"It must indeed be a great pleasure" —

"A pleasure!" interrupted he; "yes, in our hearts' simplicity we all amuse ourselves, and don't envy them in Berlin. But we have also splendid scenery, machinery, drop-curtains, and performances. On the first drop-scene we have the town fire-engine, and the jet stands just as in nature. But they are altogether painted — beautifully painted. The drop-scene representing the street is the finest: there we have our own town-market, and it is so distinct, that every one can see his own house, play whatever piece they may. The worst thing we have is the little iron chandelier: the candles drip so terribly, that if there be ever so many persons present there is always a large space under the chandelier. Another fault — for I am not the man to praise everything, — another fault is, that many of our women when they *act*, and happen to know any one on the seats, directly giggle and nod to them. But, goodness gracious, the whole is only pleasure!"

"But when there are no performances in the winter, it must be very quiet in your little town; the long evenings" —

"O, they go on quite delightfully. My wife, both the children, and the servant girl, sit down to spin; and when all the four wheels are going, I read aloud to them; so the work goes on easier, and the time flies away. On Christmas Eve we play for gingerbread-nuts and apple-fritters, whilst the poor children sing outside the doors about Christmas joys and the infant Jesus — and that brings the tears in my eyes, although I am so inwardly glad."

Thus the current of conversation ran rapidly on, whilst the vehicle moved slowly forward in the sandy road. The mountains came gradually forward from behind their misty veils, like strong proud masses, overgrown with dark fir-woods; the corn-fields wound picturesquely in between them, and Goslar, the old, free, imperial city, lay before us. All the roofs of the houses were covered with slates, in consequence of which the town, which lies inclosed between the mountains, has a strange, dark appearance. Here had once been the seat of the German kings and emperors; here the diets had been held, and the fate of the country and the kingdom decided. Now — yes, now, it is famous for its mines, and made more so by Heine's "Sketches of Travel." Here I parted company with my Hanoverian school-master, in the hope that we should again meet on Bloxbjerg.

CHAPTER V.

GOSLAR. — THE MINES. — THE SPIDER. — BEAUTIFUL MATILDA, A LEGEND. — ILSE. — THE BROCKEN.

THE air felt so singularly oppressive, I could actually smell the fumes of the mine, which has something in common with that which they tell us the devil perfumes with, when he goes angry away from a place. But as I have named the *old gentleman*, I must directly make known, before I forget it, that one of the most remarkable things in Goslar was a present from this far-famed personage. There stands in the centre of the market-place a large metal basin, constantly filled with water, through pipes, which the inhabitants use instead of the alarm-bell when there is a fire, as they beat on it so that it can be heard over the whole town. This basin, the legend says, was brought thither one night by the above named gentleman; I examined it, and found that it was very warrantable work.

The town-hall stands close by here, dark and antiquated, with all its mighty emperors disposed outside; they stand on the first floor, with crowns on their heads, sceptre in hand, and all strongly illuminated, like a Nuremberg image. I saw an old miner pointing out these doughty heroes to his little granddaughter, who would ever after imagine all the kings and emperors of the earth to be such serious looking stone men, with sword and crown. That little intelligent being could already see that it is not a life of flowers to be a king, and stand with the heavy crown, day and night, outside the town-hall, to watch over law and justice.

As I walked through the streets I saw several houses on which stood the Madonna and Child; but in many places they were whitened over, like the walls. There appeared something sad in thus seeing these half-ruined stone images, which stood here like mummies of a past age; they, also, once lived and ruled, though now obscured in this dead stone. It seemed to me as though they whispered: "It is not now as before, when the emperor and the people bent the knee before us! neither is Goslar as it was before: the crown has fallen from mine and the emperor's head!"

"These dead masses have a greater durability," thought I, as the town lay behind me, and I stood for the first time by a mountain. It was Rammelsberg, known for its mine, in which there is said to be more building timber than in all the houses in Goslar. The whole of the side facing the town consisted, for the most part, of schistous stone, which gave to the mountain the appearance of an immense building that had been burnt and fallen in ruins. The air itself had in it something sulphureous, and the water that came out of the mountain, through a drain, looked quite of an ochreous yellow.

The Norwegian peasant calls the thick, blue-white mist, which so often remains stationary between the sides of the mountains, "*Ulddotter;*"[1] and I know no name that is more characteristic: it actually looked as if an immense mass of the finest carded wool had been blown into the deep ravine, and hung there above the dark pines.

Where we descend the mine there was a number of young men rolling the rough masses of ore into a recess dug out for the purpose. We got a guide; he lighted his lamp, then opened a large door, and — I felt quite strange about the heart — we entered. The passage was of brickwork for a short distance, but the angular pieces of rock soon showed themselves in the arches round about: we descended deeper and deeper. Miners, with their lamps, met us; "Glück auf!"[2] was the mutual greeting, whilst all round about was still as in the grave. The passages here seemed to be of bronze; the ore shone forth in the stones, sometimes green, sometimes copper-colored.

A merchant from Goslar acccompanied me. We had only a narrow plank to walk on, and were often obliged to stoop quite low, on account of the pieces of rock which hung down. One passage crossed the other, and the guide often seemed to

---

[1] Carded wool.   [2] A pleasant voyage.

be far away from us. All at once there was a roaring sound over our heads ; it was as if the whole mountain was falling in. I said not a word, but held fast by my companion, who told me that it was a sluice they had opened above, and which set a wheel in motion, whereby the pieces of ore were hoisted up from the nethermost mine. An abyss opened to our view at one side of us. We could not, by the light of the lamp, distinctly perceive the whole of the large wheel which the water rushed over. I know not rightly if this, or the large grottoes where the ore is worked loose by means of fire, was the more picturesque. The red flames shot up high in the air, and, as it were, illuminated the dark miners round about. I leaned against the rocky wall, and began to accustom myself to this strange world, which had a beauty in it, though it was terrible.

It is a strange contrast, that which exists between the mariner's varied, and the miner's monotonous life. With swelling sails the seaman flies over the glorious sea, from coast to coast ; the foreign harbors swarm with life and bustle. Sometimes it blows a storm, so that the mast falls, and the ship is tossed about like a plaything by the fierce billows ; then it is again a dead calm — he sits up aloft in the main-top, and looks over the boundless space between sea and sky.

To the miner, on the contrary, one day glides on like the other. Here he sits, with his lamp, far down in the black pit, and hammers the ore out of the rock: in semi-darkness he sits, body and mind. Sunday alone brings some change : he then puts on a better dress, goes to church, and sees the sun shine mildly into it, and feels it in his heart. Perhaps, also, he goes in the afternoon to Goslar, hears the newspapers read there, and thinks how strangely people struggle and strive in the world ; he will, perhaps, also, if he be still young, unbend himself, and play and be merry with the rest ; but on Monday he is again to be found sitting far down in the pit, and plying the hammer — and thus it goes on, until a strange hand strikes the last blow with the hammer on his coffin.

When we again ascended from the mine, the sun shone beautifully over the young pine-trees, where the rain-drops lay like pearls on the light green shoots. It seemed to me that

I had never seen anything more charming than these sunlit mountain sides and the clear sky — so great was the transition from the dark mine to the fair summer scene.

A narrow footpath led us round Goslar; high grass grew in the moat, and the thick city walls were almost hidden behind bushes and underwood. We then ascended "Der Zwinger," a large round tower dating from the emperors' time; the walls are twenty-two feet thick. In later times they had blown up the walls of the first story, and arranged habitable rooms in the wall itself. At the very top there was a large saloon, where the citizens of Goslar used to hold balls and festivities. A large spider had spun its web close by the door, and looked at me and a noisy fly that buzzed about my nose as I came in. I cannot say that this hexagon weaver was any beautiful object on the wall, yet if one view it poetically, it may serve for a picture to hang up in one's gallery of travels.

THE SPIDER.

Canst thou remember, pretty fly?
   Here were candles set in sconces;
   Minuets, and English dances,
Were danced in this room so high.

Great and small, and weak and strong,
   All whirled here, a merry crew;
   Whilst thou in eddying circles flew,
And wert prettiest of the throng.

Under the beam there, I sat still,
   My heart within me glowed the while;
   But now the dance, the jest, the smile,
Are o'er, and hushed the music's thrill.

The dance! it is thy greatest pleasure!
   I, a dancing-room have wrought,
   See, 'tis light as fancy's thought!
Wilt thou with me tread a measure?

Joy and festive mirth shall be
   Once more in this famous tower;
   Come, lively fly, come to my bower,
Thy partner, I will dance with thee!

The principal church in Goslar is a ruin; there is only a

chapel standing now, and in it vestiges of the church's former glories. An old woman conducted us over the chapel, and gave us an explanation of these treasures. Close to the door, inside, was a painting of St. Christopher, of a colossal size, where he stood in the water with the infant Jesus on his shoulders. "They were what one may call *men* at that time," said the old woman, who really believed that " der grosser Christoph " had actually been as tall and stout as he appeared here.

A female figure, formed of sandstone, lay in an open coffin; it is said to be that of the beautiful Matilda, a daughter of the Emperor Henry III. She was so handsome that her own father fell in love with her; therefore she prayed to God that he would at once make her very ugly. The devil then appeared to her, and promised that he would change her father's love to hate, if she would be his forever. She agreed to the contract, on condition that if he did not find her sleeping the first three times he came to her, she should then be free from him.

In order to keep herself awake, she took her needle and silk, and embroidered a costly robe, whilst her little dog Qvedl sat by her side. Every time she fell asleep, and the devil approached, the faithful dog barked, and she was again awake and actively at work. As the devil now saw himself duped, and obliged to fulfill his promise, he passed his ugly claw over her face, so that her beautiful arched brow was pressed down, and the royal nose made broad and flat : her little mouth he extended till it reached her ears, and he breathed on her beautiful eyes, so that they appeared like lead and mist. The Emperor was now disgusted with her; and she then built an abbey, which, after her faithful dog Qvedl, she called Qvedlingburg, where she herself was the first abbess.

The old woman who showed us this stone image knew not rightly if it were intended to represent her in her days of beauty, or in the following time, when the devil had laid his fingers on her : I was most inclined to the latter opinion.

The Emperor Henry III.'s pew has also a place here; his effigy, and those of the other two emperors, in the stained-glass windows, looked so fresh and life-like as the light played through the many colored paintings, that I was induced to sit down in the pew and regard them attentively.

There was an ancient inscription in the wall, which none of us could rightly decipher. "Yes," said my companion, "if my brother, the doctor, were only here, he would explain all that stands there to us! He is a learned man; yes," said she to me, "he is just as learned as you are!"

"Poor fellow!" thought I, but I did not say it.

In the evening I again went the same tour round the town, but I was not alone. It was moonlight; the streets were still, and the houses cast strong shadows. The water plashed monotonously in the large copper basin, and the old emperors stood seriously, with their hands on their swords, and looked forth into the moonlight. It seemed to me as if I stood in one of the enchanted cities, which when a child I had read of in many a fairy tale: the mountain mists that lay around the town appeared like a magic circle that encompassed it, and when the mists were dissipated, methought everything would again awake to its former life. There would then be mirth and noise again in the streets; the old emperors would step out from their places in the walls, and address the assembled people, who bent before the Madonna, as she sat in a halo of burning lamps. The sandstone image of the Princess Matilda would rise from its fragile coffin, and become flesh and blood, and her faithful dog Qvedl would again bark merrily, so that no one should fall asleep when the evil powers approached.

It was as if the monotonous plashing of the water murmured the powerful words of enchantment that could absolve the city from its magical transmutation, and I understood that mighty hieroglyphic, — "When thou hast slept, this will awake." And it was true; for when I sallied out into the street the next morning the sun shone brightly on the houses — which looked by no means spectral — and from the window opposite the smiling face of a girl peeped forth, which, better than thousands of printed proclamations, announced that no magical transmutation lay over old Goslar.

At the opera-house in Berlin they perform a ballet called "Die Neue Amazone," in which, amongst other scenes, there appears a vessel sailing down a river. The vessel itself rocks but does not proceed, but the scene behind glides continually forward over the stage, thus showing how the country changes as they sail along. When one has looked at it for some moments, it quite deceives the eye, and we imagine that we are sailing too. If the same experiment could be made here, you, my dear reader, should likewise see how the beautiful scenery changed as I wandered on.

Goslar now lay behind me; between the mountains the road led past a mill, where the merry journeyman was struggling in the doorway with a girl, to get a kiss.

A steep bank, where the yellow ochreous earth shone forth, rose close by, with the ruins of an old watch-tower. The prospect now became more extensive; Ockerdalen (the Ochre-dale), with its smelting-huts, lay around us. The black smoke curled in the air, and contrasted strangely with the blue-white mist about the mountains. The fierce red fire burnt within the huts, and the smelted ore ran down, like lava, with green and white flames, into a gutter over the floor.

A little path led us over field and meadow, into the green leafy wood, which, however, soon changed for the old dark pines. Round about were several springs of water, so that the earth in several places was a marsh, and my guide plumped in to the knees. We met several wandering students, in white travelling blouses, and with flowers in their caps: another party had three or four large dogs with them, and looked not unlike Carl Moor's troopers. The forest resounded with whistling and shouting; but I neither saw nor heard any birds in that large and quiet forest.

We came up with a wandering postman, who was going to Blankenburg; he told us that on this road, until within the last two years, there had been many "Spitzbuben" (knaves and robbers), and that even now it was not always safe at night; and strange enough it was, that as he told this, the forest at once became thicker, much darker, and consequently also far more solemn.

A thunder-cloud gathered over us, and the first discharge of heaven's artillery rolled between the mountains as we entered the village of Ilsenburg.

The baronial castle here is finely situated, but appeared somewhat ruinous. The nettles grew up high before the walls, whence the red fragments of stone had fallen down into the river.

The Brocken was quite enveloped in the large thunder-cloud, which darted its lightning down amongst the pine-trees; yet, after a rest of a few hours, I determined to ascend the mountain.

A fresh guide announced himself, the thunder was past, and we set off through the beautiful valley Ilsedal. "Beautiful!" How little does there not lie in the mere word? Yet the painter himself cannot, with his living colors, represent nature in all its greatness; how, then, should the poet be able to do it with words? No; could tones become corporeal; could we paint with tones, as with pen and ink, then we should be able to represent the spiritual, — that which seizes the heart when the bodily eye sees a new and wondrously charming scene of nature.

The river Ilse ran on with a stormy current by the side of our path; high pine covered mountains lay on both sides. The naked rock Ilsenstein, with a large iron cross on its highest point, rose perpendicularly in the air; it made one's neck ache to look up to this height; and yet when we stand on the Brocken the eye looks far down in search of it. The opposite side is a rocky wall of similar exterior; everything around indicates that these rocks, by some mighty convulsion of nature, have been riven asunder, thereby forming a bed for the river Ilse. In this mighty rock, says the legend, lives the beautiful Princess Ilse, who, with the first beams of the morning sun, rises from her couch, and bathes herself in the clear stream; happy is he who finds her here; but only few have seen her, for she fears the sight of man, though she is good and kind.

When the Deluge blotted out man from the earth, the waters of the Baltic also rose high, high up into Germany; the beautiful Ilse then fled, with her bridegroom, from the northern lands here toward the Hartz, where the Brocken seemed to offer them a retreat. At length they stood on this enormous rock, which projected far above the swelling sea; the surrounding lands were hidden under the waves; huts, human beings, and animals, had disappeared. Alone they stood, arm in arm, looking down on the waves as they broke against the rock. But the waters rose higher; in vain they sought an uncovered ridge of rock where they could ascend the Brocken, that lay like a large island amid the stormy sea. The rock on which they stood then trembled under them; an immense cleft opened itself there, and threatened to tear them away; still they held each other's hands; the side walls bent forward and backward; they fell together into the rushing flood. From her the river Ilse has obtained its name, and she still lives with her bridegroom within the flinty rock.

We proceeded further into the forest; the way began to wind upward toward the Brocken; the declining sun could not shine in between the thick pines; round about lay the huts of charcoal-burners, enveloped in a bluish smoke, so that the whole had a still, strange, and romantic character. It was a picture that attuned the soul to sadness.

THE CHARCOAL-BURNER.

Here between the forest pines
From the hut the red glare shines;
The coal-black smoke the roof ascends;
There the charcoal-burner bends.
Illumined by the fire's warm glow,
He looks half black — half crimson now;
Whilst he the glowing masses turns,
The fire brighter, deeper burns.

Leaning on his staff so long,
He chants aloud an ancient song:
"The pine-tree, year by year it grows,
Through summer's heat and winter's snows;
Like my own true love, I ween,
Always green, but darkly green!"
The song to him no comfort brings,
But the fire deepens, as he sings.

The road went more and more upward; round about lay enormous masses of rock. The river rushed over the large blocks, and formed a succession of water-falls. Sometimes the channel of the river was hemmed in between two narrow cliffs, where the black stream then boiled with a snow-white foam; sometimes it rushed on, broad and unchecked, between the fallen pines, and carried the large green branches with it.

As we continued to ascend, the bed of the river became

less — the stream diminished, as it were, to a spring; and at last we saw only the large water-drops that bubbled forth from the moss.

The Brocken gave me an idea of a northern tumulus, and that on a grand scale. Here stone lies piled on stone, and a strange silence rests over the whole. Not a bird twitters in the low pines; round about are white grave-flowers, growing in the high moss, and stones lie in masses on the sides of the mountain-top.

We were now on the top, but everything was in a mist. We stood in a cloud.

A choir of music sounded clearly from the inn up here. There were about forty travellers there; some of them had brought instruments with them, and were playing merrily from "Fra Diavolo," "Masaniello," and other popular pieces.

Three thousand five hundred feet above the level of the sea, in the midst of a cloud, but behind a five foot thick wall, — here I sat in a little room, and warmed myself by the hot stove. The mattresses of the bed were stuffed with sea-weed from Denmark: thus I could lie down to rest on Danish ground high aloft in the clouds.

The cows were driven home; they had bells on, and it sounded prettily; but out of doors everything was still in mist; it began to blow, and the wind drove the clouds onward over the mountain's top, as if they were flocks of sheep. Three ladies, with large hats on their heads, ran about and plucked the white Brocken-flowers. The clouds touched their legs, so that it looked like the witches' scene in "Macbeth."

There was a knock at my door, and in came the good school-master, with whom I had travelled from Brunswick; it seems, we were destined to meet on Bloxbjerg. In company with his old friend in Goslar, to whom he was on a visit, he had come up here two hours earlier than I, and had already made acquaintance with several of the travellers, who all, according to his account, were very genteel and polite persons. He was extremely happy, and showed me how many verses he had already written out of the books kept on the Brocken, and which he intended to take home.

It is well known that here, and in every other remarkable

place in Germany visited by strangers, a book is kept in which the travellers write their names, and sometimes a whole verse; and it was a selection of these that he had copied out.

There were a few drawings in the book; genius had shown itself in many ways: and how many have not here dreamed of immortality when they wrote their names! Now if all these be immortal, then I shall be so too; for I wrote mine.

The school-master presented me to his friend, but he did not please me at all; he appeared to me so still, and with such a say-nothing air about him, though I could see he endeavored to put some character into his face. He was one of those persons who, if he had been a doctor, and with this his usual mien when feeling a patient's pulse, had sat down and kept silence, one would have said, "He is thinking;" although I should have thought he had just made a pause in his thoughts.

We were, however, called out of doors, where the whole company were assembled. The musicians had taken their places on the top of the tower, and all the other travellers furnished themselves with broomsticks, fire-shovels, sticks, and what they could get: they invited us to take part in a great dance of witches in the declining twilight. One took the other by the hand — great and little, stout and thin, all joined in the mad-cap fun, and the merry intermezzo began:

THE INSTRUMENTS OF THE TOWER.

We are merry, merry, ho!
Each drums, and blows like a musical fellow;
Passing from "Fra Diavolo"
To the "Bride" and "Masaniello."

CHORUS.

Dolorem furca pellas ex;
   I've sung it in the heather!
I'm a witch, thou'rt a witch,
   We're witches all together!

THE ROCK.

Dance on! I lie here like a stone,
   And cannot share your game;
But when you've passed hence one by one,
   I still shall be the same.

THE ELVES.

We sit here behind the flower,
To see you dance at midnight hour!
What clowns are those upon the tower,
Making discord near our bower?

THE LOVER.

I am lifted the clouds above;
  For how deeply was I blest,
And wafted to the heaven of love,
  When her lips to mine were pressed!

CHORUS.

Dolorem furca pellas ex;
  I've sung it in the heather!
I'm a witch, thou'rt a witch,
  We're witches all together!

Toward midnight all was again still in the house.

The moon began to force her light through the mist, and cast her pale beams into the long narrow chamber. I could not sleep, and therefore ascended the tower to enjoy the prospect. Whoever has in his dreams soared over the earth, and seen lands, with towns and forests far below him, has a remote idea of this inconceivable magnificence. The pine covered mountains below me were of a pitchy darkness; white clouds, illumined by the moon, darted like spirits along the mountain's side. There was no boundary; the eye lost itself in an infinity; towns with their towers, charcoal-burners' huts, with their columns of smoke, all stood forth in the transparent veil of mist, which the moon illumined. It was Fancy's world of dreams that lay before me, full of life. In the times when might was right, many a knight with his esquire has lain here in the dark forests, lurking for the merchant as he bore his costly wares from city to city. Yonder, where not a trace now remains, on the lofty cliff, stood the baronial castle, with its high strong walls and lofty towers, and resounded with mirth in the long winter nights. The mists rose higher and higher between the dark mountains, the clouds assumed strange forms as they hurried on. There, thought I, there, in that wide circle grows the enchanted flower, the "Wunderbluhme," of the dwellers on the Hartz, which many a childish heart in its simplicity still seeks. Only one found it, but he himself knew it not before it was lost. I did not seek it here; I felt it growing in my heart; angels had sown the seed there when I still slumbered in the cradle — it grew, it extended its magic fragrance; *fancy*, this life's glorious flower, unfolded itself more in my heart, and I heard and saw a new and greater nature around me.

CHAPTER VI.

MORNING. — BAUMANN'S CAVE. — THE ANTIQUARY. — BLANK-
ENBURG.

IT was about half-past two when I was called up to see the sun rise; most of the visitors were already out of doors, wrapped up in cloaks and mantles. With handkerchiefs round their heads, there stood a motley group of persons from widely different places, all with one thought, — "The sun is now rising."

It appeared as if we stood on an island, for the clouds lay below us, as far as we could see, like a huge swelling ocean that had suddenly ceased to move. No red streak, as in the morning, showed in the blue heavens above; the sun rose without its rays, like a large ball of blood, and not until it was above the horizon did its clear light stream forth over the sea of clouds.

Our old school-master stood with clasped hands, and said not a word for a long time, but smiled with satisfaction. At length he exclaimed, "I wish I had mother and the children here; yes, and old Anne (their servant girl), it would please her to her heart's content; here is place enough for them all together. I always think of that when I see anything really fine. Here now is a good place for so many good friends, were they but here, so they also might have the good of it."

As the sun rose higher the light clouds began to evaporate — the ether, as it were, absorbed them, whilst the wind drove the heavier clouds down between the mountains, which now rose like islands in the great sea of clouds. Everything soon became clearer and clearer; we saw towns and church-towers, fields and meadows, — all appeared like the most charming miniature landscapes round about. So fine a morning there had not been that year on the Brocken. We could see Magdeburg, with its towers, quite distinctly; also Halberstadt and

Qvedlingburg, the towers of the high cathedral at Erfurt, the mountain palaces Die Gleichen, and Wilhelmshöhe, near Cassel, besides a throng of lesser places and villages round about.

I clambered up to the so-called witches' altar, and the "Teufelskanzel," ten feet in height, drank of the ice-cold water which streams from the witches' well, gathered a Brocken bouquet, which the girl fixed in my cap, and bade farewell to my new acquaintances, particularly to the good old schoolmaster, who seemed so well pleased with the whole company here, that he begged me and them to write in his scrap-book, that he might show them at home all the names of the kind good persons he had met here. We almost all wrote in it; mine was the only Danish name — and then we parted.

I had joined a family from Hamburg. The guide went on before, the caravan followed step for step, and the little ass which bore the baggage closed the troop. We had each of us got a green branch in our hands, with which we drove our slow-paced Pegasus, who now and then seemed disposed to make himself too comfortable. Sometimes the road led through the thick forest, sometimes by the edge of the rock, when we saw the lesser mountains, far below, with their dark pines: they appeared like hills where some one had planted potatoes, which raised their low green tops in the air. The strange light veil that lay over the whole scene beneath us looked as if it were a large green glass through which one saw the whole magnificent scenery. The mist stood as if pressed together in a cloud between the narrow rocky walls; one could not see the objects below it, and yet it lay so light and airy that the eye felt it must be fine as the air itself.

The birds began to sing, the dew lay in clear drops on the flowers, and the sun shone on the great and glorious landscape before us. How beautiful the world is! what endless grandeur, from the smallest flower with its fragrance, to my heart with its flaming thoughts, and again from that to the great globe, with its glorious mountains and the swelling seas!

What cares the heart about what the flower dreams, whilst it expands its odors so sweetly powerful in the morning dew? — there is something far greater, something far more important, that sets it in motion. What cares the world about the longings of a single heart, and the flower's fragrance?— mightier passions, the combats and destruction of a whole people, revolutions in nature, and the life of man, are its dreams and thoughts.

At Elbingerode, a little mountain town, I bade farewell to my fellow-travellers.

The naked rocks soon rose on both sides of a narrow path that wound along by the small river. I was in Rübeland, a name derived from "Räuberland," because, in olden times, there stood a robber's castle here on one of the cliffs, which has now almost entirely disappeared, the moat and part of the walls alone remaining.

On the other side of Rübeland — a village so called — a little mountain-path led up to the recess in the rock, where one enters Baumann's cave. Here I found two other travellers; each of us got a lighted lamp, the guide went on before, and we entered this petrified world of fancy.

The entrance was through an aperture that looked as if the foxes had dug it: we could not walk erect. It was as if we had entered the ruins of an old castle's cellar, where the walls had half fallen down. The water-drops fell with a monotonous plashing: otherwise, all was still as death. We descended the wet paths, as well as we could, lamp in hand. Round about, above, and below us, it was pitchy dark; the lamp-light showed us only the narrow paths, which seemed as if they would never end. The strange uncertainty of not knowing how deep it was below us, made it far more terrible than it really was. If we only held fast; only took care to step to the right side, first with the left, and then with the right leg; and if only the ladder did not break — or else we might break our necks — there was no danger: this was the continued assurance given us by our guide.

How unilateral men are, in fact, in the full signification of the word! We see daily the greatest precipices above us, and for a circumference of miles around us, but none of these causes us any anxiety; on the other hand, the far less precipice, when it goes downward, causes us to be giddy. Downward! — that is a side of which we all stand in dread; and yet we must all go downward — there we first find peace and rest.

From cavern to cavern, we descended deeper and deeper; it was sometimes so low and narrow that we were obliged to go singly, in a stooping position, under the overhanging masses of limestone: sometimes it was so high and wide that the light of our lamps would not reach the side walls.

We were shown six different divisions; but besides these, there was a vast number of lesser caverns, all of which have have not been explored: they probably are connected with Biel's cave, and even extend deep under the Hartz.

These deep, dark abysses yawned round about, and the most singular stalactites hung around in clusters; yet they did not all resemble the objects which the guide informed us they did. I think I possess some imagination, but I could not, nevertheless, agree with him. There were, besides, thousands of things he did not point out, in which there was far more significance. An organ, the canopy of a throne, and a banner, which the dripping stones had shaped into these forms, were the three figures that most resembled those objects; but I will not say anything against this powerful fancy of nature. Everything that one particularly admires here, is but an imitation of what shows itself more perfectly in nature. The original stalactites, to which one does not find anything similar, I should also imagine are interesting; they appeared to me as significant hieroglyphics that held the key to the greatest secrets of nature.

A well of clear water bubbled forth at our feet; we drank of the pure crystal. One of the travellers found the bone of an animal, which he regarded with much attention, and then assured us that it must certainly be the remains of an ancient animal. I had nothing to object to this supposition, for it looked very much like the bone of a cow; and cows are an old race.

The cavern has received its name from its discoverer. A miner named Baumann was the first who visited it, in 1670, to look for ore; he found nothing, and prepared, therefore, to return, but he could not find the outlet. Two days and nights he crept about, before he discovered it; but he was then so exhausted in mind and body, so affected by anxiety and hunger, that he died shortly afterward, yet not before he had informed his friends of the strange and wonderful structure of the interior of the cavern.

The fate and feelings of the unfortunate miner, Baumann, made such an impression on me here, in this labyrinth of caverns and gulfs, that my heart beat faster; I saw what he must have felt here, alone, given up to terror and death by hunger. Only when I saw the clear daylight, and the blue sky, did I again feel myself well, and amongst the living. It was as if I had awakened from a horrible dream, and as if all the strange, deformed, terrifying images lay petrified behind me: the sun again shone into my eyes and heart.

The antiquary whose acquaintance I had made in the cavern determined on going to Qvedlingburg the same evening; and as his way lay over Blankenburg, we became travelling companions. He knew a path across the fields that would spare us a couple of miles' circuit; we therefore climbed up the cliff, which here was only so high that it projected over a mill that lay beneath, and where the water rushed over the large wheel. He was a very good-natured man, whose life's happiness hung on an old coin. He took his cow-bone out every moment, and assured me that it must have been that of one of the Huns. No landscape, he confessed to me, had that smiling, that spiritual beauty in it, which was to be discerned in such an antiquity. He asked me if we also collected antique remains in Denmark? I was obliged to tell him what I knew; and when I began to speak about our barrows,[1] and sacrificial altars, whereof one sees none in Germany, he began to feel a real respect for my country, and regarded me as happy in living in this *saga* land. At last, he *would* have me with him to

[1] The barrows, or tumuli, are still numerous in many parts of Denmark, though many have been dug up and explored by members of "The Society for the Preservation of Northern Antiquities." Rich treasures have often been found, all of which are in the museum, which contains a very rich collection, consisting of many thousands of objects worthy the attention of the archæologist. By a decree of the state, it is ordered that all relics of antiquity found in digging, ploughing, or otherwise, shall be sent to "The Museum of Northern Antiquities," the finders receiving the full value of the articles found, be they coins, gold or silver ornaments, arms, dresses, or other relics; and this order has in almost every instance been complied with, so that the national collection has been considerably enriched, and continues to augment every year. The museum is in Copenhagen, in one of the wings of the palace of Christiansborg, and is open to the public three days in the week during the year.—*Translator.*

Qvedlingburg, to see the palace, the old churches, and all the many curiosities there.

Only think! — there was still one of the six jars in which Christ had changed the water into wine at the marriage in Cana; a piece of the finger of John, with which he had pointed at Christ; a bottle of Mother Mary's own milk; earth from Golgotha; a piece of our Saviour's cross, etc, etc.; and what was particularly remarkable, the comb that Heinrich the bird-catcher had used to comb his beard with. Yet all these well authenticated (?) relics did not tempt me; my longing was for majestic nature.

I arrived at Blankenburg, and asked at the gate of the city for the names of the best inns; they mentioned, amongst others, "Der Weisse Adler" (the White Eagle), and I chose that, because the eagle was Jupiter's and Napoleon's bird; an inviting sign, but which the innkeeper had scarcely thought of when he had it painted over his door. I got a room with a very picturesque prospect. Directly opposite, I had for neighbors two students, with red Greek caps and Scotch dressing-gowns. Large folios lay on the table, and the persons themselves lolled out of the window, with their long pipes, whilst the old castle of Blankenburg, built on a mountain, rose, high above the roofs of the houses, which lay like a foreground to this fine theatrical decoration.

CHAPTER VII.

THE RUINS OF REGENSTEIN. — THE TAILOR'S WIFE. — ROSZ-TRAPPE. — A TOUR TO ALEXIS BATHS.

AT four o'clock in the morning we were again on foot ; our Brocken bouquets still sat quite fresh in our "mützer" (caps), a female guide was in waiting for us, and thus we, six *studiosi*, set off from the town to the ruins of the old mountain castle of Regenstein, situated close to Blankenburg. The fields were covered with dew — it was the powerful sunlight that caused the eyes of the flowers and grass to fill with water. We passed through an avenue of cherry-trees, hopped over the wet field, and each sung his own song. The birds took example by us, so that the whole neighborhood resounded with the songs of students and the warbling of birds.

We now ascended the cliff, the topmost part of which forms the ruins of the castle of Regenstein ; the walls have disappeared, but all that is hewed out in the rock itself stands like a mighty gigantic mummy, and tells of olden times, though it cannot speak a word. It had such an imposing appearance, it was so great, that I was not myself rightly aware of it before the pencil moved in my hand, and traced the colossal image off in my note-book. I became a draughtsman without ever having had an hour's instruction in the art. The fields lay far below, like beds in a kitchen-garden ; the farmer behind his plough was like a snail in his shell, creeping along the ground. The church, which is hollowed in the rock, will remain firm for centuries, though it is only a large cave without form. The chambers, where there had been dormitories, are only recesses in the rock, where the large masses of stone project above the head ; we threw stones into the deep well, and had almost left the place ere we heard that they had reached the bottom.

"If the stones here could speak," said I, "what would

they not be able to tell us about all that has happened from the time when 'Heinrich the bird-catcher' founded the castle, until I came from Denmark and saw its ruins; then we might be able to contribute to Wallenstein's history, and to the Thirty Years' War; then we should certainly hear fine stories about the Seven Years' War, and I might get an idea for one or other chivalric poem."

As I said this, the flowers round about nodded their large heads, and looked so proud and stupid as they did so! just as if they would say, "Yes, you are right! if we were to speak we could then tell you something!" And yet they knew nothing; they were all of that year's growth, — all shot up with their stems that same spring.

We took our seats on the topmost point of the rock, which forms the ceiling of the church, and looked out into the wide world, well pleased with all around us. Beneath us masses had been chanted centuries ago, and the lamps burnt around the Madonna's sainted image; here we now sat like profane birds, but yet without thinking there was anything wrong in it, and sung opera songs, and made witticisms, as well as we could. I was obliged to tell about Denmark and the sea, — the sea, which that glorious mountain-land here knows nothing of: but how shall one describe the sea to those who have never seen it? I knew nothing better to liken it to than the great blue sky: if one could stretch it out over the flat fields to the boundaries of the horizon, it would then be a sea. It appeared as if they understood this picture.

It seemed as though I imbibed, with eye and thought, the wide prospect from the ruins of the old mountain castle. I looked down into the abyss, and shut my eyes when I had done so, as if to try whether I had conceived the whole depth, but when I again opened my eyes and looked down, it was far deeper than I had represented to myself; the extent on all sides round about was far greater than the moment's memory could embrace.

I went through the whole picture that thought had drawn, and then compared it with the reality. Towns and hamlets then rose round about in the vast extent; mountains with their woods, Blankenburg with its castle; and even the small biped and quadruped figures far below us then came forth more strongly. Regenstein itself, with its narrow chambers, its broken walls, and stairs that only led from the free air up into the same element, got, as a picture by itself, its own place in my memory's pantheon. Every ruin stands, however, as a bodily, gigantic epos, that carries us ages back, to other men and other customs; the higher the grass grows in the knight's hall, the slower the river glides over the fallen columns, and so much the greater poesy does the heart find in this stone epos. Time will come when the ruin will quite disappear; even the last trace of Regenstein's hewed rocks will moulder away and fall down; but then the legend about the place will still live, as the remembrance of many a work of the ancients that has entirely disappeared, still endures.

We bade adieu to the old castle, and turned down a little path between the cliffs, overgrown with brushwood, which brought us back to Blankenburg; whence we, part of the way, followed the main road, planted on each side with yellow roses, then in bloom.

Our female guide, with whom we shared our breakfast, became garrulous, and now told us about her domestic happiness and misery. Her husband cultivated the art of man-making — or, in other words, the profession of a tailor: but he was born to something higher than the board on which he sat. Two years before our coming there had been an execution in the neighborhood; it had awakened his slumbering abilities: he had become a poet, had written the murderer's whole life and death in mournful verse, which was penned as if it were the criminal himself who sang it during his last night, and was set to the air of, "A bridal wreath we bind for thee." "However, he gained four dollars by that," said the woman, "and last year two, for some verses over a midwife who was drowned in a horse-pond. Versemaking brings in more than the needle, but it has made him so unreasonable, and so fond of tears! Now there is nothing more to write about, and he does not care to use the needle; so that it would look bad enough, if I didn't gain something by showing travellers about. There," she exclaimed, interrupting herself as she pointed over the fields to the left, — "there lies '*The Devil's Wall*,' which he built at the time when he and our Lord disputed about the mastery of the world."

There, sure enough, rose by the side of us that strangely formed mountain-ridge which looks like the ruins of an immense intrenchment, and extends to a considerable distance. But the eye can follow it. The legend says that Satan was not satisfied with having got the mastery over half the earth, but that he renewed the dispute, for which reason he lost it entirely, and his proud barrier was hurled down: others relate that it was erected by the wicked spirits, as a wall against Christ's doctrines, that they should not be extended farther; but the stones were compelled to break before the living word.

As I further questioned the tailor's wife, if it were not possible to learn the noble art of versifying, she informed me in confidence that her husband had an old German psalm-book, out of which he took many pieces, and all of the best rhyme; therefore all his songs had something spiritual in them, which made them so affecting.

We now left the high-road, and passed over fields and meadows into the green leafy woods. I have never heard so many nightingales as here. The sun was high in the heavens, yet they did not seem to observe it within the thick bushes. God knows how it is people say about this bird's song, that there is desire and complaint in it; no, it is anything but that; the nightingale has quite the Italian manner; its note consists mostly of trills, and runs with the voice; it does not complain at all; it sings its proud bravura airs in fullest strains. There is something far deeper and more solemn in the song of the thrush: it whistles for us a northern ballad, simple, but touching, when it sits, in the morning hour, on the moss-grown cairn at home, in Denmark.

A wider prospect soon opened to our view; the beautiful Thale-dale lay before us with its wide extent: we should now ascend the mountains, and therefore rested first to gather strength. It was "Berg auf" (up the mountain); we were quite exhausted, whilst two white butterflies, that followed us the whole way up in a fluttering circular dance, seemed to mock us weak children of men. Arrived at the top, we took leave of our female guide, and got a male guide instead, who lived up here. He took his pistol; and after having tasted his "birchen wasser," which effervesces like champagne, we followed him to the so-called Rosztrappe,[1] the wildest, the most romantic point in the whole Hartz.

The high rocks go perpendicularly down into the deep abyss. We look upon a great and glorious mountain scene, where rock rises upon rock with gloomy pine forests; and in the deep, by looking into which one becomes giddy, there rushes the river Bode. We saw a crowd of travellers below, but they appeared like flowers in a garden-bed. The bridge over the river was like a plaything formed of a single willow branch. Our guide fired his pistol, and its echo resounded like the loudest thunder. We were shown a deep indentation in the rock, which had the appearance of a colossal horse-shoe and from which the place takes its name.

The little boy who accompanied the guide drank some of the rain-water that had collected there, from the hollow of his hand, whilst fancy showed him, perhaps clearer than us, the legend about the fugitive princess, the beautiful Emma of Reisengebirge. In time he will succeed his father in his office as guide, and also quietly relate how there — many thousand years since — lived giants and wizards here, who tore up the ancient oaks on the mountains, and used them as clubs with which they murdered women and children. He will tell about great Bodo, who loved the beautiful Emma, and pursued her hither, where she made her horse spring over; but then he will not, as now, himself see that great glorious picture with childish fancy's colors. He now sees her with the heavy gold crown and fluttering dress, flying with her horse from mountain to mountain, from rock to rock, through valley and forest, and the wild Bodo behind, — the fire-sparks fly from the stony rocks and shine round about in the valleys. Now she is here by the precipice; she sees the deep before her, where the river rushes frothing on over fragments of rock, and yet the opposite point of rock appears more distant from her than this immense depth. She hears Bodo's horse behind, and in dread desperation she calls on the Eter-

[1] The Horse-stairs.

nal to protect her, strikes the sharp spurs into the sides of her steed, who sets his foot so firmly on the rock that its impress stands for centuries. With one spring she bounds over the deep abyss — and is saved; the golden crown alone falls from her head into the deep, whirling stream, where the wild Bodo follows, and lies crushed on the flinty cliffs.

All these dreams of fancy will vanish: the little boy will also, like the father, stand quietly and fire his pistol off, and perhaps calculate how great his receipts may be to-day from the travellers. Dreams are, however, flowers; there are good and bad! Flowers must decay, but there will come new ones from the old stem! The princess with the golden crown and flying horse will also hurry past the new throng of children; they will also look with fixed eyes, as the little boy now does, into the river Bode, and think they see the yellow gold shining through the water once so great and deep that a diver went down before the assembled people and found the golden crown, which he raised so high that they saw the points above the surface. It was large and heavy; twice it fell from his hands; they shouted to him that he should once more descend to the bottom, and he did so. A stream of blood shot up through the water: they never saw him or the golden crown more.

Here I left the merry students, and went further on into the great and beautiful world. Close under the cliff lay Blechhütterne, which I must pass, consequently I required no guide. They waved their hats and handkerchiefs when they saw me half way down, as a farewell token: it was strange to receive their "Live well" thus, certainly the last in this life, — for how should we all be again assembled in this world? There lies something very interesting in this: to meet, to know, and then to part forever!

I was soon under Rosztrappe: the river Bode rushed on before me over the great stones, and on the other side the highway ran past the red-roofed houses; but I saw no bridge. Over I must go, but how? I ran along by the river side, but as far as I could see on both sides there was no passage over, except by wading, or springing from stone to stone. I chose the latter course, but got no farther than the middle, where the current foamed on both sides of the large stone block on which I stood.

When I reached Blechhütterne, and approached the inn, I thought that a hostile army had taken up their quarters there; there was as much noise as if the chairs and tables had all been thrown down and broken. I entered the large room, and found that the whole invading host consisted of — four students from Jena. They were in complete sporting dresses, and had each a green oak wreath around his head, with hair hanging down in long locks over the white embroidered shirt-collar. They sang most lustily, and drummed on the table with the bottles, so that the glasses and plates danced again. They appeared very good-natured, and made a pause in their musical exercise as I entered. We soon got into conversation together; they had resolved upon making a journey to the Brocken, and had wandered on foot from Jena.

When they heard that I was a Dane, and a student, they put many questions to me: they asked me if we had no "Burschenschaften," and what color I bore; and when I assured them that we knew nothing of the kind, they showed me their caps, and told me that they bore Sand's color. Did I know Sand? — and their eyes sparkled as they told me what a brave and glorious man he had been. They were children when he was executed, but they remembered him well, and recollected when his head fell under the sword of the executioner.

Their ideas about Denmark were, however, very imperfect. Thus, they thought that the lower classes alone spoke the Danish language, and that French was the language of the court and the well-informed classes of the community.

When I mentioned the name of Oehlenschläger, they asked me if we had any of his works translated. I answered that we had them in the original; and they were not a little astonished to hear that he was a Dane, that he lived in Denmark, and wrote there. I had to describe to them his appearance, to tell them about him and his works; and when they heard that I was personally acquainted with the poet, and that he was at that time in Germany, they looked quite kindly on me; and when we separated, one of them presented me his oak wreath, which he took off his head and set on my cap, probably for Oehlenschläger's sake.

My way was now to Gernrode; but if a travelling female harpist had not taken the peaceful wanderer under her guidance, I should have lost my way in the green forest. I asked her if she were not from Reisengebirge, but she was from another part, and not at all related to Lafontaine. When she had brought me into the right road, she sat down on a stone under a large hazel-bush, and played a piece for me into the bargain; and then we parted, she with her harp on her back, and I with the harp in my heart, both with the intention of singing for the world.

Woods and meadows varied the scene: I saw the ruins of an old castle through the trees, and above the high bushes in which it lay embosomed; it looked very frail, and yet it was a great ornament on account of its decayed state. It was as if Ossian meant this place when he sang, "The thistle shook there its lonely head: the moss whistled to the wind. The fox looked out from the windows; the rank grass of the wall waved round its head." It was the last remains of the castle of Lauenborg.

Gernrode is a little quiet village. I saw scarcely a soul in the street, but the window of a small house stood open, and I heard a female voice sing prettily of love. I listened, and as the invisible one did not appear, I took the oak wreath from my cap — which the student had placed there — and after having taken off one of the leaves, I laid it by her door as "thanks for the song," and wandered out of the place.

The road went up the steep side of a mountain: the clayey, yellow earth contrasted strongly with the violet-blue sky. Some old women and ragged children came down the mountain with burdens of sticks they had gathered in the forest. I sat down and wrote in my note-book; a bee hummed in a flower close by me; and thus all the figures in that picture were occupied.

As I approached Mägdesprung, the sun went down; it was quite twilight on the way between the sides of the mountains, but the light fell so much the stronger on the tops of the trees, which cast long, dark shadows. I here overtook two school-boys whom I had seen on the Brocken. One was from Berlin, and the other from Magdeburg; they had during the vacation fluttered about the wide world and enjoyed the romantic scenery.

We also met a trooper on the high-road, who looked as if he had just sprung forth alive from some robber story; but he did nothing to us, as he found we were so strong a body! — nor did we do anything to him, so that politeness was preserved.

We soon saw the black iron cross on the cliff above us, whence, as the legend says, a young girl threw herself when her princely lover pursued her; yet she did not meet her death here, for God caused the wind to bear her gently down where the wild brambles grow between the rocks. Whether the place takes its name, Mägdesprung,[1] from this legend or not, I cannot say. Ottomar tells us that two giant girls played here on the steep ridge of the mountain; the one hopped over the great abyss where the road now passes, but the other thought that such a jump required some consideration: she tarried awhile, but then made the spring, so that there was the impress of her foot in the stone she stood on. A peasant, ploughing in the valley, saw it, and laughed at the great lady; when she took him up in her apron, together with his oxen and plough, and carried him home with her to the mountain.

It is not alone the immense masses of rock with their forests, which exceed the range of vision, the tall bushes that bent over the foaming river, nor the dead stone masses of a half-ruined building, that make a country romantic; it is when the place has, by this its particular character, one or other legend connected with it, that the whole gets its perfect magic light, which raises it in the mind's eye. The dead masses then become animated; it is no longer an empty decoration; there is action. Every leaf, every flower then stands as a speaking bird, and the well as a singing fountain, which strikes its eternally murmuring chords to the spirit's melodrama.

The country round about became doubly beautiful to me on account of its legend; there was likewise life and motion

[1] The Maiden's Leap.

on the road. We met some charcoal-burners with dark, characteristic faces, and peasant girls who looked like milk and blood. The river Silke rushed noisily past; it certainly related what we saw so well that the whole was very agreeable.

We soon heard the noise of the numerous workshops. We ascended to that remarkable iron obelisk which the Duke of Brunswick erected, in 1812, to his deceased father's memory. It is entirely of iron, and is said to be the highest in all Germany. We wrote our names on it with pencil, as many others had done before us.

"To become immortal," is a thought which, even in the most childish, shines forth from the poor human breast!

The rain and snow will soon obliterate these pencil marks of immortality, and a new race will write their names instead, till the obelisk itself be obliterated by time. Thus we also seek, through life's pilgrimage, to write our names on the world's great obelisk, where the one name must make way for the other, until this great writing-slate itself goes to rubbish. God knows what name will stand as the last! Probably the architect's, who raised it to his own honor, and the improvement of the whole.

No guests had yet arrived at Alexis Baths, as they generally make their first appearance in the warm summer months. The well here was in a temple-shaped building, into which one descended by a flight of broad stairs. There sat a young girl with her clay pitcher — she was Rachel at the well; and the man who handed us the water was what we in Denmark call a long Laban. The school-boys and I stood like thirsty camels, tired with the day's heat and wandering, so that we altogether formed a complete Biblical picture.

CHAPTER VIII.

PICTURES ON WANDERING TO EISLEBEN. — MARTIN LUTHER.

TO be in a strange haste with everything, is, in reality, my chief characteristic! The more interesting a book is, the more do I hasten to read it through, that I may at once get the whole impression of it: even in my travels it is not that which is present that pleases me; I hasten after something new, in order to come to something else. Every night when I lie down to rest, I hanker after the next day, wish that it was here, and, when it comes, it is still a distant future that occupies me. Death itself has in it something interesting to me — something glorious, because a new world will then be opened to me. What can it in reality be that my uneasy self hastens after?

Fresh with life, and glorious, stood Nature's vernal green around us, and breathed gladness and quiet, whilst there lay, as it were, a dark veil over my heart; yet, thought I, why envy the fresh variegated flowers? Let them exhale their perfume, they will in a few months be withered: the well that now bubbles so merrily, passes away into the sea; and the sea itself, that swells so in its greatness, will evaporate. Let the sun play with his hot beams; he also, — the heavens, — will grow old as a garment, when my heart, which now melts with sadness over its own dreams, will exult in its ascending flight toward infinity!

This morning I had no quiet in my mind. I left Hartzgerode, — one picture made way for another. One of them will certainly appear very insignificant to many, and yet it stands just as lively before me as the view from the Brocken and Rosztrappe — nay almost more so — and it was about four miles [1] from this latter place.

[1] The distances are here given in English miles. — *Translator.*

At Klaus, a little hamlet which consists of, I believe, three or four houses, I went into the inn, one of the three or four. Everything here was exceedingly picturesque, but yet quite of the Dutch school, so much so that I would rather have wished to see it on the canvas. A young kitten rolled itself about before my legs; two cock chickens were fighting on the floor; and the servant girl — who was very pretty, dressed in full peasant's costume and full of ruddy health — reached me a glass of milk with supreme indifference, as though she were performing an act of charity; and then heeded me so little, that she stepped up to the glass and made her toilet, loosened her long hair, and let it fall down over her shoulders and back. I see this picture still, and wish that you, dear reader, could see it too, for it was not so bad.

I went on for one, two, three hours, without meeting a soul. Sometimes the road was as broad as ten others; sometimes so narrow that only one wagon could go upon it. I began to be quite bewildered, and therefore asked two respectable-looking beeches, that seemed to look like fellow-countrymen, about the way, but they only shook their tops, and knew nothing about it.

The path led me to a little village, where, on a great open space before a house, there was dancing and merriment. The dancers were young half-grown girls, who waltzed with each other to the tones of a violin, played by an old bow-legged Orpheus. The mothers, and all the oldest women of the place, sat on benches round about, their hands resting on their laps, and looking at the dancers without noticing the stranger who stood close by. The eldest there, with a little black cap on her gray hair, thought perhaps of her blooming youth, when she also jumped about to the violin under the blue sky. Now these springings were past; yes, the best dancer probably died long ago, and sleeps under the cool turf.

But picture after picture tires; even the child becomes wearied of turning over the most varied picture-book, therefore we will not for the present look at more, although the next was extremely interesting. I should like to describe the picturesque town of Leimbach, which lay close by in the valley, almost enveloped in smoke, and hid behind the high banks of black dross. I should like to show the steep ravine which almost went precipitously down toward the church-tower, yet where, however, a large carrier's wagon with four horses was toiling slowly upward; but as I have said, it might be tedious. This time I will relate my story quite in the common way, that the reader and I may both rest ourselves.

"Leimbach is an open middling town with about seven hundred inhabitants, smelting furnaces, silver refiners, town-hall," etc. etc.

We will take the next place in the same way — it is very convenient! "Mansfeldt, half a mile from Leimbach, has above sixteen hundred inhabitants and an inn: '*Zum Braunen Hirsch*' (The Brown Stag)."

Now I have rested! I know not if the reader has. We are, however, near Eisleben.

> Here, the high green hills between,
>   The little town arises proud,
> The sun now casts his brightest sheen
>   Athwart yon brown-tinged summer cloud;
> It shines upon the lofty spire,
>   While the bells ring clear and strong,
> And in the street, in best attire,
>   The people stand, a silent throng.
> The monks with song, and flag unfurled,
>   March through the town with solemn **pace;**
> Stern censors of their little world:
>   Is't fast or festival they grace?
> See yonder men on prancing steeds,
>   The Bishop and the Duke are they;
> Famed far and near for noble deeds,
>   And they're the townsmen's guests **to-day.**
> On the ramparts, there they throng,
>   By the gate, a motley crowd
> Of men and women, old and young,
>   Who stand, or sit, or talk aloud.
> See, a miner quiet stands,
>   With his wife, the crowd among;
> Their little boy holds by their hands,
>   His flaxen hair is fine and long.
> In mute surprise to see their lord,
>   His eyes are fixed, with childish stare;
> The bishop's robe, and Prince's sword,
>   Please him most of all things there.

The boy stands bound, as by a spell,
  His thoughts now hither, thither flee.
Those who beyond the mountain dwell
  Here have come, this sight to see,

Here, the high green hills between,
  The little town arises proud;
The sun now casts his brightest sheen,
  Athwart you brown-tinged summer cloud;
It shines upon the lofty spire;
  But all is silent now, and drear,
No Bishop, Duke, nor lordly squire,
  Makes his stately entry here,
How strangely doth the fancy grant
  Images that woo belief!
What here do I or others want? —
  Is't to see the princely chief?
The Bishop's robe, and Prince's sword,
  In rot and rust have passed away;
And we who journeyed hitherward,
  See but a desert place to-day.
Narrow is the little street,
  'Tis silent, as if all were dead:
Here, where trod the miner's feet,
  His little son was born and bred.
Duke and Bishop are forgot,
  The ramparts are a heap of clay;
Yet everything around this spot
  Recalls to mind that glorious day.

The town had in it something extremely pleasing. A little boy played outside the old church, and drew figures on the large stones; perhaps they were also Luther's writing-slates, when he played here. The town-hall has an angular, gloomy appearance, like the age in which he lived; it was probably the same in his time, as now. The house where he was born has, on the contrary, undergone great changes since then. It is now used as a school. On a window of painted glass, stand Luther and Melancthon; and over the door, around an illuminated bass-relief, with Luther's portrait, we read, —

"Gottes werck es Luthers Lehr,
  Darum weyht sie nimmer mehr!"[1]

[1] These are what Luther taught — God's works and word;
Therefore his doctrine lives, as doth the Lord.

There stood an old peasant, with his wife, in the street; he spelt the verse for her, and I could see on their faces what a mass of deep and glorious poesy there was for them in every word, for their looks cleared up surprisingly; and when he uttered the last word, it was as if he had spoken the revelation of an angel, and they believed it.

"Luther!" says Jean Paul, "thou resemblest the fall of the Rhine! How mightily dost thou storm and thunder. But as the rainbow hovers immovably on its stream, so rests also the bow of grace, peace with God and man, in thy breast: thou shakest only thy earth, but not thy heaven!"

This is poetically fine; but yet there lay something in the tone and the expression with which the old man said to his wife, of Luther, "*That was a man!*" — something far greater, more just and sublime. I believe that Jean Paul himself would have said the same thing if he had heard the old man.

Luther! — "*That was a man!*" — therefore he broke the yoke of popedom, and therefore he sang, —

"Wer nicht liebt Wein, Weiber und Gesang,
Der bleibt ein Narr sein Leben lang!"[1]

Therefore he threw the inkstand at the head of the Prince of Darkness; for, as a German poet (I think it is Börne) says: "Writing-ink and printing-ink are the best weapons to use against the Devil; they will in time chase him entirely from the world."

[1] He who loves not wine, women, and song,
Will be a fool his whole life long.

CHAPTER IX.

A JOURNEY THROUGH HALLE AND MERSEBURG TO LEIPSIC. — THE BLIND MOTHER. — ST. NICHOLAS CHURCH. — GELLERT'S GRAVE. — AUERBACH CELLAR.

IT was midnight when I rolled out of old Eisleben — in the Saxon, "Eilwagen," the quick post. The first green vine hills greeted me with the rising sun. The postilion played one fine piece after another. We passed two large lakes, and the green mountains and the red clouds were reflected on their quiet surface. There stood, also, an old baronial castle, with angles and towers, high walls, and ditches. Here was a glorious echo: we halted for a moment; the postilion blew his horn, and the mountains reëchoed almost the whole piece. I have never heard so many tones repeated by an echo, nor shall I ever forget that beautiful morning; but then it is set to music in my memory's picture-gallery. The postilion and the echo gave to the whole neighborhood a higher sense of beauty, whereby it is probable that the learned city of Halle afterward lost in my estimation — it appeared to me so narrow, so uncomfortable. The river Saale was a dirty yellow water; and the streets, — some, at least, — I think, were not paved.

The road to Merseburg was planted with cherry-trees; the town itself is dark and narrow, like Halle, but yet worth a visit, on account of its old Gothic cathedral.

They told me a popular tradition here — quite a history *à la "Gazza Ladra."* A bishop had caused an innocent servant of his to be executed; but as he afterward discovered that a favorite raven was the thief, he became melancholy, had the bird imprisoned in an iron cage, and exposed to mockery and abuse. Nay, he even invested a sum of money, that the Council of Merseburg should forever be in possession of a raven, and that it should be taught to cry out the servant's name, "Jacob!" So that, as soon as a raven dies, it happens, as it does on the death of a pope — a council is immediately convened, and another chosen.

I was told, though I could not find it, that such a poor innocent bird was then sitting imprisoned, and cried "Jacob!" without dreaming why it had free board and lodging, and, perhaps, without being related to the episcopal thief to whose infamous memory the legacy was founded.

We now left the town of Merseburg for the German library, Leipsic. The country round about looked quite Danish; here was still a woody district; afterward everything was lost in an immense plain, which human blood has terribly immortalized.

THE BLIND MOTHER.

"The drum is beating, they are near!
    The banners whistle in the breeze."
"Mother, 'tis the wind that here
    Rushes through the forest trees."
"Hearest thou not the horses' tread?
    The wagons follow close each other."
"The road it passes through this mead;
    They're travellers thou hear'st, my mother!"

"Silence, child! they near our post:
    'Tis not the trees i' the wind that mourn.
Seest thou not the imperial host?
    Thy father's pennon's proudly borne.
No, 'tis not the night's harsh blast,
    Nor stranger men that travel; for
On his steed, before his host,
    There rides the mighty Emperor!

" Before my eyes 'tis dark and dreary,
    But yet I know him in the gloom;
Child, I feel myself so weary, —
    Fold my old hands for the tomb!
The banner whistles in the breeze,
    Mildly thy father beckons now;
O set me, child, by yonder trees,
    For death, I feel, is on my brow!"

It was a strange feeling that seized me as I drove over the great, extended plain of Leipsic, where every village is so remarkable in the history of the wars. Here Napoleon had been — here that great General had thought and felt. The corn waved luxuriantly over the immense battle-field; no wound heals so easily as that of Nature's. One spring alone is sufficient to adorn the oldest ruins with flowers and verdure.

Some laborers were making a new road: I saw human bones and bullets found in digging. There sat an old man under a tree, with a wooden leg; he had certainly seen a little more here than the corn that now waved before him — heard a louder song than that which the birds warbled on the branches above him: he was now resting here, with his pipe in his mouth, and thinking of old times.

Leipsic itself made an agreeable impression on me; it is a large and pleasant city. There are two or three book-sellers in every street; everywhere were to be seen book-cases filled with volumes; and, in the large bright glass windows, engravings and pictures innumerable. Students, with long pipes in their mouths, and books under their arms, were to be seen running about in the streets; some had their original German costume — large white trousers, short frock coats, and long locks hanging down over their white collars.

I visited the church of St. Nicholas, where there are some paintings by Oeser. They showed us an old pulpit, in a little closet here, in which Luther is said to have preached; I stood on my toes to reach up, that I might lay my hands where he had laid his.

From the old church, I wandered out of the town, to Gellert's grave. A flat, plain stone, with his name and the year of his death, lay above it. By the side was planted a rose-tree, and round about stood a low paling, where the many who had visited the poet's grave had written and cut their names; I followed the example, and wrote mine.

Round about were many finer ornamented tombs, which certainly contained persons of far greater distinction than Gellert, but no strange hand had written its memorial there: even the iron-railed chapels around looked merely as a wall that served to inclose the simple poet's grave. Here the poet was the greatest; by his death, this place had acquired an interest. The Duke of Weimar has determined that Goethe's and Schiller's bodies shall stand in the royal chapel, on each side of his; thus, a man may have a rainbow over him, when his body stands between the sun and the foaming cataract.

The other fresh graves were strangely ornamented: besides flowers and wreaths, they had placed on them oranges and lemons, some of which were cut in pieces. Long ribbons, with gold and silver fringes, fluttered about, so that, when all this finery was a little old, it made an ugly appearance. Verses were, in general, printed on the ribbons, some *home-made*, some chosen from the works of celebrated poets; thus, I found on one, Hölty's:—

> "Heute hüpft im Frühlings-Tanz,
> Noch der frohe Knabe,
> Morgen weht der Todtenkranz
> Schon auf seinem Grabe!"[1]

I think that a grave, ornamented with a single wreath, is pretty and significant. The carpenter sets his wreath, with ribbons and gilt papers, on the roof of the house, when the whole building is erected;[2] why should we not, then, like him, also place a wreath here? the grave is the roof over our earthly life's building, and when it is first smoothed by the sexton, the mansion is perfect.

As I wandered through the streets, alone, in the evening, to find the Hôtel de Bavière, I lost my way in this strange town, and lighted upon the "Auerbacher-Keller," which is remarkable from its connection with Dr. Faust, who, as the legend states, flew out of a window here, riding on a wine-cask. I went down, that I might say I had been in that famous room where this event is said to have taken place. It was very small, and had but one window, through which Faust

---

[1] "To-day the boy, so blithe and brave,
    Gambols in childish glee;
    To-morrow o'er his silent grave
    The waving death-wreath see!"

[2] Such is the custom in Denmark, when the workmen generally pass the evening in the new house, with music, dance, and song. — *Translator.*

rode. The whole story was painted on the canvas of the walls, only it is a pity the figures were so dark and indistinct.

Here sat three old fellows in a deep dispute; I think it was about the impossibility of a triangle being in fact half a square; it appeared as if they would fly much further, with the fumes of the wine, than out of the window. At last, they began to sing like *Frosch* and *Brander* in Goethe's "Faust," "*Es var cine Ratt' in Kellernest!*" — that is, they did not precisely sing this, but the situation was the same; so that I every moment peeped toward the door, to see if *Mephistopheles* were not coming with the Doctor.

I went to Reichenbach's garden, to see the place where Poniatowsky found a watery grave in the river Elster. The owner, a rich merchant, takes payment from those who wish to see the place.

Here, between these high trees, rushed the wounded hero, pursued by superior numbers. It is almost incredible that any one could drown in this insignificant narrow water! A weeping-willow was planted on the spot whence he sprang with his horse; and a few paces further, where they had found his body, stood a small plain column, which was covered with names, particularly those of his countrymen.

CHAPTER X.

THE DEPARTURE. — MEISSEN. — THE FIRST DAY IN DRESDEN. — DAHL AND TIECK.

AFTER a stay of three days I left the friendly city of Leipsic, where I had made acquaintance with several excellent men.

We passed the hunting palace of Hubertsburg, with its large gardens, in the gloom of evening. Mengs' pencil, it is said, attracts many to the palace chapel. We had no time, nor did we want pictures; for one gave place to the other when we looked through the open window of the carriage. Here was an inn, with travellers: the ostler stood in the doorway with his large lantern; this was a night-scene, — a style which Rembrandt is said to have done justice to. Now we saw a swampy meadow in the morning light; a few wild ducks splashed amongst the green rushes, — a style Ruysdael has imitated. There lay a hamlet, with a half broken-down wall; in the foreground, under a large tree, sat a couple of young folks, and kissed each other — that was a style I myself would like to imitate.

As we approached Meissen the country assumed a more romantic character. Rocks began to show themselves, and they had quite another appearance than those in the Hartz. They hung over our heads in reddish-yellow masses, and were overgrown with young beeches; on the other side of the road lay the green vine hills, with their red-roofed houses; and below was the Elbe, winding in picturesque curves. Vessels were towed up the river with horses and men, whilst others rushed down the stream with swelling sail.

Meissen itself has narrow streets, and to me appeared an uncomfortable town: one must manage with it, as with every other charming picture, not bring the eye too close to it, but regard the whole at a distance.

The cathedral is a fine Gothic building: the sun shone in through the high windows, and a little bird, that had come in, flapped and beat its wings against the panes to get out. It was the world of my own childhood that I saw! Childhood also is such a holy Gothic church, where the sun shines sweetly through the variegated windows, where every gloomy nook awakens a powerful feeling, and where the simplest images, from its light and legend, have a far deeper signification! Every-day life shows itself in childhood in its Sunday clothes; God and the world lie much nearer to each other, and yet the heart beats and flutters, like the little bird here in the church, after the new future without, where, perhaps, the hunter waits behind the bush to fire a shot through its wings.

The road from Meissen to Dresden is planted with Egyptian thorn and pear-trees; the fields are covered with cabbages and potatoes: it is a complete kitchen-garden! Charming vine hills and leafy woods lie on both sides and behind. Meissen itself, which lies high, forms, with its palace and its Gothic cathedral, the finest point in the whole picture. A stone bridge rises over the Elbe, below the town, where people drive and walk, without thinking, much less priding themselves, on the life they thereby give to the whole.

The farther we recede from here, the higher do the mountains become; and we soon see, as through a bluish veil, the German Florence. Dresden lies before us, with its high towers and cupolas.

When I reached Augustus Bridge, which I knew so well from engravings, it appeared to me as if I had, in a dream, been here once before. The Elbe poured its yellow waves under the proud arches; there were life and bustle on the river, but still more on the bridge; carriages and horsemen went rapidly over it, and on both sides there was a great variety of foot-passengers. About the middle of the river, on one of the piers which form the single arches, stood a Christ on the Cross; I think it is of bronze. We now came to Alstadt (the old city) or Dresden Proper; the Brühlian terraces, with their broad stairs, lay to the left, and the Catholic church, with its towers, to the right; and in the centre the gate, through which we entered the city itself.

Dresden appeared to me to be the point of transition between North and South Germany, and it has also a mixed character of both; it was the last great city I should see in Germany toward the south, so that it was with a feeling of sadness that I entered this dear Dresden.

There was something in the city that at once attached me to it, and I felt myself at home directly. My first visit was to our celebrated landscape-painter, Dahl.[1] I had no letter of introduction to him, but, as a Dane, I was extremely welcome. How much interest did he not show, and how much sacrifice of time did he not make for me and his countrymen, who were there at the same time as myself! In the evening he was going with two Norwegians to visit Tieck, for the great poet was on that evening to read to a party of friends. Having a letter of introduction to him from Ingemann,[2] and having besides previously written to the poet, Dahl invited me to accompany him, but at the same time begged me not to waste my time with him then, but to go to the Catholic church, as on that day it was the festival of *Corpus Christi.*

I soon found the way over the Brühlian terraces, which were crowded with promenaders: it was beautiful to see the great Augustus Bridge, with its throng of passengers, the Elbe, with its vessels, and the green vine hills along it; but I had no time to stay.

Now I stood in the Catholic church. How vast and light! The music-choir resounded over my head; lights burnt on all the altars, and people knelt in the side chapels and the vast aisles. The royal family were present, and the king appeared to pray with much zeal. Three priests, in robes of gold tissue, stood by the altar; and as many boys in red mantles, with a short white surplice above, swung the censer. There was a continual movement at the high altar, which disturbed the impression the whole ceremony would otherwise have made

---

[1] Dahl is a Norwegian, residing in Dresden, where he is Professor of Painting in the academy. — *Translator.*

[2] Ingemann is a Danish author, who has acquired some celebrity as a poet, but more particularly as a novelist; his writings are chiefly historical, of which the majority have been translated into German. His "Waldemar Seier," and "Kong Erik og de Fredlose," have also been translated into English, by Miss Jane Frances Chapman. — *Translator.*

on me. The singing boys came and went with large lighted tapers, and the priests bowed every moment and rung their silver bells. The attendants of the church, in yellow clothes, with large silver sticks in their hands, went up and down the aisles to keep order, and to take care that the goats were separated from the sheep. People came and went, but all passed in silence. I saw Bohemian women and girls, who had certainly been at market with their wares; they came into the church with their baskets or bundles, knelt down in the aisles, counted their beads, and then went away in the greatest haste. Men and women knelt in the chapels before the image of the Madonna, and in many a face I saw the most sincere piety and adoration. The sun shone through the windows, and united strangely with the gleam of the many lights, and the smoke of the fragrant incense; there was a something in the whole that, together with the flood of music, soon found its way to the heart.

At seven in the evening I went, with Dahl and the two young Norwegians, to visit the poet who stands next to Goethe in age, worth, and estimation amongst his countrymen — Germany's Tieck. The room we were ushered into was not large. Here the family sat around the tea-table with a number of strangers, mostly foreigners. Dahl presented the two Norwegians and myself to him as his countrymen, and the poet gave us a hearty welcome.

What expression was there not in his look! I have never seen a more open face. The tone of his voice was so good-natured; and when one looked in his large clear eyes there was a feeling of confidence toward him. It was not the poet that I loved — the man himself now became dear to me! He was just as I had pictured him to myself when I read his "Elves;" but my dreams have so often proved false, that I sometimes could not help thinking, "In reality he is, perhaps, a stiff courtier;" and this would have repulsed me quite. Such is, also, my conception of Goethe, and this overcame my desire to see that great poet, who, I imagine, rises in his full grandeur when one sees him, like the church-towers, at a distance. This is not the case with Tieck; if one has been with him for half an hour, one forgets the poet for the man.

Tieck is very fond of Holberg, whose works he has in an old German translation, from which he sometimes reads aloud to his friends, and that excellently. That evening I heard him read the second part of Shakespeare's " Henry IV." He does not name the characters when reading, but he plays every part so well that one can tell directly who it is. The comic scenes, in particular, he gave in a masterly manner; and it was impossible to resist laughing at *Falstaff* and *Dame Quickly*.

When the party broke up in the evening, Tieck invited me to come and see him often during my stay in Dresden, and prepared me for the treat that was still remaining for me, in Saxon Switzerland and the picture-gallery; this place was, however, unfortunately closed, as the paintings were being arranged anew, but Dahl promised to take me next morning where the best things were already hung up. I bade Tieck good-night, Dahl put me on the right way homeward, and this was my first day in Dresden.

CHAPTER XI.

THE PICTURE-GALLERY. — "DAS GRÜNE GEWÖLBE." — THE ARMORY. — A TOUR TO SAXON SWITZERLAND. — PILLNITZ. — LOHMEN. — OTTOWALDER GRUND. — BASTEI. — WOLF'S GORGE. — HOHENSTEIN. — KUHSTALL.

WITH Dahl, our Danish Ambassador, and the two young Norwegians, I went to the picture-gallery. In some of the rooms the paintings lay on the floor, but in most of them they were already arranged and hung up. What a mass of works of art! One picture superseded the other; a few only remained in the memory.

What shall I say first about the great productions that made the deepest impression on me; yet, can there be a question? Raphael's "Madonna!" I hurried through the rooms in search of this painting, and when I stood before it, it did not surprise me at all. It appeared to me as a friendly female face, but not more beautiful than many I had seen. Is this the world's far-famed picture? thought I, and wished to be surprised on seeing it, but it remained the same. It even appeared to me that several paintings of the Madonna, several female faces here in the gallery, were far prettier. I returned to them again, but then the veil fell from my eyes; they now appeared to me as painted human faces, for I had seen the divine one itself. I again stood before her, and then I first felt the endless truth and glory in this picture. There is nothing in it that strikes, nothing that blinds; but the more attentively one regards her and the infant Jesus, the more divine do they become. Such a superhuman, child-like face, is not found in woman, and yet it is pure nature. It appeared to me as if every pious, innocent girl's face had some resemblance to this, but that this was the ideal after which the others strove. Not love, but adoration, called forth that look. It now became intelligible to me how a rational Catholic can kneel to an image. It is not the colors on the canvas that he worships, it is the spirit, the divine spirit that reveals itself here in a corporeal form to the bodily eye, whilst the powerful tones of the organ peal above him and chase away the discords of the soul, so that there becomes harmony between the earthly and the eternal.

Time has paled the colors of the painting, but yet all the figures seem to live: the great halo of angels' heads behind develop themselves more and more, and in the look of the infant Jesus we see the whole grand expression comprised. Such a look, such a wise eye, is not to be found in any child; and yet here it is natural childishness that seizes so powerfully on us. And then the angel children below; they stand as a beautiful type of earthly innocence; the younger look forward in childish calmness, whilst the elder raise their eyes to heavenly figures above them. This single picture would make the gallery famous, just as it has been sufficient to make its master immortal. There hung three masterpieces in this room: here was Correggio's "Night," a poetical idea charmingly conceived and executed. The light streams forth from Jesus and extends over all the other figures around. What struck me most was, a female figure holding her hand before her eyes, and turning partly away from the strong dazzling light. Most connoisseurs place this piece first amongst that great master's works; yet I prefer the "St. Sebastian," which is in the same room. What a glorious group of angels! They hover down on the light clouds around the pious martyr with his quiet, inspired look. There was still another piece which I dare call the fourth of these divine, animated paintings, "A Christ," by Carlo Dolce: greatness and suffering were blended together in that noble, resigned face.

I went from room to room, and saw that great collection of art, yet always returned to these four treasures —to Raphael's "Madonna," and Correggio's group of angels. Yet I still preserve the impression of the other glorious treasures, from my first visit to the gallery.

"The Day of Judgment," painted by Rubens, where he has introduced the portraits of his three wives, attracted me. Two are angels rising to heaven; the third, on the contrary, is dragged by devils down into the deep. Rubens himself sits on his grave. No one appears to notice him: he is in deep thought; he is probably meditating where he is to go, and quietly awaits his destiny.

In a painting by Bassano, representing the Ark, it was comical to see that a sow was the first animal that was led in, and thus got the best place.

Tired in a spiritual sense with the enjoyment of all these glories, and bodily so from so long a stay, I left the gallery to visit it again.

What a change did not every day bring me, nay, every hour, in that dear city! What a mass of ideas and feelings did there not flow through me during the nine days I passed here! I roamed about from morning till evening, and every moment saw something new.

I was advised to see "Das grüne Gewölbe," the guide procured me company, and we then proceeded to the palace. "Das grüne Gewölbe" is a suite of rooms which are not at all green, and no one knew rightly whence they had got that name. There were many large tables of mosaic work, with flowers and fruit; full-length portraits of the kings of Saxony hung on the walls; there were cups and vessels of different kinds, of gold and silver, and a whole chamber full of playthings of pearls and precious stones.

I saw Luther's ring, and whole cases full of gems and jewels, which lay here so dead and insignificant with all their lustre, that I almost began to be in despair on account of all this wealth that in no way interested me. Had the walls not been covered with mirrors, so that I could by way of change see my own face, with all its tedium expressed therein, and thus amuse myself contentedly, it would have been bad indeed.

The armory amused me much more than "Das grüne Gewölbe." Arms were piled on arms in the large chambers. Many a famed war-horse that had borne a royal prince on its back, stood here carved out in wood, painted and caparisoned, with saddle and bridle; but although the man who showed us about often declared that it was a Danish horse which the figure represented, it affected me not a whit the more. Wax figures of kings and knights stood like enchanted yeomen round about by the doors, and stared at us with their dead eyes. There were whole closets filled with arrows and pistols: I saw a drum covered with human skin. There was the armor that Gustavus Adolphus had worn the day before he fell at Lützen, and a saddle that Napoleon had ridden on, with many other things "too numerous to mention within the limits of a bill of entertainment," as the showman says.

The whole of that night I dreamt of nothing but swords and daggers, immense wax figures, and large wooden horses, so that I had no easy night of it.

I also longed to see Saxon Switzerland; the next day was, therefore, fixed for that excursion.

It was a beautiful morning! I went into the Catholic church; the tapers on the altar were lighted, and in one of the side chapels there was a group of sweet children, boys and girls, who sang with childish voices, whilst the sun shone in on the Madonna's image. I leaned against a pillar, whilst the song and the organ's tones pealed above me. A poor old man, clothed in rags, but with the deepest contrition in his dark, rigid face, knelt, deeply dejected, in the aisle, as if he had not courage to approach the altar. It was sincere repentance that stood painted in his features; he looked toward the ground and counted his beads; whilst the throng of children, piously innocent, sang their morning hymn, I, also in my heart, knelt before my God. It was to me as if the song and the organ's tones melted together in mighty pictures of life which glided past me. If, now, the whole be but a dream! thought I; if, now, I am really at home in Denmark, sleeping, and dreaming that I am in this foreign city between mountains; dreaming these organ-tones and the children's pious song, whilst the poor beggar kneels by my side before the holy Mother! No, I did not dream it, and yet the heart dreamt, — it also dissolved itself in tones; for the heart is a world where the feelings — those warbling birds — build their nests, where love's light humming-bird sings, but sings only once, and then the heart becomes a Memnon's pillar, where the tones are always awakened by music's strong morning light. In love was man created; love is our home, and therefore all music becomes an echo, that awakens the remembrance of home! I tore myself away from my dreams; my friends waited for me by the Elbe, where our gondola lay. The excursion to Saxon Switzerland was now to begin; the sail soon swelled in the breeze, and the rapid strokes of the oar cleft the watery mirror. My companions sang and laughed; I was compelled to laugh too, whilst the awakened remembrances of life in my heart were broken in jarring discords by this sudden transition from dreams to reality.

We passed several large boats filled with villagers — girls and women who had been to Dresden with milk; they lay in various groups, and shaded themselves from the sun whilst the wind gently touched the sail. The women's faces were quite of a yellow brown; the girls', on the contrary, red and white, with lively dark eyes; I thought of the naiads of the Danube, and imagined to myself these rustic beauties as the ruling spirits of the Elbe. I looked into the large dark-blue eyes of one of the kindliest, and directly a whole dozen of songs and ballads came rushing into my head. The vine hills assumed a fresher green; the pine woods were somewhat more gloomy, and all the red-roofed buildings on the sides of the mountains stood before me as brownies who had lost their lives in the bright sunshine.

We landed at the palace of Pillnitz, the summer residence of the King of Saxony.

>Here let us pause upon our way!
> There's not a better place to see;
>By the mill here we will stay,
> Under this old linden-tree.
>O'er the wheel the foaming water
> Rushes like the troubled main!
>And there's the miller's pretty daughter
> Peeping through the window-pane.
>Innocence dwells on her brow,
> Faith's in her mildly beaming eye!
>She regards us closely now,
> And the smiling landscape nigh.
>Stately rocks of gray and red
> Stretch the river's shores along,
>The sun shines bright, the birds have sped
> O'er bush and brake, with merry song.

What a landscape! Let us tarry,
  Everything invites to gladness;
And yet I feel at heart so weary,
  I must weep for very sadness.
Hark! the bird bewails its fate:
  "My young ones they have from me torn,
And they have shot my tender mate,
  And left me here bereft, forlorn."
Behold these rocks' majestic height!
  And yet into the vale of late
One thundered down in hideous might,
  And sealed a hapless father's fate.
Brightly shines the morning sun,
  With equal warmth, on all mankind;
His bright beams gladden every one, —
  The rich, the poor, the halt, the blind.
'Tis just as if the mill-wheel's rush
  Sang as it roared with rapid whirl:
"Did I not an infant crush,
  And in the treacherous water hurl
The girl herself?" And yet to grieve
  O'er woes unreal, sure is vain;
My fancy is too skilled to weave
  These horrors from a sickly brain.

In nature and the world there is no dissonance; the one dissolves itself in the other, and in our own breasts we must seek the last, which can only be dissolved by the great Master.

We passed by the high declivity of rock, and looked down into the valley, which lay, like a mighty picture of my own heart, still and gloomy, with its foaming river, whilst the sun shone bright and warm over our heads, on the waving corn-fields and on the road where the children played and romped.

We descended the rocky path at Mühlsdorf, where there was a bridge over the river Wesenitz, and we were in Lohmen. In former times it had been a little city, and still enjoys the rights of many corporate towns; the castle stands on a projecting cliff, high above the river. The two principal buildings are united by a balcony, which is laid over a point of rock, whence one looks out over the charmingly romantic environs. There is an inscription in rhyme, on a tablet here, which states that, above sixty years since, a young countryman, who had laid himself down to sleep in the balcony, fell down though he fell from a height of seventy-six feet, he, through God's help, escaped uninjured.

Not far from here is a church, said to be one of the handsomest village churches in all Saxony. There was something strikingly fine about it. A fresh grave had just been covered, and the white sand strewed on it, but the wind had torn the flowers from the grave. I gathered them together, made a wreath of them, and laid it on the grave again. A little bird twittered in a tree close by, as if it would thank me: it must have seen and known the silent sleeper that here rested his tired head in the cool earth.

From the resting-place of the dead we went to that of the living. The inn stood close by a pond, where there was a number of quacking ducks; we entered the guests' room — yes, here was something for a painter! A number of peasants sat in groups, and played cards; O! there were characteristic faces! The girl came down the high stairs which led from the side-room into this, with a candle in her hand; the flame of the candle fell on her fresh young face as she cast a side glance on the strangers. Two women were playing the harp and singing; they seized the strings like a storm-wind, and sang with squeaking voices: "Herz, mein Herz, warum so traurig?"[1] so that we were all made quite sad and melancholy by it. The supper was soon steaming on the table; it consisted of roasted ducks, which were quite remarkable for their age; the landlord stood in a fine, serious position, with folded arms, and looked at us and the ducks with a mien which indicated that neither the ducks nor we were to his taste. We went to rest, — but let us spring over that night! I had enough of it in reality. Nature and art had here played a trick; the first had made me too long, and the last the bedstead too short. In desperation I was obliged to play the part of a night wanderer, and descended into the large guests' room; but here it looked too romantic! Some wild looking fellows, with thick black beards, were slumbering round about on bundles of straw; an ugly black bull-dog, that looked like a worn-out hair trunk, sprang toward me with a howling war-song, so that, like a prudent general, I turned

---

[1] O heart, my heart, wherefore so sad?

my back toward him. The rain poured down in torrents out of doors, and lashed the ground, as much as to say, "See, this was the way it came down at the Deluge." The day began to break, but there was no hope of getting to the mountains. This was the first bad weather I had as yet had on my travels, and therefore I found it very interesting. It will be better in the course of the day, thought I; and scarcely had an hour passed before the rain abated. We took courage, and having got a little peasant boy, of about ten years' old, as guide, we set out on our way, through Ottowalder Grund, and to Bastei, which place we were to ascend. I looked a little suspiciously at our small edition of a guide, as he hopped on before us so merrily, with his hazel stick in his hand. He was barefooted, and laughed and chattered away without ceasing; and it almost appeared to me as if he had a trick in his head, — as if he were the living Cupid who had become our guide. If he be not our seducer, thought I — and then many of that young rogue's tricks came into my head. "That little rascal who runs about with arrows," Wessel calls him; and it is, in truth, vexatious that such a little whelp has the right to shoot great, full-grown persons. Yet it is said that those who get each other soon draw the arrows out again, and then all love is gone; but the others keep the arrows in their hearts, and then it is often mortal.

We descended, step by step, deeper and deeper into the valley; this was Ottowalder Grund. The rocky walls arose on both sides in the strangest forms, and richly grown with wild plants, roots, and various colored mosses; the trees and bushes stood in picturesque groups between the clefts of the rocks; far below rushed a little streamlet, and above us we saw but once a small piece of the gray sky.

The rocky walls were soon so close together that there was only space for one at a time; three immense blocks of stone had fallen from above and formed a natural arch, under which we had to pass: here it was quite gloomy.

The vale suddenly became broader, and then narrow again. We entered "Die Teufelskuche,"[1] — a wild cleft in the rock, where the masses of fallen blocks have formed a long chim-

[1] The devil's kitchen.

ney-like opening. I looked up through it; clouds hurried past, above us, and it looked as if some ghostly being was flying away in the open air.

We soon left the rocks behind, and a wide vale extended itself before us. The bluish white mist hung in light clouds around the mountains' tops, and the heavens and the earth seemed as if they would melt together in one great mass of rock. We continued our progress, and Nature's great panorama around us continually changed. Little Cupid knew his business; he would not lead us astray: one is apt to judge too severely of Love's propensities.

A fine large building lay before us: it was the inn on "Bastei" (the bastion) — for here it is exceedingly high. Could you place a couple of church-towers one on the other, and not be giddy by standing on the extreme point, you would then have some idea of its height. There is a railing so that you cannot fall. That long, pale-yellow ribbon down there, which to your eye does not look broader than the curb-stones in the street, is the river Elbe; that brown-yellow willow leaf which you think is floating on it, is a long river-vessel; you can also see the men on it, but they are only dots! Try to throw a stone into the Elbe — you must use your whole strength — yet it will fall here on this side, in the grass. The villages lie down there like playthings on a stall. Yonder Königstein and Lilienstein rise half way up into the cloud of mists; but see, the cloud is breaking; the sun's rays fall on Pfaffenstein and "the Cupola Mountains;" the whole curtain rolls up, and in the azure distance you see the Bohemian Rosenberge and Geisingberge in Erzgebirge. Close by us, toward the left, there are only wild rocks which rise from the abyss, and from the deep a walled pillar lifts itself, on which rests a bridge that unites "Bastei" with "Das Felsenschloss." It is quite dark in the rocky ravine under us; our guide pointed out traces in the rock which show that men have lived here before. It looks as if this huge mass of rock had been riven asunder, — as if some mighty power had here tried to split our proud globe in two.

The road wound along the deep abyss; rocks and clefts succeeded each other alternately.

The whole scene was to me like a great lyrical, dramatic poem, in all possible metres. The rivulet brawled, in the choicest iambics, over the many stones that lay in the way; the rocks stood as broad and proud as respective hexameters; the butterflies whispered sonnets to the flowers as they kissed their fragrant leaves; and all the singing birds warbled, in Sapphic and Alcaic strains: I, on the contrary, was silent, and will also be so here.

We now bent our steps toward Hohenstein, but first made a little detour in order to see that strange freak of nature, "Teufelsbrücke" (the devil's bridge). The devil really has taste. Every place that bears his name, or alludes to him, has in it something piquant: the most romantic places are those which they have placed in connection with him. As I have said, he has taste, and that is one good quality.

Teufelsbrücke is just as if thrown over a ravine between two perpendicular cliffs; the rock is split from its topmost summit down to the green meadow, but the whole extent of the opening is not more than three or four yards in breadth. At a few paces from it there is a similar cleft, but the chasm is a strange zigzag, and forms a sort of passage. This place has obtained a peculiar interest from the poet Kind having laid the incantation scene in "Der Freischutz" here.

From the topmost verge of the cliff we descend through this cleft into the valley. One can only go singly, the rocks being so near each other: sometimes we scramble down a ladder, sometimes we find ourselves nearly wedged in the rock itself, and at the very bottom we stand in a narrow cavern, where there is not room for more than three or four persons.

"Help, Zamiel!" we shouted, when we were about half-way down; for it appeared to be a fathomless pit. Every time we rounded a piece of rock which we thought concealed the entrance, there still lay a deeper abyss below us.

By way of Hohenstein and Schandau we now pursued our course through the free and open country. A broad carriage-road by the shore of a small river between the green forests, led us into a wild, rocky region. The ladies were now carried up the path in a sort of sedan chair, we others carried ourselves; and thus we reached about the same time the end of this day's tour. A lofty, arched, rocky hall lay before us; it was Kuhstall.[1] At first sight it appears as if it had been built by human hands; but when we approached nearer to this proud mass, we felt that Nature alone can erect such a gigantic building. The inhabitants of the environs are said to have sought a refuge here in the Thirty Years' War; here they had a great number of their cattle, whence the place has derived its name.

It began to rain, but we sat high and dry, as seamen say, under the huge portal, whilst a rainbow extended its glorious arch over the forest, and between the opposite rocks. I cannot remember ever having seen such bright colors, or such a splendid rainbow; it was not alone in the air that it showed itself; no, it passed down the side of the rocky wall, and rounded itself far below us on the top of the dark pine forest, forming a complete circle. An old man in a worn-out gray frock-coat sat on a stone block at the entrance of the hall, and played to us; several strings of his harp were broken; discord followed discord; but when one looked at the old man, whose life certainly must have resembled his harp-playing, there was harmony again in the whole.

A narrow road, like a cavern through the rock, led us to a third side of this rocky portal. Bare stone walls rose on both sides; we were obliged to go up ladders and stairs to get to the summit of the cliff. The first cavern is called " Das Wochen-bett," [2] because unhappy mothers brought their children into the world here in the time of the war.

The path wound close by the deep abyss; we passed over a small bridge, and came to another group of rocks. Here a pair of large shears was painted on the rock; the place is called Schneiderloch," [3] and is said to have been a place of refuge for a band of robbers, whose leader had learnt the trade of tailoring, but afterward found pleasure in ripping up men instead of old coats. In order to get in and out of this cavern we were obliged to crawl on hands and feet; there was something really frightful in it to see one after the other creep out of that deep hole, so far above two yawning abysses. Here was, however, a splendid echo which repeated our words six or seven times.

[1] Cow-stall.   [2] Child-bed.   [3] Tailor's hole.

Close by is "Pfaffenloch,"[1] an aperture through which a priest was cast down, during the times of religious persecution. I looked down into its depth, but it was perfect night there, whilst the sky above us was red with the setting sun. Before we descended we were obliged to creep on hands and feet through "Die krümme Caroline,"[2] a very winding hole, that led us back to the path in the cliffs. I have never seen such a number of names in any place as here in Kuhstall; not even in the Directory are there so many! The whole rocky hall, inside and outside, on every spot, was a variegated picture of names alone: some were even carved in the stone, and then tarred and burnt in afterward — so that this kind of immortality must have cost no little trouble.

[1] Priest's hole.   [2] Crooked Caroline.

CHAPTER XII.

A TOUR INTO BOHEMIA. — THE RETURN BY WAY OF PIRNA. — SONNENSTEIN. — MY LAST DAYS IN DRESDEN.

WE were all on foot again by early dawn. The birds warbled merrily, but they had most assuredly slept better than we had — at least, they had had the bed they were accustomed to. The misty clouds hung like sleep in Nature's eyes, so that the good lady did not look so very well pleased. At length the sun burst through the veil; but I was quite tired of the eternal pine forests, which even in the best light appeared to me cold and stiff. Our way was now in a continued zigzag upward, and over pieces of basalt rock; thus we reached " Kleine Winterberg."[1] Here the Elector Augustus of Saxony, in 1558, is said to have pursued a powerful stag to the very verge of the precipice. The Elector stood on the narrow path under the rock, the animal above him, pursued by the dogs; the stag was about to spring down on him, when it must have hurled him into the abyss below. There was but one chance of escape: he took aim at the animal, fired, and was successful. His son afterward erected a hunting-lodge on that spot: it is still standing, and the roof is ornamented with the antlers of this same stag.

After a somewhat fatiguing walk, we came to the end of the pine forest, and stood amongst beautiful green beeches; round about were numerous springs, which bubbled forth from the luxuriant soil; a few paces further, and we stood 1780 feet above the level of the sea. What an infinity stretched around us! Far below, in the wood-grown abyss, was the Elbe, winding its way like a ribbon, which lost itself near Dresden, whose towers and cupolas rose before the blue mountains of Meissen. Yet it was grandest toward Bohemia. I had never imagined

[1] The little winter-mountain.

that the mountains could assume such a dark-blue tinge — they lay before me like a petrified sea, and in the distant horizon rose Riesengebirge, with their snow-clad summits, like an airy cloud-land, where one could see to Colmberg, although there are twenty-four German miles between. Heavy clouds passed along the mountains' sides; a part lay quite in shadow, whilst another rose in the clear sunshine.

The sun shone also into my heart, whilst heavy clouds sailed over this inner world. There is something powerfully touching in thus surveying a great tract of land as with a bird's eye. How many a heart is there not beating with desire or joy far below in the valley! how many a scalding tear is there not shed on the proud mountains that lift their heads above the clouds! Could one but read the heart of that stranger who sits here amongst the heather, what an idyl or an epos should we not find there! he looks down on the charming landscape beneath the wild rocks, and on the waving clouds that sometimes conceal, then divide, and disclose this paradise of peace.

> Aloft on the mountain, where the clouds ride,
> While the dark pines groan on its rocky side,
> Where the well bubbles forth beneath the stone,
> I sat alone.
> The rock is an island unto me,
> And the clouds pass by, like the waves of the sea;
> Now the heavy masses break,
> And the sun shines, as on a glassy lake.
> I see below me the green mead,
> Where my steps were wont to tread, —
> There, where the birds are singing clear,
> And the nuts have the tint of the falling year;
> Where the blue-white smoke-clouds ride,
> And whirl about the mountain side;
> Then did I find a home, and one —
> My heart and soul were hers alone.
> She loved me — she was constant ever,
> But Fate compelled us twain to sever.
> She was a bride, — below they dwell,
> Where the old oaks shade the lonely dell;
> Where the smoke-clouds hang, and their tops **conceal**:
> She her thoughts must not reveal.
> Thou must not think of me,
> Yet this heart dreams but of thee!

> In my pain I heap sin on sin,
> While my heart thou dwellest in.
> Thou sea of clouds, more thickly spread, and prove
> A veil to hide from me my grave of hope and love!

A single melody we have heard but once, often makes so powerful an impression on our minds that it seems to sound in our ears again, amidst the bustle of the world, without our being able to sing it aloud, however clearly it echoes in our memory. It is even so with me also with regard to the beautiful in nature. This piece of music, brought forth in colors, with light and shade, I learned during a few hours' wandering in the Bohemian mountains. There was, perhaps, also something in this circumstance — that here was the most southern part of the continent that I had fixed on seeing during my peregrination, and accordingly that hence I must bend my steps again toward the North. The whole of that charming landscape, seen in the brightest sunshine, lives in my remembrance; I see every point, and, like old melodies, it often sounds in my mind, without my having the power to express it in tones and song. I see the large plain in the forest with the felled pines, where they told us that we had now passed the frontiers; I see the sun-burnt Bohemian girl, with the white linen head-dress and bare feet, whom we met in the dark pine forest; and now that wild group of rocks, " Prebischthor," where we stood under the proud rocky arch which the mighty spirit of nature had so grandly raised above our heads   I see the far-extended forests deep below us, and the distant mountains, with their snows, illumined by the bright rays of the sun. " Only down into that valley, and then no further!" thought I; and yet a a still more beautiful valley discloses itself to view beyond yonder mountains, where one can see the frontiers of Tyrol, where one already breathes the air of Italy on the high mountains. Only down into that valley, and then homeward — homeward toward the North, perhaps never to return — never more to see these mountains, with their gloomy forests, aloft in the light-blue clouds.

We ran down the steep mountain declivity, where the path wound round in large curves: through " Die heiligen Hallen,"[1]

[1] The holy hall.

a romantic rocky group under the mountain, we came to the broad highway in the forest. Bohemian peasants drove past us; large, strong-built oxen drew the wagons; the forest resounded with the woodman's axe, several of whom we passed, as, with their lively songs and tra-la-las, they kept time to the strokes of the axe. The Bohemians have an innate bent for music; almost every peasant plays the violin or flute. This alone makes me love the people; for whoever loves music must have an open and good heart. Musical sounds form, however, that Iris which unites heaven with earth. Color, tone, and thought are, in fact, the trinity of nature. The earthly expresses itself in the value of different colors; and these again reveal themselves spiritually in the mighty tones, which again hold the key of the heart's deepest recess. It is melody alone that has sufficient strength to solve the deep enigmas of thought often awakened in our souls.

We went past a pleasant little house, with red-painted wood-work and vines growing up the walls; there sat a little sunburnt boy, with silvery-white hair, practicing on an old violin. Perhaps that little fellow will one day be a great virtuoso, astonish the world with his playing, be admired and honored, whilst a secret worm gnaws all the green leaves off his life's tree.

The forest now receded more and more; the road lay between wild rocks; a small river contributed to vary the whole scene; water-mill succeeded water-mill, where large planks and stones were sawn through; in several places we only found a narrow board, without any railing, that served as a bridge over the river. At length we entered the Bohemian frontier-town Herrnskretschen.

Everything around me had quite a new character. The whole bore a strange and peculiar stamp. I still see so clearly, under the yellow-gray cliffs, with their greenwood sides, the neat red-painted houses, with their wooden balconies, high stairs, and palisades, and with a picture of Christ or the Madonna over the door, which, however badly it was painted, nevertheless gave the whole a touch of interest. I still see the many women, the lively girls and boys, who stood with naked feet by the river side, and dragged to land with long poles the large pieces of wood that floated down the stream. I see the tawny old woman by the open window, who greeted us in the names of Joseph and Mary. I see that strange parti-colored picture, with the fresh garland of flowers, there, in the centre of the market-place, where an old peasant kneels and says his " Ave Maria," and where the pretty young girls go past, courtesy low, and make the sign of the cross.

It was the picture of St. Nepomuck, the Bohemians' tutelary saint, that I saw here. It was strange to think that I was now in a land where I was regarded as a heretic. The Catholic church in Dresden, with its music and its ceremonies, did not draw me so near the Papal chair, however, as this picture of a saint in the open air, and the old woman's Catholic greeting.

We walked some distance along the shores of the Elbe, where we met with some Austrian soldiers, who kept guard on their frontiers. Three Bohemian watermen waited for us with a sailing-boat, to conduct us back again to Saxony. The wind blew and filled the sails; wood-covered mountains rose on both sides; we passed several large vessels with timber and planks from the interior of Bohemia. Close by the shores of the Elbe we saw a large stone-quarry, which has a particular interest for Danes, as the stones used in the building of Christiansberg Palace (in Copenhagen) were brought from this place. Not far from hence, over the path along by the Elbe, there stands a rock which, at a distance, forms a striking likeness to the bust of Louis XVI., and is called after him. There was the whole expression of the face, and the large peruke hung round the gigantic head; if one got close under the rock, then the whole was indistinct, and one saw only the wild rocks one above the other, with green bushes in the deep clefts.

We landed at Schandau, that we might be in Dresden the same evening; but we had still another rocky group to visit, the well-known Lilienstein. The stately cliffs rose perpendicularly; we stood at their feet, under the ancient linden-trees, which also afforded shade to Frederick II. A number of footpaths intersected each other here; sometimes we sank down in the deep sand; sometimes we had to ascend almost perpendicularly up steps that were hewn in the rock. A little wooden bridge lay across a yawning gulf; the path curved more and more; at length we stood on the topmost point, which is a large flat surface, almost the circumference of the whole rock, and grown with pines and firs. Here is a most charming prospect over Schandau and to the Bohemian Mountains. The river Elbe, far below, wound its way between the sunlit meadows; and on the other side lay the hamlet of Königstein, under the noble rocks on which the fortress itself is situated.

A little path along one side of the Elbe, under the lofty rocks, leads down toward Pirna and the palace of Sonnenstein, an institution for insane persons.

A strange feeling must seize every one that pays a visit within these walls, which inclose a world within themselves, — a world that is warped out of its natural career, where the green germ of life either withers, or develops itself in a spiritual deformity. Imagination, this life's best cherub, that conjures up an Eden for us in the sandy desert, — that lifts us in its strong arms over the deepest abyss, over the highest mountain, into God's glorious heaven, — is here a frightful chimera, whose Medusa-head petrifies reason and thoughts, and breathes a magic circle around the unfortunate victim, who is then lost to the world.

Seest thou that little square room, with the iron-grated window up there? There, on the floor, in the middle of the straw, sits a naked man with a black beard, and with a wreath of straw around his head — that is his crown; a withered thistle he found in the straw is his sceptre. He strikes at the flies that buzz about him; for he is a king, he is a despot; the flies are his subjects; he says they have rebelled, they will have his head, they have forced their way in to him, but he cannot tell how; yet they storm in, but they cannot tear his head off his shoulders.

A woman approaches us; she has been pretty, but pain has contorted her features. "I am Tasso's Leonora; Heine has sung about me! Ha! there are many poets who have sung my charms, and that can flatter a woman's heart finely! It is my triumph; there was likewise one, but he could not celebrate me in song, and so he shot himself through the heart, and that was quite as good as a song. Now the whole world is mad for love of me, and, therefore, I have come to this foreign palace; but now they have all become mad here from looking at me; but I can do nothing for them; I cannot help it!"

Look at that open window: there sits a pale young man; he leans his head on his arm, and looks out at the red evening sky and the ships which, with outstretched sails, glide up the Elbe. Our approach does not disturb his meditation; he regards his whole existence as a dream, recalls to mind a happier time in which he has lived, and regards us and the whole scene before him as a vision.

Here is one who has a monomania: he believes he can hear the pulsations of every beating heart, that he can hear it burst its strings in death — in his ears they burst with the wildest tones, so that he becomes furious. He is then bound fast in a chair which is whirled round by means of a wheel. With a wild scream he rushes round until consciousness leaves him, when the wheel is stopped.

But away with these frightful pictures: the carriage is already waiting, and in a few hours we shall be again in Dresden.

I had only three days to remain here, and there were many things yet to be seen, many that I wished to see again. Those pictures hurried past my mind like clouds in a stormy night; every hour brought with it something interesting to me. I revisited the picture-gallery, saw the works of the great masters once more, and imprinted the glorious subjects in my mind. I then heard mass in the Catholic church, and once more ascended, and took leave of the mountains in "Plauenschen Grund," — a romantic landscape close to Dresden, which reminded me of Rübeland, although it is far richer in variety than the latter. The way lay between steep cliffs: there was a river which formed a water-fall, and close by lay a mill. Charcoal-burners drove into the forest, and up on the declivity of the rock there sat a little boy watching goats: there was not a painting in the whole picture-gallery at Dresden where the figures could be better placed than these were here. A refreshing quiet lay over the charming landscape; it was as if rocks, forests, and flowers dreamt of a more southern sky, whilst the river bubbled on between the stones, and sang a loud, somniferous lullaby to the whole scene around. Dresden itself lay pleasantly embosomed between the green vine hills; the whole landscape was a picture of childish peace, of the innocent heart's romantic dreams.

Many prefer Tharand to Plauenschen Grund; others, the latter to the former: I know not which party I shall join; both had in them something peculiar, something that made one feel one's self comfortable here. Plauenschen Grund, with its winding road under the cliffs, where there is life and bustle, appeared to me more lively, and seems to show a more manly character; whilst Tharand, with its ruin, its smooth lake, and its deep solitude, has in it something more passive, something more feminine.

The old school-master came into my mind, and I said with him, "Here is room enough; many persons might here profit by all this grandeur!" but how few are they who see all the beautiful things with which God has adorned our earth! In reality there is but little difference between man and the dog, which, chained to his kennel, is only able to make a few springs on his usual place of exercise.

That Dresden can display its character as a point of transition between northern and southern Germany, I had a perfect idea of, the last forenoon I stayed here. It was as cold as winter. The rained poured down, and everything assumed a dark, northern aspect. Porters ran through the streets with sedan-chairs, where the ladies peeped out from behind the red curtains. The Elbe looked like thick yellow coffee. Only a few showed themselves in the streets.

Later in the day it was again clear weather, and warm as in summer; crowds of persons were again seen moving about on the Brühlian terraces, where the trees, refreshed by the rain, now gave a pleasant scent. Music sounded up there, and gondolas, boats, and ships crossed each other on the Elbe.

The last morning in Dresden now greeted me. I must go out once more to hear the glorious tones under the vaulted roof of the church, to see once more the green vine hills in the morning light. The day was fine; the whole country by the Elbe lay in the most glorious sunshine — it appeared to me as if everything had put on its Sunday clothes, to say adieu to me! but on this account I felt it the more. There was no mass that day in the Catholic church; the organ alone played its simple melodies; but they were the farewell songs, the last deep tones that I should probably hear in Dresden during my life. I saw an old priest, in one of the confessionals, with a venerable face; a young girl was kneeling on the other side of the grating at confession. I also wished for a father, a friend, to whom I could pour out the feelings that rushed into my heart on taking leave of a dear, yet foreign spot, which was no longer alien to the heart.

I now went to take leave of Dahl, who gave me some drawings and a sketch in oil, that I might be able to say I had something he had painted. "Next summer," said he, "I shall certainly visit Denmark, and see all friends and acquaintances." He then shook hands with me as a "Live-well!" saying, "That is in Danish; and that," added he, as he kissed me on the cheek, "is in German!"

I could not just now bid farewell to Tieck. I was obliged to walk about in the open air until the parti-colored pictures round about again began to reflect themselves in the heart and mind; for these worldly pictures are like the sea in a storm, no star can be reflected there; but when one sees the green coasts, and the every-day life's red-roofed houses show themselves on the surface, then it is quiet again.

Tieck received me in his study, and looked so kindly in my face with his large wise eyes, that I made myself strong again, for I felt a lately suppressed sadness creeping over me with renewed power. He showed much kindness toward me, praised what things he knew of mine, and as I had no album with me, he wrote on a loose sheet of paper the following lines in remembrance of himself: —

"Gedenken Sie auch in der Ferne meiner; wandeln Sie wohlgemüth und heiter auf dem Wege der Poesie fort, den Sie so schön und muthig betreten haben. Verlieren Sie nicht den Muth, wenn nüchterne Kritik Sie ärgern will. Grüssen Sie uns bald einmal frisch gesund und reichbegabt von den Musen nach Deutschland zurück.

"Ihr wahrer Freund,   LUDWIG TIECK.[1]
"DRESDEN, 10*de Juni*, 1831."

[1] "Remember me also at a distance: may you wander, elevated with joy,

I bade him farewell. No stranger saw us, and therefore I feared not to give vent to my feelings. He pressed me to his bosom, predicted a fortunate career for me as a poet, and certainly thought that I was a far better man than I am. His kiss glowed on my brow: I know not what I felt, but I loved all mankind. "May I, if for only once, as a poet," thought I, "be able to present something to the world whereby I may show the great poet that he did not make a mistake in his estimation of the stranger!"

It was six o'clock in the evening when I left Dresden by the "Schnelpost;" I now saw the Catholic church and the Brühlian terraces for the last time, as we hurried past.

Neustadt also was soon left behind; fields and meadows stretched away on both sides. We were nine in the diligence, and I sat in the middle of that game of nine-pins; God knows, thought I, which of us Death will hit the first? All of us it will not be at once; but, perhaps, the corner pin. In the one corner sat a young Russian Woiwod; he came from Paris, was going, by way of Dresden and Berlin, to Bremen, and would go from thence to Italy; he did not like the shortest road! In another corner sat an Englishman, who praised Denmark, where he had been, very much; and said that it wanted nothing else but to belong to England to be the chief pearl in Europe's crown. In the third was a travelling comedian, but whence he came I know not; and in the fourth a young wool-merchant, with his still younger wife. They came from a town on the Rhine, and he was going to establish himself in Berlin: they had been married but fourteen days, and, therefore, they kissed each other continually, played with each other's hands, and made quotations from "Don Carlos." Town followed town, whilst the whole country changed by degrees from a stout, healthy, blooming nature, to a personified consumption. Only a few pictures stand out clearly from that dreamy chaos. Thus, I and happy in mind, on the path of poesy, which you have begun so fairly and courageously. Let not your spirits sink when degenerate criticism vexes you. Send us soon a greeting, healthy and richly gifted; send a greeting from the Muses back to Germany.

"Your true friend, L. T.

"DRESDEN, *June* 10*th*, 1831."

see a flat country, in the dusky summer night, where there lay a market town — they called it Grosenhain; there was a church where all the doors and windows were walled up, so that the whole formed a hollow stone vault, where no one could enter, and we were told that this was done in the time of the plague; the sick were brought here, and when the last closed his eyes, they stopped up the church entirely, and have since then not dared to open it again.

I see distinctly the fat hostess in Jüterborg, with her significant smile at my ignorance, when I pointed to the figure of a knight carved in stone, which is placed outside the townhall. Every child, she thought, knew *"Der alte Mauritius;"* I was certainly the first who had put this singular question to her.

I see the far-famed mill near Sans-souci, which turned its large wings so slowly, as if it could no longer go round like other respectable mills, on account of its renown. Here, however, was a little verdure to relieve the eye, — aye, and a lake too; and light boats, with white sails, rocked about on the river Havel. Sans-souci stood proudly on its terraces, and stared at the stiff city of Potsdam.

It was already evening when we rolled into the streets of Berlin, which stretched interminably before and on both sides of us. It was imposing from its greatness; everything was riches and splendor; even the inhabitants seemed to be dressed out. "It is not Sunday to-day?" I asked. No, it was Saturday in the almanac, but Berlin always looks as if it were Sunday afternoon. Where should I take up my quarters? was the next question; the old king and "Drei Tage aus dem Leben eines Spielers," which we all know from the chapter about Brunswick, came into my mind. Louis Angely, the translator of "Drei Tage," etc., etc., and author of several vaudevilles, was owner of "Der Kaiser von Rusland," one of the first hotels in Berlin; how could I, then, be in doubt as to where I should choose my quarters?

CHAPTER XIII.

ADALBERT VON CHAMISSO. — THE THEATRES IN BERLIN. — THE THIERGARTEN. — THE PICTURE-GALLERY. — SPANDAU. — AN ADVENTURE. — THE BIRD. — THE JOURNEY'S END.

WITH a letter of introduction from our Örsted[1] I set out to visit the poet Chamisso. He is by birth a Frenchman, and has been an officer in the army. Afterward, as a naturalist, he made a voyage round the world, and was, when I was in Berlin, one of the directors of the Botanical Garden there. I was extremely anxious to see the author of Peter Schlemil's "Wundersame Geschichte." I entered, and Peter Schlemil himself stood living before me — at least the selfsame figure that stands in the book — a tall meagre figure, with long gray locks hanging down over his shoulders, and with an open good-natured face; he had on a brown dressing-gown, and a crowd of rosy-cheeked children played about him. He bade me welcome with the heartiest good-will, and I had now one acquaintance in this strange city.

In the evening I went to the Opera-house, where Weber's opera, "Oberon," was performed, and right glad I was, and though I only got a spare seat, I was yet one of the first. Here it was that I was to have a proper idea of an opera — to see the scenery and decorations treated as an art by themselves, and what machinery can be. The overture was received with *da capo*, the curtain rolled up, and whilst the overture was repeated I had an opportunity of regarding the splendid decorations and the charming groups. *Oberon* did not lie, as with us, in a solid bed: the whole airy hall was overgrown with lilies, and he lay in the rocking cup of one of them. Round about in the other lilies stood smiling genii,

[1] The celebrated Danish chemist, Hans Christian Örsted.

whilst the larger ones hovered about in a light and airy dance. Every decoration was thus a work of art, as also the arrangement of the whole; but the machinery — *mirabile dictu!* — the machinery was, in proportion to the means, bad. I call it bad, when the clouds remain stationary half-way, so that the genii must help to slide them on; when in the otherwise magnificent sea-decoration in the second act, where the air was so deceitfully true, one could see into the lofts over the air curtains if one sat on the second bench in the pit opposite to it The whole airy scenery was charming here — one saw the stars peep gradually forth: if the ceiling had not come forward at the same time, it would have been beautiful. The changes were also managed rather clumsily; and in the Sea of Astrachan we saw a scene-shifter pass over the surface of the water, which surprised me much, although I knew that experiment at home. I was, however, told it had never been managed so awkwardly as on that evening — that the machinery here was a real work of art: we must, therefore, regard it as a misfortune that evening, yet I cannot refrain from mentioning it.

In a large city it is always pleasant when there are several theatres to choose amongst; but when good pieces are performed in them all the same evening, one cannot agree with one's self; for more than two a man cannot well go to the same evening. This I felt on the second evening of my stay, when I had to choose between the "French Theatre," the "Charlottenberg Theatre," "Königstatisches Theatre," and the "Opera-house." Added to this, Chamisso had invited me to accompany him to the Thiergarten, where he would introduce me to the *beaux esprits* of Berlin. I stood like Hercules on the cross-road, and — accompanied Chamisso. I, however, found no wild animals in the Thiergarten;[1] they were all tame, very good-natured, and friendly persons. A little festival was arranged here in consequence of the poet Hölty's return home from Darmstadt, where he had been giving readings.

Here I also met with the poet Hoffman's friend, Hitzig, and made acquaintance with Wilibald Alexis (Häring), who spoke with much warmth about Denmark, and the happy hours he had passed with Oehlenschläger.

[1] The Deer Park.

It is quite a peculiar and pleasant feeling, when in a strange land, to hear our own spoken well of; then we feel truly that we are "bone of its bone, and flesh of its flesh," so that every praise and every reproach that is pointed at it also seem to fall on us, who are, however, but a small part thereof; yet I suppose it is in this case as in most others, we set our native land in the one scale and ourselves in the other.

Here was, however, much that reminded me of home, and carried me back to Denmark, particularly the warm affection with which they named their king, whose health was one of the first we drank.

It was late in the evening when we separated. The night brought sleep and rest, and the next day new things to be seen.

The Museum is only open on certain days in the week, but strangers are permitted to view it at all times on showing their passports to the keeper.

The building has in it something imposing. A high flight of steps occupies almost the whole breadth of the façade; columns and arches rise prettily above us. Where we enter a rotunda, decorated with antiques, a suite of rooms opens with these glorious remains of past ages. Taste and elegance distinguish the whole. Some steps higher lead us into the great picture-gallery, which in royal magnificence surpasses both that in Dresden and Copenhagen, but in value is far inferior to either of them.

The floors were polished, and the attendants, in new silver-laced liveries, stood by the doors. For the rest, there were paintings here by the first masters, only I was astonished at the number of horrifying ideas I found executed here. For instance, there were three pieces, hanging together, by Jeronimus Bosch, representing the Creation, the Day of Judgment, and Hell — where the Day of Judgment represented such disgusting images that I do not like to refer to them in all their ugliness. I found more than one Christ's head by Hughe van d'Goes, which might certainly be considered as masterpieces, if taken directly from nature; but here they were executed to perfect ugliness. The crown of thorns was pressed deep into the head of the Redeemer, so that the large blood-drops gushed forth: every vein was swelled; the lips were of a dark blue; and the heavy sweat-drops lay in loathsome truthfulness over the whole face. There was something in it, to me at least, revolting. It is the poetical in pain that 'the painter should express, and not its prosaic repulsiveness. I cannot forget the vampire-looking pictures: they stand before me now far more living than Guido Reni's "Fortune," Vandyke's "The Descent of the Holy Ghost," and Michael Angelo's "Burial of Christ," which I saw here.

Five days in Berlin depart like a sneeze; one only knows, in fact, the beginning and the end.

Chamisso was the last to whom I bade farewell! Before we parted, the poet wrote the following little impromptu, as a remembrance, which I here add to my recollections of Berlin: —

"O lasset uns, in dieser, düstern, bangen Zeit,
Wo hochanschwellend donnernd der Geschichte Strom,
Die starre, langgehegte Eisesdecke sprengt,
Das neue Leben unter Trümmern bricht hervor,
Und sich in Stürmen umgestalten will die Welt,
O lasset uns, ihr Freunde — rings verhallt das Lied
Und unserm heitern Saitenspiele lauscht kein Ohr —
Dennoch die Göttergabe des Gesanges treu
In reinen Busen hägen, wehren, dass vielleicht
Wir hochergraute Barden einst die Sonne noch
Mit Hochgesang begrüssen, welche das Gewölck
Zertheilend die verjüngte Welt bescheinen wird.
Prophetisch, Freunde, bring ich dieses volle Glas,
Der fernen Zukunft einer andern Liederzeit."

My way home lay through Brandenborg-Thor. I bade farewell to the Goddess of Victory, who, with her proud bronze horses, had seen other scenes than I. In her younger days she was placed as if she drove out of Berlin; but when she did so in reality, and even went direct to Paris, she was transported back and placed with her face toward the city; and it is certainly better that Victory make her entry into a city than that she should go out of it.

My travelling companions this time were, a baker, two miller's children, that is to say, a he and a she — the latter one might call "Die schöne Müllerin" — an old governess, and a poetical tailor.

The sun burnt like fire, and the country began to put its worst face on as we left Spandau: it was just as if we drove over a map, the whole was so flat. At last the beautiful scenery crept into a blade of grass that peeped forth here and there.

The baker, who suffered much from the heat and fear of the cholera, puffed and groaned. He had five or six bottles of wine with him, in which there was something he called cholera-drops; and, as he emptied one after the other, he began to sing, as if from despair. It sounded like a broken wail. At last, when the bottles became lighter, he grew quite poetical, and began to recite. They were "terrible recitatives," about death, the devil, the white lady, and all given in one tone.

The sun now looked into the diligence to see all this. The road began to be so dusty that we were obliged to draw the windows up. Here we now sat, six souls in six bodies and a half, — for the baker's could pass very well for one and a half. He now came out with effect: the clear water-drops stood on his face. His neighbor, the young poetical tailor, sat quite pale and warm, and exclaimed at the close of every verse, "*jöttlich!*" The old governess looked so stately, and kept smelling continually of a lemon, whilst I tried all possible ways to stretch my poor legs, which I at length bored in between "Die schöne Müllerin" and her brother, who slept, and nodded in their sleep, like two marsh marigolds when it blows a little. The baker took them for approving nods, and raised his voice still louder, when a coal-black head darted out of the governess's reticule, with a bark and a scream. Here she had concealed her dog, as no dogs are permitted in the diligence. It had kept still the whole time previously, but now it lost all patience: it gave a few short barks, so that the sleeping brother and sister, and we other half-dead beings, sprang up in the vehicle, and thrust our heads into the large net that hung from the roof, for our sticks, umbrellas, and other small articles. "Die schöne Müllerin" had also stuck a large paper in the net full of white powdered-sugar, which was broken, and overwhelmed the poor baker, whose face now looked like a living spring. Fortunately we were near a town — Peesin.

I think they called it. Here he found comfort, and we other preliminaries toward resting ourselves; that is to say, we had just time to sit down, when the postilion blew his horn, and we were again crammed into our wandering prison. The baker no longer recited verse; but, by an association of ideas, he passed from the governess's dog to Goethe's "Faust," where the dog in particular had been so devilish good. He had seen this piece in Berlin, and placed it equally as high as "Rolla's Death," which was his favorite piece, for he had once performed in it in his youth as a young savage. "Die schöne Müllerin" and I passed the time in talking about the different sorts of cheese, and I rose considerably in her esteem when I told her the way to prepare Funen's sour-milk cheese. We, however, went forward at a rapid rate, and every time I peeped out of the window I saw nothing but white sand and dark fir woods.

The tailor, who sat between the baker and governess, cast a look now and then to the window, but it required a swan's neck to look out; and as we just happened to pass a large thistle, that stood here as a symbol of fertility, he lisped, with a look at the baker, to whom he wished to show his acquaintance with literature, —

"Röslein, Röslein, Röslein roth,
Röslein auf der Haiden;"

but then stopped short, quite perplexed, and looked at his handkerchief, which he played with, as he probably feared that the baker would regard this outburst as an allusion to himself; for he also sat here in the sand with a face round and red as a "Röslein roth, Röslein auf der Haiden."

We drove continually forward; it was just as if an ever green piece of calico with white spots had been extended before the windows of our vehicle — not a change in the whole country. I wished now that I had the last act of "Drei Tage aus dem Leben eines Spielers," which I went away from in Brunswick. It would have done some good.

The dark night, however, brought us an incident, or rather a comic scene, only it is a pity that it was more dramatic than epic, and therefore cannot so well be told as performed. We stopped to change horses before one of those pretty two-storied inns, with fluted columns in the walls, and handsome façades, that one finds on the way between Berlin and Hamburg. We all got out, except the old governess and her lap-dog, which she still had in a bag, to refresh ourselves in the neat and prettily ornamented guests'-room. The old lady fell asleep in the mean time, and perhaps dreamt of her youth, when she also was a rose ; for every wild brier has been such a flower. At length she awakes ; there is no one but herself and the dog in the carriage — she looks out, all is dark and still as death — no light shines through the windows of the house. The horses are taken from the carriage ; she screams out, for her traveling companions have travelled on, and forgotten her : she sits alone here in the middle of the high-road, in the Prussian sands, in the depth of night !

We were all in the guests'-room, on the other side of the house, as there were some minutes to spare before the horses would be put to. We heard the scream, ran out of the house to render assistance, and opened the carriage door ; but her terror was now greater than before, as she thought it was some one who would rob her. She screamed, the dog barked, and we shouted to each other in order to get an explanation, which even then it was not very easy to obtain.

We were now soon off again. The Prussian roads are excellent ; they are as if one drove over a chamber floor.

At length we came to the frontiers of Mecklenburg. The land here is a smiling oasis in the midst of the desert. Here we again saw noble trees, oaks and beeches : the corn waved in the fields, and I dreamt I was in the middle of Sealand. Ludwigslüst, with its palace, its large gardens, and broad avenues, lay before us. A window stood open in the inn yard where we stopped ; a sparrow sat on it and chirped merrily. I know not what it was, but both the bird itself and the voice seemed familiar to me. It was certainly the same little person that chirped outside my window the last morning I was in Denmark, but who I did not then understand.

At Lauenburg there were enormous sand banks in succession ; it looked as if the sea had lately receded and left them behind.

The road soon became so broad that it scarcely knew where

its own end was. Sometimes it ran in between those white mountains, where the carriage sank so deep that the horses could scarcely drag it from the place ; and then think that it was moonlight, and that we neither saw nor heard a living being but ourselves ! I have said I would depict this, that I would paint Hamburg and Lubeck on my return tour, now that I am quiet within the wall of Copenhagen ; but as I take the pen, that little bird sits again outside my window and chirps as before I travelled, and as it chirped at Ludwigslüst. I really think it says the self-same words as then, and it is the third time. It *must* be a critic, for it puts me in a bad humor ! Therefore there will be no more rambling sketches — not even of the glorious sea, which was also out of humor when I came home ; but that dark look suited it well, as did the fresh breeze that filled the sail and whirled the black smoky column up into the air. The towers of Copenhagen rose before us : they appeared to me pointed and satirical, as if they were a type of that pen which, perhaps, would scratch out my sketches.

Many a little bird that sings in the woods, if it were corrected every time it sang, would certainly soon be quiet, and grieve itself to death behind the green hedges ; but the poet, —

> Nor praise, nor blame, must stop his free pursuit ;
> With storm and sun the flower becomes a fruit !

PICTURES OF SWEDEN.

PICTURES OF SWEDEN.

I.

WE TRAVEL.

IT is a delightful spring; the birds warble, but you do not understand their song? Well, hear it in a free translation.

"Get on my back," says the stork, our green island's sacred bird, "and I will carry thee over the Sound. Sweden also has fresh and fragrant beech woods, green meadows, and corn-fields. In Scania, with the flowering apple-trees behind the peasant's house, you will think that you are still in Denmark."

"Fly with me," says the swallow; "I fly over Holland's mountain ridge, where the beech-trees cease to grow; I fly further toward the north than the stork. You shall see the vegetable mould pass over into rocky ground; see snug, neat towns, old churches and mansions, where all is good and comfortable, where the family stand in a circle around the table and say grace at meals, where the least of the children says a prayer, and, morning and evening, sings a psalm. I have heard it, I have seen it, when little, from my nest under the eaves."

"Come with me! come with me!" screams the restless sea-gull, and flies in an expecting circle. "Come with me to the Skjärgaards, where rocky isles by thousands, with fir and pine, lie like flower-beds along the coast; where the fishermen draw the well-filled nets!"

"Rest thee between our extended wings," sing the wild swans. "Let us bear thee up to the great lakes, the perpetually roaring elvs (rivers), that rush on with arrowy swiftness; where the oak forest has long ceased, and the birch-tree becomes stunted. Rest thee between our extended wings: we fly up to Sulitelma, the island's eye, as the mountain is called; we fly from the vernal valley, up over the snow-drifts, to the mountain's top, whence thou canst see the North Sea, on yonder side of Norway.

"We fly to Jemteland, where the rocky mountains are high and blue; where the Foss roars and rushes; where the torches are lighted as *budstikke*,[1] to announce that the ferryman is expected. Up to the deep, cold, running waters, where the midsummer sun does not set; where the rosy hue of eve is that of morn."

That is the birds' song. Shall we lay it to heart? Shall we accompany them — at least a part of the way? We will not sit upon the stork's back, or between the swans' wings. We will go forward with steam, and with horses — yes, also on our own legs, and glance now and then from reality, over the fence into the region of thought, which is always our near neighbor land; pluck a flower or a leaf, to be placed in the note-book — for it sprung out during our journey's flight: we fly and we sing. Sweden, thou glorious land! Sweden, where, in ancient times, the sacred gods came from Asia's mountains! land that still retains rays of their lustre, which streams from the flowers in the name of "Linnæus;" which beams for thy chivalrous men from Charles XII.'s banner; which sounds from the obelisk on the field of Lutzen! Sweden, thou land of deep feeling, of heartfelt songs! home of the limpid elvs, where the wild swans sing in the gleam of the Northern Lights! Thou land, on whose deep, still lakes Scandinavia's fairy builds her colonnades, and leads her battling, shadowy host over the icy mirror! Glorious Sweden! with thy fragrant Linnæus, with Jenny's soul-enlivening songs! To thee will we fly with the stork and the swallow, with the restless sea-gull and the wild swans. Thy birch woods exhale refreshing fragrance under their sober, bending branches; on the tree's white stem the harp shall hang: the North's summer wind shall whistle therein!

[1] A chip of wood in the form of a halberd, circulated for the purpose of convening the inhabitants of a district in Sweden and Norway.

II.

TROLLHÄTTA.

WHOM did we meet at Trollhätta? It is a strange story, and we will relate it.

We landed at the first sluice, and stood as it were in a garden laid out in the English style. The broad walks are covered with gravel, and rise in short terraces between the sunlit greensward: it is charming, delightful here, but by no means imposing. If one desires to be excited in this manner, one must go a little higher up to the older sluices, which, deep and narrow, have burst through the hard rock. It looks magnificent, and the water in its dark bed far below is lashed into foam. Up here one overlooks both elv and valley; the bank of the river on the other side rises in green, undulating hills, grouped with leafy trees and red-painted wooden houses, which are bounded by rocks and pine forests. Steamboats and sailing vessels ascend through the sluices; the water itself is the attendant spirit that must bear them up above the rock, and from the forest itself it buzzes, roars, and rattles. The din of Trollhätta Falls mingles with the noise from the saw-mills and smithies.

"In three hours we shall be through the sluices," said the captain: "in that time you will see the Falls. We shall meet again at the inn up here."

We went from the path through the forest: a whole flock of bare-headed boys surrounded us. They would all be our guides; the one screamed longer than the other, and every one gave his contradictory explanation, how high the water stood, and how high it did not stand, or could stand. There was also a great difference of opinion amongst the learned.

We soon stopped on a ling-covered rock, a dizzying terrace. Before us, but far below, was the roaring water, the

Hell Fall, and over this again, fall after fall, the rich, rapid, rushing elv — the outlet of the largest lake in Sweden. What a sight! what a foaming and roaring, above — below! It is like the waves of the sea, but of effervescing champagne — of boiling milk. The water rushes round two rocky islands at the top, so that the spray rises like meadow dew. Below, the water is more compressed, then hurries down again, shoots forward and returns in circles like smooth water, and then rolls, darting its long sea-like fall into the Hell Fall. What a tempest rages in the deep — what a sight! Words cannot express it!

Nor could our screaming little guides. They stood mute; and when they again began with their explanations and stories, they did not come far, for an old gentleman whom none of us had noticed (but he was now amongst us) made himself heard above the noise, with his singularly sounding voice. He knew all the particulars about the place, and about former days, as if they had been of yesterday.

"Here, on the rocky holms," said he, "it was that the warriors in the heathen times, as they are called, decided their disputes. The warrior Stärkodder dwelt in this district, and liked the pretty girl Ogn right well; but she was fonder of Hergrimmer, and therefore he was challenged by Stärkodder to combat here by the falls, and met his death; but Ogn sprung toward them, took her bridegroom's bloody sword, and thrust it into her own heart. Thus Stärkodder did not gain her. Then there passed a hundred years, and again a hundred years: the forests were then thick and closely grown; wolves and bears prowled here summer and winter; the place was infested with malignant robbers, whose hiding-place no one could find. It was yonder, by the fall before Top Island, on the Norwegian side — there was their cave: now it has fallen in! The cliff there overhangs it!"

"Yes, the Tailor's Cliff!" shouted all the boys. "It fell in the year 1755!"

"Fell!" said the old man, as if in astonishment that any one but himself could know it. "Everything will fall once, and the tailor directly. The robbers had placed him upon the cliff and demanded that if he would be liberated from them, his ransom should be that he should sew a suit of clothes up there; and he tried it; but at the first stitch, as he drew the thread out, he became giddy and fell down into the rushing water, and thus the rock got the name of 'The Tailor's Cliff.' One day the robbers caught a young girl, and she betrayed them, for she kindled a fire in the cavern. The smoke was seen, the caverns discovered, and the robbers were imprisoned and executed. That outside there is called 'The Thieves' Fall,' and down there under the water is another cave; the elv rushes in there and returns boiling; one can see it well up here, one hears it too, but it can be heard better under the bergman's loft."

And we went on and on, along the Fall, toward Top Island, continuously on smooth paths covered with saw-dust, to Polham's Sluice. A cleft had been made in the rock for the first intended sluice-work, which was not finished, but whereby art has created the most imposing of all Trollhätta's Falls,— the hurrying water falling here perpendicularly into the black deep. The side of the rock is here placed in connection with Top Island by means of a light iron bridge, which appears as if thrown over the abyss. We venture on to the rocking bridge over the streaming, whirling water, and then stand on the little cliff island, between firs and pines, that shoot forth from the crevices. Before us darts a sea of waves, which are broken by the rebound against the stone block where we stand, bathing us with the fine spray. The torrent flows on each side, as if shot out from a gigantic cannon, fall after fall: we look out over them all, and are filled with the harmonic sound, which, since time began, has ever been the same.

"No one can ever get to the island there," said one of our party, pointing to the large island above the topmost fall.

"I however know one!" said the old man, and nodded with a peculiar smile.

"Yes, my grandfather could!" said one of the boys; "scarcely any one besides has crossed during a hundred years. The cross that is set up over there was placed there by my grandfather. It had been a severe winter, the whole of Lake Wener was frozen; the ice dammed up the outlet, and for many hours there was a dry bottom. Grandfather has told about it: he went over with two others, placed the cross up, and returned. But then there was such a thundering and cracking noise, just as if it were cannons. The ice broke up and the elv came over the fields and forest. It is true, every word I say!"

One of the travellers quoted Tegnér: —

> "Vildt Göta störtade från Fjällen,
>   Hemsk Trollet från sat Toppfall röt!
>   Men Snillet kom och sprängt stod Hällen,
>   Med Skeppen i sitt sköt!"

"Poor mountain sprite," he continued, "thy power and glory recede! Man flies over thee — thou mayst go and learn of him."

The garrulous old man made a grimace, and muttered something to himself — but we were just by the bridge before the inn. The steamboat glided through the opened way, every one hastened to get on board, and it directly shot away above the Fall, just as if no Fall existed.

"And that can be done!" said the old man. He knew nothing at all about steamboats, had never before that day seen such a thing, and accordingly he was sometimes up and sometimes down, and stood by the machinery and stared at the whole construction, as if he were counting all the pins and screws. The course of the canal appeared to him to be something quite new; the plan of it and the guide-books were quite foreign objects to him: he turned them and turned them — for read I do not think he could. But he knew all the particulars about the country — that is to say, from olden times.

I heard that he did not sleep at all the whole night. He studied the passage of the steamboat; and when we in the morning ascended the sluice terraces higher and higher, from lake to lake, away over the high-plain — higher, continually higher — he was in such activity that it appeared as if it could not be greater — and then we reached Motala.

The Swedish author Tjörnerös relates of himself, that when a child he once asked what it was that ticked in the clock, and they answered him that it was one named "*Bloodless.*" What brought the child's pulse to beat with feverish throbs and the hair on his head to rise, also exercised its power in Motala, over the old man from Trollhätta.

We now went through the great manufactory in Motala. What ticks in the clock, beats here with strong strokes of the hammer. It is *Bloodless*, who drank life from human thought, and thereby got limbs of metals, stone, and wood; it is *Bloodless*, who by human thought gained strength which man himself does not physically possess. *Bloodless* reigns in Motala, and through the large foundries and factories he extends his hard limbs, whose joints and parts consist of wheel within wheel, chains, bars, and thick iron wires. Enter, and see how the glowing iron masses are formed into long bars. *Bloodless* spins the glowing bar! see how the shears cut into the heavy metal plates; they cut as quietly and as softly as if the plates were paper. Here where he hammers, the sparks fly from the anvil. See how he breaks the thick iron bars; he breaks them into lengths; it is as if it were a stick of sealing-wax that is broken. The long iron bars rattle before your feet; iron plates are planed into shavings; before you rolls the large wheel, and above your head runs living wire — long heavy wire! There is a hammering and buzzing, and if you look around in the large open yard, amongst great up-turned copper boilers for steamboats and locomotives, *Bloodless* also here stretches out one of his fathom-long fingers, and hauls away. Everything is living; man alone stands and is silenced by — *stop!*

The perspiration oozes out of one's fingers' ends: one turns and turns, bows, and knows not one's self, from pure respect for the human thought which here has iron limbs. And yet the large iron hammer goes on continually with its heavy strokes: it is as if it said: " Banco, Banco! many thousand dollars; Banco, pure gain! Banco! Banco!" Hear it, as I heard it; see, as I saw!

The old gentleman from Trollhätta walked up and down in full contemplation; bent and swung himself about; crept on his knees, and stuck his head into corners and between the machines, for he would know everything so exactly; he would see the screw in the propelling vessels, understand its mechanism and effect under water — and the water itself poured like hail-drops down his forehead. He fell unconscious, backward into my arms, or else he would have been drawn into the machinery, and crushed: he looked at me, and pressed my hand.

"And all this goes on naturally," said he; "simply and comprehensibly. Ships go against the wind, and against the stream, sail higher than forests and mountains. The water must raise, steam must drive them!"

"Yes," said I.

"Yes," said he, and again *yes*, with a sigh which I did not then understand; but, months after, I understood it, and I will at once make a spring to that time, and we are again at Trollhätta.

I came here in the autumn, on my return home; stayed some days in this mighty piece of nature, where busy human life forces its way more and more in, and, by degrees, transforms the picturesque to the useful manufactory. Trollhätta must do her work; saw beams, drive mills, hammer and break to pieces: one building grows up by the side of the other, and in half a century hence here will be a city. But that was not the story.

I came, as I have said, here again in the autumn. I found the same rushing and roaring, the same din, the same rising and sinking in the sluices, the same chattering boys who conducted fresh travellers to the Hell Fall, to the iron bridge island, and to the inn. I sat here and turned over the leaves of books, collected through a series of years, in which travellers have inscribed their names, feelings, and thoughts at Trollhätta — almost always the same astonishment, expressed in different languages, though generally in Latin: *Veni, vidi, obstupui.*

One has written: "I have seen nature's masterpiece pervade that of art;" another cannot say what he saw, and what he saw he cannot say. A mine owner and manufacturer, full of the doctrine of utility, has written: "Seen with the greatest pleasure this useful work for us in Värmeland, Trollhätta." The wife of a dean from Scania expresses herself thus. She has kept to the family, and only signed in the remembrance book as to the effect of her feelings at Trollhätta. "God grant my brother-in-law fortune, for he has understanding!" Some few have added witticisms to the others' feelings; yet as a pearl on this heap of writing shines Tegnér's poem, written by himself in the book on the 28th of June, 1804, —

"Götha kom i dans från Seves fjällar," etc.

I looked up from the book and who should stand before me, just about to depart again, but the old man from Trollhätta! Whilst I had wandered about, right up to the shores of the Silja, he had continually made voyages on the canal; seen the sluices and manufactories, studied steam in all its possible powers of service, and spoke about a projected railway, in Sweden, between the Hjalmar and Wener. He had, however, never yet seen a railway, and I described to him these extended roads, which sometimes rise like ramparts, sometimes like towering bridges, and at times like halls of miles in length, cut through rocks. I also spoke of America and England.

"One takes breakfast in London, and the same day one drinks tea in Edingburgh."

"That I can do!" said the man, and in as cool a tone as if no one but himself could do it.

"I can also," said I; "and I have done it."

"And who are you, then?" he asked.

"A common traveller," I replied; "a traveller who pays for his conveyance. And who are you?"

The man sighed.

"You do not know me: my time is past; my power is nothing! *Bloodless* is stronger than I!" and he was gone.

I then understood who he was. Well, in what humor must a poor mountain sprite be, who only comes up every hundred years to see how things go forward here on the earth!

It was the mountain sprite and no other, for in our time every intelligent person is considerably wiser; and I looked with a sort of proud feeling on the present generation, on the gushing, rushing, whirling wheel, the heavy blows of the hammer, the shears that cut so softly through the metal plates, the thick iron bars that were broken like sticks of sealing-wax, and the music to which the heart's pulsations vibrate: " Banco, Banco, a hundred thousand Banco!" and all by steam — by mind and spirit.

It was evening. I stood on the heights of Trollhätta's old sluices, and saw the ships with outspread sails glide away through the meadows like spectres, large and white. The sluice gates were opened with a ponderous and crashing sound, like that related of the copper gates of the secret council in Germany. The evening was so still that Trollhätta's Fall was as audible in the deep stillness as if it were a chorus from a hundred water-mills — ever one and the same tone. In one, however, there sounded a mightier crash that seemed to pass sheer through the earth; and yet with all this the endless silence of nature was felt. Suddenly a large bird flew out from the trees, far in the forest, down toward the Falls. Was it the mountain sprite? We will imagine so, for it is the most interesting fancy.

III.

THE BIRD PHŒNIX.

IN the garden of Paradise, under the tree of knowledge, stood a hedge of roses. In the first rose a bird was hatched; its flight was like that of light, its colors beautiful, its song magnificent.

But when Eve plucked the fruit of the tree of knowledge, when she and Adam were driven from the garden of Paradise, a spark from the avenging angel's flaming sword fell into the bird's-nest and kindled it. The bird died in the flames, but from the red egg there flew a new one — the only one — the ever only bird Phœnix. The legend states that it takes up its abode in Arabia; that every hundred years it burns itself up in its nest, and that a new Phœnix, the only one in the world, flies out from the red egg.

The bird hovers around us, rapid as the light, beautiful in color, glorious in song. When the mother sits by the child's cradle, it is by the pillow, and with its wings flutters a glory around the child's head. It flies through the chamber of contentment, and there is the sun's radiance within: the poor chest of drawers is odoriferous with violets.

But the bird Phœnix is not alone Arabia's bird: it flutters in the rays of the Northern Lights on Lapland's icy plains; it hops amongst the yellow flowers in Greenland's short summer. Under Fahlun's copper rocks, in England's coal mines, it flies like a powdered moth over the hymn-book in the pious workman's hands. It sails on the lotus-leaf down the sacred waters of the Ganges, and the eyes of the Hindoo girl glisten on seeing it.

The bird Phœnix! Dost thou not know it? The bird of Paradise, song's sacred swan! It sat on the car of Thespis, like a croaking raven, and flapped its black, dregs-besmeared wings ; over Iceland's minstrel-harp glided the swan's red, sounding bill. It sat on Shakespeare's shoulder like Odin's raven, and whispered in his ear : " Immortality ! " It flew at the minstrel competition, through Wartzburg's knightly halls.

The bird Phœnix! Dost thou not know it ? It sang the " Marseillaise " for thee, and thou didst kiss the plume that fell from its wing : it came in the lustre of Paradise, and thou perhaps didst turn thyself away to some poor sparrow that sat with merest tinsel on its wings.

Bird of Paradise ! regenerated every century, bred in flames, dead in flames ; thy image set in gold hangs in the saloons of the rich, even though thou fliest often astray and alone. " The bird Phœnix in Arabia " — is but a legend.

In the garden of Paradise, when thou wast bred under the tree of knowledge, in the first rose, our Lord kissed thee and gave thee thy proper name — Poetry.

IV.

KINNAKULLA.

KINNAKULLA, Sweden's hanging gardens! Thee will we visit. We stand by the lowest terrace in a wealth of flowers and verdure; the gray pointed wooden tower of the ancient village church leans as if it would fall; it produces an effect in the landscape; we would not even be without that large flock of birds, which just now chance to fly away over the mountain forest.

The high-road leads up the mountain with short palings on either side, between which we see extensive plains with hops, wild roses, corn-fields, and delightful beech woods, such as are not to be found in any other place in Sweden. The ivy winds itself around old trees and stones — even to the withered trunk green leaves are lent. We look out over the flat, extended woody plain to the sunlit church-tower of Mariestad, which shines like a white sail on the dark green-sea: we look out over Wener Lake, but cannot see its further shore. Skjärgaards' wood-crowned rocks lie like a wreath down in the lake; the steamboat comes — see! down by the cliff under the red-roofed mansions, where the beech and walnut-trees grow in the garden.

The travellers land; they wander under shady trees away over that pretty light-green meadow, which is enwreathed by gardens and woods: no English park has a finer verdure than the meadows near Hellekis. They go up to "the grottoes," as they call the projecting masses of red stone higher up, which, being thoroughly kneaded with petrifactions, project from the declivity of the earth, and remind one of the mouldering colossal tombs in the Campagna of Rome. Some are smooth and rounded off by the action of the water, others bear the moss of ages, grass, and flowers, nay, even tall trees.

The travellers go from the forest road up to the top of Kinnakulla, where a stone is raised as the goal of their wanderings. The traveller reads in his guide-book about the rocky strata of Kinnakulla: "At the bottom is found sandstone, then alum-stone, then limestone, and above this red-stone, higher still slate, and lastly, trap." And, now that he has seen this, he descends again, and goes on board. He has seen Kinnakulla: yes, the stony rock here, amidst the swelling verdure, showed him one heavy, thick stone finger; and most of the travellers think they are like the devil: if they lay hold upon one finger, they have the body — but it is not always so. The least visited side of Kinnakulla is just the most characteristic, and thither will we go.

The road still leads us a long way on this side of the mountain, step by step downward, in long terraces of rich fields: further down, the slate-stone peers forth in flat layers, a green moss upon it, and it looks like threadbare patches in the green velvet carpet. The high-road leads over an extent of ground where the slate-stone lies like a firm floor. In the Campagna of Rome, one would say it is a piece of *via appia*, or antique road; but it is Kinnakulla's naked skin and bones that we pass over. The peasant's house is composed of large slate-stones, and the roof is covered with them; one sees nothing of wood except that of the door, and above it, of the large painted shield, which states to what regiment the soldier belongs who got this house and plot of ground in lieu of pay.

We cast another glance over Wener, to Lockö's old palace, to the town of Lindkjöping, and are again near verdant fields and noble trees, that cast their shadows over Blomberg, where, in the garden, the poet Geijer's spirit seeks the flower of Kinnakulla in his granddaughter, little Anna.

The plain expands here behind Kinnakulla; it extends for miles around, toward the horizon. A shower stands in the heavens; the wind has increased: see how the rain falls to the ground like a darkening veil. The branches of the trees lash one another like penitential dryads. Old Husaby church lies near us, yonder; the shower lashes the high walls, which alone stand, of the old Catholic bishop's palace. Crows and ravens fly through the long glassless windows, which time has made larger; the rain pours down the crevices in the old gray walls, as if they were now to be loosened stone from stone: but the church stands — old Husaby church — so gray and venerable, with its thick walls, its small windows, and its three spires stuck against each other, and standing, like nuts, in a cluster.

The old trees in the church-yard cast their shade over ancient graves. Where is the district's "Old Mortality," who weeds the grass, and explains the ancient memorials? Large granite stones are laid here in the form of coffins, ornamented with rude carving from the times of Catholicism. The old church-door creaks in the hinges. We stand within its walls, where the vaulted roof was filled for centuries with the fragrance of incense, with monks, and with the song of the choristers. Now it is still and mute here: the old men in their monastic dresses have passed into their graves; the blooming boys that swung the censer are in their graves; the congregation — many generations — all in their graves; but the church still stands the same. The moth-eaten, dusty cowls, and the bishops' mantle, from the days of the cloister, hang in the old oak presses; and old manuscripts, half eaten up by the rats, lie strewed about on the shelves in the sacristy.

In the left aisle of the church there still stands, and has stood time out of mind, a carved image of wood, painted in various colors which are still strong; it is the Virgin Mary with the child Jesus. Fresh flower wreaths are hung around hers and the child's head; fragrant garlands are twined around the pedestal, as festive as on Madonna's birthday feast in the times of Popery. The young folks who have been confirmed, have this day, on receiving the sacrament for the first time, ornamented this old image — nay, even set the priest's name in flowers upon the altar; and he has, to our astonishment, let it remain there.

The image of Madonna seems to have become young by the fresh wreaths: the fragrant flowers here have a power like that of poetry — they bring back the days of past centuries to our own times. It is as if the extinguished glory around the head shone again; the flowers exhale perfume: it is as if incense again streamed through the aisles of the church; it shines around the altar as if the consecrated tapers were lighted — it is a sunbeam through the window.

The sky without has become clear: we drive again in under Cleven, the barren side of Kinnakulla: it is a rocky wall, different from almost all the others. The red stone blocks lie, strata on strata, forming fortifications with embrasures, projecting wings, and round towers; but shaken, split, and fallen in ruins — it is an architectural, fantastic freak of nature. A brook falls gushing down from one of the highest points of the Cleven, and drives a little mill. It looks like a plaything which the mountain sprite had placed there and forgotten.

Large masses of fallen stone blocks lie dispersed round about; nature has spread them in the forms of carved cornices. The most significant way of describing Kinnakulla's rocky wall is to call it the ruins of a mile-long Hindostanee temple: these rocks might be easily transformed by the hammer into sacred places like the Ghaut Mountains at Ellora. If a Brahmin were to come to Kinnakulla's rocky wall, he would recognize the temple of Cailasa, and find in the clefts and crevices whole representations from Ramayana and Mahabharata. If one should then speak to him in a sort of gibberish — no matter what, only that, by the help of Brockhaus's "Conversation-Lexicon" one might mingle therein the names of some of the Indian spectacles, — Sakantala, Vikramorwasi, Uttaram Ramatscheritram, etc., — the Brahmin would be completely mystified, and write in his note-book: "Kinnakulla is the remains of a temple, like those we have in Ellora; and the inhabitants themselves know the most considerable works in our oldest Sanskrit literature, and speak in an extremely spiritual manner about them." But no Brahmin comes to the high rocky walls — not to speak of the company from the steamboat, who are already far over Lake Wener. They have seen wood-crowned Kinnakulla, Sweden's hanging gardens — and we also have now seen them.

V.

GRANDMOTHER.

GRANDMOTHER is so old, she has so many wrinkles, and her hair is quite white; but her eyes! they shine like two stars, nay, they are much finer — they are so mild, so blissful to look into. And then she knows the most amusing stories, and she has a gown with large, large flowers on it, and it is of such thick silk that it actually rustles. Grandmother knows so much, for she has lived long before father and mother — that is quite sure.

Grandmother has a psalm-book with thick silver clasps, and in that book she often reads. In the middle of it lies a rose, which is quite flat and dry; but it is not so pretty as the roses she has in the glass, yet she smiles the kindliest to it, nay, even tears come into her eyes!

Why does Grandmother look thus on the withered flower in the old book? Do you know why?

Every time that Grandmother's tears fall on the withered flower the colors become fresher; the rose then swells, and the whole room is filled with fragrance; the walls sink as if they were but mists; and round about it is the green, the delightful grove, where the sun shines between the leaves. And Grandmother — yes, she is quite young; she is a beautiful girl, with yellow hair, with round red cheeks, pretty and charming — no rose is fresher. Yet the eyes, the mild, blissful eyes, — yes, they are still Grandmother's! By her side sits a man, young and strong; he presents the rose to her and she smiles. Yet grandmother does not smile so, — yes; the smile comes, — he is gone. Many thoughts and many forms go past. That handsome man is gone; the rose lies in the psalm-book, and grandmother, — yes, she again sits like an old woman, and looks on the withered rose that lies in the book.

Now grandmother is dead!

She sat in the arm-chair, and told a long, long, sweet story. "And now it is ended!" said she, "and I am quite tired: let me now sleep a little!" And so she laid her head back to rest. She drew her breath, she slept, but it became more and more still; and her face was so full of peace and happiness — it was as if the sun's rays passed over it. She smiled, and then they said that she was dead.

She was laid in the black coffin; she lay swathed in the white linen: she was so pretty, and yet the eyes were closed — but all the wrinkles were gone. She lay with a smile around her mouth: her hair was so silvery white, so venerable, one was not at all afraid to look on the dead, for it was the sweet, benign grandmother. And the psalm-book was laid in the coffin under her head (she herself had requested it), and the rose lay in the old book — and then they buried grandmother.

On the grave, close under the church wall, they planted a rose-tree, and it became full of roses, and the nightingale sang over it, and the organ in the church played the finest psalms that were in the book under the dead one's head. And the moon shone straight down on the grave — but the dead was not there: every child could go quietly in the night-time and pluck a rose there by the church-yard wall. The dead know more than all we living know — the dead know the awe we should feel at something so strange as their coming to us. The dead are better than us all, and therefore they do not come.

There is earth over the coffin, there is earth within it; the psalm-book with its leaves is dust, the rose with all its recollections has gone to dust. But above it bloom new roses, above it sings the nightingale, and the organ plays: we think of the old grandmother with the mild, eternally young eyes. Eyes can never die! Ours shall once again see her, young and beautiful, as when she for the first time kissed the fresh red rose which is now dust in the grave.

VI.

THE PRISON-CELLS.

BY separation from other men, by solitary confinement, in continual silence, the criminal is to be punished and amended; therefore were prison-cells contrived. In Sweden there were several, and new ones have been built. I visited one for the first time in Mariestad. This building lies close outside the town, by a running water, and in a beautiful landscape. It resembles a large, white washed summer residence, window above window.

But we soon discover that the stillness of the grave rests over it. It is as if no one dwelt here, or like a deserted mansion in the time of the plague. The gates in the walls are locked: one of them is opened for us: the jailer stands with his bunch of keys: the yard is empty, but clean — even the grass weeded away between the stone paving. We enter the waiting-room, where the prisoner is received: we are shown the bathing-room, into which he is first led. We now ascend a flight of stairs, and are in a large hall, extending the whole length and breadth of the building. Galleries run along the floors, and between these the priest has his pulpit, where he preaches on Sundays to an invisible congregation. All the doors facing the gallery are half opened: the prisoners hear the priest, but cannot see him, nor he them. The whole is a well-built machine — a nightmare for the spirit. In the door of every cell there is fixed a glass, about the size of the eye: a slide covers it, and the jailer can, unobserved by the prisoner, see everything he does; but he must come gently, noiselessly, for the prisoner's ear is wonderfully quickened by solitude. I turned the slide quite softly, and looked into the closed space, when the prisoner's eye immediately met mine. It is airy, clean, and light within the cell, but the window is placed so high that it is impossible to look out of it. A high stool, made fast to a sort of table, and a hammock, which can be hung upon hooks under the ceiling, and covered with a quilt, compose the whole furniture.

Several cells were opened for us. In one of these was a young and extremely pretty girl. She had lain down in her hammock, but sprang out directly the door was opened, and her first employment was to lift her hammock down, and roll it together. On the little table stood a pitcher with water, and by it lay the remains of some oatmeal cakes, besides the Bible and some psalms.

In the cell close by sat a child's murderess. I saw her only through the little glass in the door. She had heard our footsteps; heard us speak; but she sat still, squeezed up into the corner by the door, as if she would hide herself as much as possible: her back was bent, her head almost on a level with her lap, and her hands folded over it. They said this unfortunate creature was very young. Two brothers sat here in two different cells: they were punished for horse stealing; the one was still quite a boy.

In one cell was a poor servant girl. They said: "She has no place of resort, and is without a situation, and therefore she is placed here." I thought I had not heard rightly, and repeated my question, "why she was here," but got the same answer. Still I would rather believe that I had misunderstood what was said — it would otherwise be abominable.

Outside, in the free sunshine, it is the busy day; in here it is always midnight's stillness. The spider that weaves its web down the wall, the swallow which perhaps flies a single time close under the panes there high up in the wall — even the stranger's footstep in the gallery, as he passes the cell-doors, is an event in that mute, solitary life, where the prisoners' thoughts are wrapped up in themselves. One must read of the martyr-filled prisons of the Inquisition, of the crowds chained together in the Bagnes, of the hot lead chambers of Venice, and the black, wet gulf of the wells — be thoroughly shaken by these pictures of misery, that we may with a quieter pulsation of the heart wander through the gallery of the prison-cells. Here is light, here is air; here it is more humane. Where the sunbeam shines mildly in on the prisoner, there also will the radiance of God shine into the heart.

VII.

BEGGAR BOYS.

THE painter Callot—who does not know the name, at least from Hoffmann's "in Callot's manner?"—has given a few excellent pictures of Italian beggars. One of these is a fellow on whom the one rag lashes the other: he carries his huge bundle and a large flag with the inscription, "Capitano de Baroni." One does not think that there can in reality be found such a wandering rag-shop, and we confess that in Italy itself we have not seen any such; for the beggar-boy there, whose whole clothing often consists only of a waistcoat, has in it not sufficient costume for such rags.

But we see it in the North. By the canal road between the Wener and Wigen, on the bare, dry, rocky plain there stood, like beauty's thistles in that poor landscape, a couple of beggar-boys, so ragged, so tattered, so picturesquely dirty, that we thought we had Callot's originals before us, or that it was an arrangement of some industrious parents, who would awaken the traveller's attention and benevolence. Nature does not form such things: there was something so bold in the hanging on of the rags, that each boy instantly became a Capitano de Baroni.

The younger of the two had something round him that had certainly once been the jacket of a very corpulent man, for it reached almost to the boy's ankles; the whole hung fast by a piece of the sleeve and a single brace, made from the seam of what was now the rest of the lining. It was very difficult to see the transition from jacket to trousers, the rags glided so into one another. The whole clothing was arranged so as to give him an air-bath: there were draught holes on all sides and ends; a yellow linen clout fastened to the nethermost regions seemed as if it were intended for a shirt. A very large straw hat, that had certainly been driven over several times, was stuck sideways on his head, and allowed the boy's wiry, flaxen hair to grow freely through the opening where the crown should have been: the naked brown shoulder, and upper part of the arm which was just as brown, were the prettiest of the whole.

The other boy had only a pair of trousers on. They were also ragged, but the rags were bound fast into the pockets with packthread; one string round the ankles, one under the knee, and another round about the waist. He, however, kept together what he had, and that is always respectable.

"Be off!" shouted the captain, from the vessel; and the boy with the tied-up rags turned round, and we — yes, we saw nothing but packthread, in bows, genteel bows. The front part of the boy only was covered: he had only the foreparts of trousers — the rest was packthread, the bare, naked packthread.

VIII.

WADSTENA.

IN Sweden, it is not only in the country, but even in several of the provincial towns, that one sees whole houses of grass turf, or with roofs of grass turf; and some are so low that one might easily spring up to the roof, and sit on the fresh greensward. In the early spring, whilst the fields are still covered with snow, but which is melted on the roof, this turf affords the first announcement of spring, with the young sprouting grass where the sparrow twitters, "Spring comes!"

Between Motala and Wadstena, close by the high-road, stands a grass-turf house — one of the most picturesque. It has but one window, broader than it is high, and a wild rose branch forms the curtain outside.

We see it in the spring. The roof is so delightfully fresh with grass, it has quite the tint of velvet; and close to it is the chimney, nay, even a cherry-tree grows out of its side, now full of flowers: the wind shakes the leaves down on a little lamb that is tethered to the chimney. It is the only lamb of the family. The old dame who lives here lifts it up to its place herself in the morning, and lifts it down again in the evening, to give it a place in the room. The roof can just bear the little lamb, but not more — this is an experience and a certainty. Last autumn — and at that time the grass turf roofs are covered with flowers, mostly blue and yellow, the Swedish colors — there grew here a flower of a rare kind. It shone in the eyes of the old Professor, who on his botanical tour came past here. The Professor was quickly up on the roof, and just as quick was one of his booted legs through it, and so was the other leg, and then half of the Professor himself — that part where the head does not sit; and as the house had no ceiling, his legs hovered right over the old dame's head, and that in very close contact. But now the roof is again whole; the fresh grass grows where learning sank; the little lamb bleats up there, and the old dame stands beneath, in the low doorway, with folded hands, with a smile on her mouth, rich in remembrances, legends, and songs, — rich in her only lamb, on which the cherry-tree strews its flower-blossoms in the warm spring sun.

As a background to this picture lies the Wetter — the bottomless lake as the commonalty believe — with its transparent water, its sea-like waves, and in calm, with "Hegring," or *Fata Morgana*, on its steel-like surface. We see Wadstena palace and town, "the city of the dead," as a Swedish author has called it — Sweden's Herculaneum reminiscence city. The grass turf house must be our box, whence we see the rich mementos pass before us — memorials from the chronicle of saints, the chronicle of kings, and the love songs that still live with the old dame, who stands in her low house there, where the lamb crops the grass on the roof. We hear her, and we see with her eyes; we go from the grass turf house up to the town, to the other grass turf houses, where poor women sit and make lace, once the celebrated work of the rich nuns here in the cloister's wealthy time.

How still, solitary, and grass-grown are these streets! We stop by an old wall, mouldy-green for centuries already. Within it stood the cloister; now there is but one of its wings remaining. There, within that now poor garden, still bloom St. Bridget's leek, and once rare flowers. King John and the Abbess, Ana Gylte, wandered one evening there, and the King cunningly asked, "If the maidens in the cloister were never tempted by love?" and the Abbess answered, as she pointed to a bird that just then flew over them: "It may happen! One cannot prevent the bird from flying over the garden; but one may surely prevent it from building its nest there!"

Thus thought the pious Abbess, and there have been sisters who thought and acted like her. But it is quite as sure that in the same garden there stood a pear-tree, called the tree of death; and the legend says of it, that whoever approached and plucked its fruit would soon die. Red and yellow pears weighed down its branches to the ground. The trunk was unusually large; the grass grew high around it, and many a morning hour was it seen trodden down. Who had been here during the night?

A storm arose one evening from the lake, and the next morning the large tree was found thrown down; the trunk was broken, and out from it there rolled infants' bones — the white bones of murdered children lay shining in the grass.

The pious but love-sick sister Ingrid, this Wadstena's Heloise, writes to her heart's beloved, Axel Nilsson, — for the chronicles have preserved it for us, —

"Broderne og Systarne leka paa Spil, drikke Vin och dansa med hvarandra i Tradgården!"

(The brothers and sisters amuse themselves in play, drink wine, and dance with one another in the garden.)

These words may explain to us the history of the pear-tree: one is led to think of the orgies of the nun-phantoms in "Robert le Diable," the daughters of sin on consecrated ground. But "Judge not, lest ye be judged," said the purest and best of men that was born of woman. We will read Sister Ingrid's letter, sent secretly to him she truly loved. In it lies the history of many, clear and human to us: —

"I dare not confess to any other than to thee that I am not able to repeat my Ave Maria or read my Paternoster, without calling thee to mind. Nay, even in the mass itself thy comely face appears, and our affectionate intercourse recurs to me. It seems to me that I cannot confess to any other human being — the Virgin Mary, St. Bridget, and the whole host of heaven will perhaps punish me for it. But thou knowest well, my heart's beloved, that I have never consented with my free will to these rules. My parents, it is true, have placed my body in this prison, but the heart cannot so soon be weaned from the world."

How touching is the distress of young hearts! It offers itself to us from the mouldy parchment, it resounds in old songs. Beg the gray-haired old dame in the grass turf house to sing to thee of the young, heavy sorrow; of the saving angel — and the angel came in many shapes. You will hear the song of the cloister robbery; of Herr Carl who was near to death when the young nun entered the dark chamber, sat down by his feet and whispered how sincerely she had loved him, and the knight rose from his bier and bore her away to marriage and pleasure in Copenhagen. And all the nuns of the cloister sang: "Christ, grant that such an angel were to come, and take both me and thee!"

The old dame will also sing for thee of the beautiful Agda and Oluf Tyste; and at once the cloister is revived in its splendor, the bells ring, stone houses arise — they even rise from the waters of the Wetter: the little town becomes churches and towers. The streets are crowded with great, with sober, well-dressed persons. Down the stairs of the town-hall descends, with a sword by his side and in fur-lined cloak, the most wealthy citizen of Wadstena, the merchant Michael. By his side is his young, beautiful daughter Agda, richly dressed and happy; youth in beauty, youth in mind. All eyes are turned on the rich man — and yet forget him for her, the beautiful. Life's best blessings await her; her thoughts soar upward, her mind aspires; her future is happiness! These were the thoughts of the many — and amongst the many there was one who saw her as Romeo saw Juliet, as Adam saw Eve in the garden of Paradise. That one was Oluf, the handsomest young man, but poor as Agda was rich. And he must conceal his love; but as only he lived in it, only he knew of it; so he became mute and still, and after months had passed away, the town's-folk called him Oluf Tyste (Oluf the silent).

Nights and days he combated his love; nights and days he suffered inexpressible torment; but at last — one dewdrop or one sunbeam alone is necessary for the ripe rose to open its leaves — he must tell it to Agda. And she listened to his words, was terrified, and sprang away; but the thought remained with him, and the heart went after the thought and stayed there; she returned his love strongly and truly, but in modesty and honor; and therefore poor Oluf came to the rich merchant and sought his daughter's hand. But Michael shut the bolts of his door and his heart too. He would neither listen to tears nor supplications, but only to his own will; and as little Agda also kept firm to her will, her father placed her in Wadstena cloister. And Oluf was obliged to submit, as it is recorded in the old song, that they cast

> "den svarta Muld
> Alt öfver skön Agdas arm."[1]

She was dead to him and the world. But one night, in tempestuous weather, whilst the rain streamed down, Oluf Tyste came to the cloister wall, threw his rope-ladder over it, and however high the Wetter lifted its waves, Oluf and little Agda flew away over its fathomless depths that autumn night.

Early in the morning the nuns missed little Agda. What a screaming and shouting — the cloister is disgraced! The Abbess and Michael the merchant swore that vengeance and death should reach the fugitives. Lindkjöping's severe bishop, Hans Brask, fulminated his ban over them, but they were already across the waters of the Wetter; they had reached the shores of the Wener, they were on Kinnakulla, with one of Oluf's friends, who owned the delightful Hellekis.

Here their marriage was to be celebrated. The guests were invited, and a monk from the neighboring cloister of Husaby was fetched to marry them. Then came the messenger with the bishop's excommunication, and this — but not the marriage ceremony — was read to them.

All turned away from them terrified. The owner of the house, the friend of Oluf's youth, pointed to the open door and bade them depart instantly. Oluf only requested a car and horse wherewith to convey away his exhausted Agda; but they threw sticks and stones after them, and Oluf was obliged to bear his poor bride in his arms far into the forest.

Heavy and bitter was their wandering. At last, however, they found a home: it was in Guldkroken, in West Gothland. An honest old couple gave them shelter and a place by the hearth: they stayed there till Christmas, and on that holy eve there was to be a real Christmas festival. The guests were invited, the furmenty set forth; and now came the clergyman of the parish to say prayers; but whilst he spoke he recognized Oluf and Agda, and the prayer became a curse upon the

[1] The black mould over the beautiful Agda's arm.

two. Anxiety and terror came over all; they drove the excommunicated pair out of the house, out into the biting frost, where the wolves went in flocks, and the bear was no stranger. And Oluf felled wood in the forest, and kindled a fire to frighten away the noxious animals and keep life in Agda — he thought that she must die. But just then she was stronger of the two.

"Our Lord is almighty and gracious; He will not leave us!" said she. "He has one here on the earth, one who can save us, one who has proved, like us, what it is to wander amongst enemies and wild animals. It is the King — Gustavus Vasa! He has languished like us! — gone astray in Dalecarlia in the deep snow! he has suffered, endured, knows it — he can and he will help us!"

The King was in Wadstena. He had called together the representatives of the kingdom there. He dwelt in the cloister itself, even there where little Agda, if the King did not grant her pardon, must suffer what the angry Abbess dared to advise: penance and a painful death awaited her.

Through forests and by untrodden paths, in storm and snow, Oluf and Agda came to Wadstena. They were seen: some showed fear, others insulted and threatened them. The guard of the cloister made the sign of the cross on seeing the two sinners, who dared to ask admission to the King.

"I will receive and hear all," was his royal message, and the two lovers fell trembling at his feet.

And the King looked mildly on them; and as he long had had the intention to humiliate the proud Bishop of Lindkjöping, the moment was not unfavorable to them; the King listened to the relation of their lives and sufferings, and gave them his word that the excommunication should be annulled. He then placed their hands one in the other, and said that the priest should also do the same soon; and he promised them his royal protection and favor.

And old Michael, the merchant, who feared the King's anger, with which he was threatened, became so mild and gentle, that he, as the King commanded, not only opened his house and his arms to Oulf and Agda, but displayed all his riches on the wedding-day of the young couple. The marriage ceremony took place in the cloister church, whither the King himself led the bride, and where, by his command, all the nuns were obliged to be present, in order to give still more ecclesiastical pomp to the festival. And many a heart there silently recalled the old song about the cloister robbery, and looked at Oluf Tyste: —

"Krist gif en sadan Angel
Kom, tog bâd mig och dig!"[1]

The sun now shines through the open cloister-gate. Let truth shine into our hearts; let us likewise acknowledge the cloister's share of God's influence. Every cell was not quite a prison, where the imprisoned bird flew in despair against the window-pane; here sometimes was sunshine from God in the heart and mind; from hence also went out comfort and blessings. If the dead could rise from their graves they would bear witness thereof: if we saw them in the moonlight lift the tombstone and step forth toward the cloister, they would say, "Blessed be these walls!" if we saw them in the sunlight hovering in the rainbow's gleam, they would say, "Blessed be these walls!"

How changed the rich, mighty Wadstena cloister, where the first daughters of the land were nuns, where the young nobles of the land wore the monk's cowl. Hither they made pilgrimages from Italy, from Spain: from far distant lands, in snow and cold, the pilgrim came barefooted to the cloister door. Pious men and women bore the corpse of St. Bridget hither in their hands from Rome, and all the church-bells in all the lands and towns they passed through, tolled when they came.

We go toward the cloister — the remains of the old ruin. We enter St. Bridget's cell — it still stands unchanged. It is low, small, and narrow; four diminutive panes form the whole window, but one can look from it out over the whole garden and far away over the Wetter. We see the same beautiful landscape that the fair saint saw as a frame around her God, whilst she read her morning and evening prayers. In the

[1] Christ, grant that such an angel were to come, and take both me and thee!

tile-stone of the floor there is engraved a rosary : before it, on her bare knees, she said a Paternoster at every pearl there pointed out. Here is no chimney — no hearth, no place for it. Cold and solitary it is, and was, here where the far-famed woman dwelt, — she who by her own sagacity, and by her contemporaries was raised to the throne of female saints.

From this poor cell we enter one still meaner, one still more narrow and cold, where the faint light of day struggles in through a long crevice in the wall. Glass there never was here: the wind blows in. Who was she who once dwelt in this cell?

In our times they have arranged light, warm chambers close by: a whole range opens into the broad passage. We hear merry songs ; laughter we hear, and weeping: strange figures nod to us from these chambers. Who are these? The rich cloister of St. Bridget's, to which kings made pilgrimages, is now Sweden's mad-house. And here the numerous travellers write their names on the wall. We hasten from the hideous scene into the splendid cloister church, — the blue church, as it is called, from the blue stones of which the walls are built, — and here, where the large stones of the floor cover great men, abbesses, and queens, only one monument is noticeable, that of a knightly figure carved in stone, which stands aloft before the altar. It is that of the insane Duke Magnus. Is it not as if he stepped forth from amongst the dead, and announced that such afflicted creatures were to be where St. Bridget once ruled ?

Pace lightly over the floor ! Thy foot treads on the graves of the pious: the flat, modest stone here in the corner covers the dust of the noble Queen Philippa. She, that mighty England's daughter, the great-hearted, the immortal woman, who with wisdom and courage defended her consort's throne, — that consort who rudely and barbarously cast her off! Wadstena's cloister gave her shelter — the grave here gave her rest.

We seek one grave. It is not known — it is forgotten, as she was in her life-time. Who was she ? The cloistered sister Elizabeth, daughter of the Holstein Count, and once the bride of King Hakon of Norway. Sweet creature! she proudly — but not with unbecoming pride — advanced in her bridal dress, and with her court ladies, up to her royal consort. Then came King Valdemar, who by force and fraud stopped the voyage, and induced Hakon to marry Margaret, then eleven years of age, who thereby got the crown of Norway. Elizabeth was sent to Wadstena cloister, where her will was not asked. Afterward when Margaret — who justly occupies a great place in the history of Scandinavia, but only comparatively a small one in the hearts — sat on the throne, powerful and respected, she visited the then flourishing Wadstena, where the Abbess of the cloister was St. Bridget's granddaughter, her chilhood's friend: Margaret kissed every monk on the cheek. The legend is well known about him, the handsomest, who thereupon blushed. She kissed every nun on the hand, and also Elizabeth, her, whom she would only see here. Whose heart throbbed loudest at that kiss? Poor Elizabeth, thy grave is forgotten, but not the wrong thou didst suffer.

We now enter the sacristy. Here, under a double coffin lid, rests an age's holiest saint in the North, Vadstene cloister's diadem and lustre — St. Bridget.

On the night she was born, says the legend, there appeared a beaming cloud in the heavens, and on it stood a majestic virgin, who said: "Of Birger is born a daughter whose admirable voice shall be heard over the whole world." This delicate and singular child grew up in the castle of her father, Knight Brahe. Visions and revelations appeared to her, and these increased when she, only thirteen years of age, was married to the rich Ulf Gudmundsen, and became the mother of many children. "Thou shalt be my bride and my agent," she heard Christ say, and every one of her actions was, as she averred, according to his announcement. After this she went to Nidaros, to St. Oluf's holy shrine: she then went to Germany, France, Spain, and Rome.

Sometimes honored and sometimes mocked, she travelled, even to Cyprus and Palestine. Conscious of approaching death, she again reached Rome, where her last revelation was that she should rest in Wadstena, and that this cloister especially should be sanctified by God's love. The splendor of the

Northern Lights does not extend so far around the earth as the glory of this fair saint, which now is but a legend. We bend with silent, serious thoughts before the mouldering remains in the coffin here — said to be those of St. Bridget and her daughter St. Catherine; but even of these the remembrance will be extinguished. There is a tradition amongst the people, that in the time of the Reformation the real remains were carried off to a cloister in Poland, but this is not certainly known. Wadstena, at least, is not the repository of St. Bridget and her daughter's dust.

Wadstena was once great and glorious. Great was the cloister's power, as St. Bridget saw it in the prospect of death. Where is now the cloister's might? It reposes under the tombstones — the graves alone speak of it. Here, under our feet, only a few steps from the church door, is a stone in which are carved fourteen rings: they announce that fourteen farms were given to the cloister, in order that he who moulders here might have this place, fourteen feet within the church door. It was Boa Johnson Grip, a great sinner; but the cloister's power was greater than that of all sinners: the stone on his grave records it with no ordinary significance of language.

Gustavus, the first Vasa, was the sun — the ruling power: the brightness of the cloister star must needs pale before him.

There yet stands a stone outline of Wadstena's rich palace which he erected, with towers and spires, close by the cloister. At a far distance on the Wetter, it looks as if it still stood in all its splendor; near, in moonlight nights, it appears the same unchanged edifice, for the fathom-thick walls yet remain; the carvings over the windows and gates stand forth in light and shade, and the moat round about, which is only separated from the Wetter by the narrow carriage road, takes the reflection of the immense building as a mirrored image.

We now stand before it in daylight. Not a pane of glass is to be found in it; planks and old doors are nailed fast to the window frames; the balls stand only on two of the towers, broad, heavy, and resembling colossal toad-stools. The iron spire of the one still towers aloft in the air; the other spire is bent: like the hands on a sun-dial it shows the time — the time that is gone. The other two balls are half fallen down ; lambs frisk about between the beams, and the space below is used as a cow-stall.

The arms over the gateway have neither spot nor blemish : they seem as if carved yesterday ; the walls are firm, and the stairs look like new. In the palace yard, far above the gateway, the great folding door was opened, whence once the minstrels stepped out and played a welcome greeting from the balcony, but even this is broken down : we go through the spacious kitchen, on whose white walls a sketch of Wadstena Palace, ships, and flowering trees, in red chalk, still attract the eye.

Here where they cooked and roasted, is now a large empty space : even the chimney is gone ; and from the ceiling where thick, heavy beams of timber have been placed close to one another, there hangs the dust-covered cobweb, as if the whole were a mass of dark-gray dropping stones.

We walk from hall to hall, and the wooden shutters are opened to admit daylight. All is vast, lofty, spacious, and adorned with antique chimney-pieces, and from every window there is a charming prospect over the clear, deep Wetter. In one of the chambers in the ground-floor sat the insane Duke Magnus (whose stone image we lately saw conspicuous in the church), horrified at having signed his own brother's death-warrant ; dreamingly in love with the portrait of Scotland's queen, Mary Stuart ; paying court to her, and expecting to see the ship, with her, glide over the sea toward Wadstena. And she came — he thought she came — in the form of a mermaid, raising herself aloft on the water : she nodded and called to him, and the unfortunate Duke sprang out of the window down to her. We gazed out of this window, and below it we saw the deep moat in which he sank.

We enter the yeoman's hall, and the council-hall, where, in the recesses of the windows, on each side, are painted yeomen in strange dresses, half Dalecarlians and half Roman warriors.

In this once rich saloon, Svanta Steenson Sture knelt to Sweden's queen, Catherine Léjonhufvud : she was Svanta Sture's love, before Gustavus Vasa's will made her his Queen. The lovers met here : the walls are silent as to what they said, when the door was opened and the King entered, and saw the kneeling Sture, and asked what it meant. Margaret answered craftily and hastily: "He demands my sister Martha's hand in marriage!" and the King gave Svanta Sture the bride the Queen had asked for him.

We are now in the royal bridal chamber, whither King Gustavus led his third consort, — Catherine Steenbock, also another's bride, — the bride of the Knight Gustavus. It is a sad story.

Gustavus of the three roses was in his youth honored by the King, who sent him on a mission to the Emperor Charles V. He returned adorned with the Emperor's costly golden chain — young, handsome, joyous, and richly clad, he returned home, and knew well how to relate the magnificence and charms of foreign lands: young and old listened to him with admiration, but young Catherine most of all. Through him the world in her eyes became twice as large, rich, and beautiful; they became dear to each other, and their parents blessed their love. The love-pledge was to be drunk, — when there came a message from the King, that the young Knight must, without delay, again bear a letter and greeting to the Emperor Charles. The betrothed pair separated with heavy hearts, but with a promise of mutual inviolable troth. The King then invited Catherine's parents to come to Wadstena Palace. Catherine was obliged to accompany them; here King Gustavus saw her for the first time, and the old man fell in love with her.

Christmas was kept with great hilarity; there were song and harp in these halls, and the King himself played the lute. When the time came for departure, the King said to Catherine's mother that he would marry the young girl.

"But she is the bride of the Knight Gustavus!" stammered the mother.

"Young hearts soon forget their sorrows," thought the King. The mother thought so likewise, and as there chanced to come a letter the same day and hour from the young Knight Gustavus, Frau Steenbock committed it to the flames. All the letters that came afterward and all the letters that Catherine wrote were burnt by her mother, and doubts and evil reports were whispered to Catherine, that she was forgotten abroad by her young lover. But Catherine was secure and firm in her belief of him. In the spring her parents made known to her the King's proposal, and praised her good fortune. She answered seriously and determinedly, "No!" and when they repeated to her that it should and must happen, she repeatedly screamed in the greatest anguish, "No, no!" and sank exhausted at her father and mother's feet, and humbly prayed them not to force her.

And the mother wrote to the King that all was going on well, but that her child was bashful. The King now announced his visit to Torpe, where her parents, the Steenbocks, dwelt. The King was received with rejoicing and feasting, but Catherine had disappeared, and the King himself was the successful one who found her. She sat dissolved in tears under the wild rose-tree, where she had bidden farewell to her heart's beloved.

There were merry song and joyous life in the old mansion; Catherine alone was sorrowful and silent. Her mother had brought her all her jewels and ornaments, but she wore none of them: she had put on her simplest dress, but in this she only fascinated the old King the more, and he would have it that their betrothal should take place before he departed. Frau Steenbock wrested the Knight Gustavus's ring from Catherine's finger, and whispered in her ear: "It will cost the friend of thy youth his life and fortune; the King can do everything!" And the parents led her to King Gustavus, showed him that the ring was from the maiden's hand; and the King placed his own golden ring on her finger in the other's stead. In the month of August the flag waved from the mast of the royal yacht which bore the young Queen over the Wetter. Princes and knights in costly robes stood by the shore, music played, and the people shouted. Catherine made her entry into Wadstena Palace. The nuptials were celebrated the following day, and the walls were hung with silk and velvet, with cloth of gold and silver   It was a festival and rejoicing. Poor Catherine!

In November, the Knight Gustavus of the three roses returned home. His prudent, noble mother, Christina Gyllenstjerne, met him at the frontiers of the kingdom, prepared him, consoled him, and soothed his mind: she accompanied him by slow stages to Wadstena, where they were both invited by the King to remain during the Christmas festival. They accepted the invitation, but the Knight Gustavus was not to be moved to come to the King's table or any other place where the Queen was to be found. The Christmas approached. One Sunday evening, Gustavus was disconsolate; the Knight was long sleepless, and at daybreak he went into the church, to the tomb of his ancestress, St. Bridget. There he saw, at a few paces from him, a female kneeling before Philippa's tomb. It was the Queen he saw; their eyes met, and Gustavus hastened away. She then mentioned his name, begged him to stay, and commanded him to do so.

"I command it, Gustavus!" said she: "the Queen commands it."

And she spoke to him; they conversed together, and it became clear to them both what had been done against them and with them; and she showed him a withered rose which she kept in her bosom, and she bent toward him and gave him a kiss, the last — their eternal leave-taking — and then they separated. He died shortly afterward, but Catherine was stronger, and yet not strong enough for her heart's deep sorrow. Here, in the bed-chamber, in uneasy dreams, says the story, she betrayed in sleep the constant thought of her heart, her youth's love, to the King, saying: "Gustavus I love dearly; but the rose — I shall never forget."

From a secret door we walk out on the open rampart, where the sheep now graze; the cattle are driven into one of the ruined towers. We see the palace yard, and look from it up to a window. Come, thou birch-wood's thrush, and warble thy lays; sing, whilst we recall the bitterness of love in the rude, the chivalrous ages.

Under that window there stood, one cold winter's night, wrapped in his white cloak, the young Count John, of East Friesland. His brother had married Gustavus Vasa's eldest daughter, and departed with her to his home: wherever they came on their journey, there was mirth and feasting, but the greatest splendor was at Wadstena Palace. Cecilia, the King's younger daughter, had accompanied her sister hither, and was here, as everywhere, the first, the most beautiful in the chase as well as at the tournament. The winter began directly on their arrival at Wadstena; the cold was severe, and the Wetter frozen over. One day Cecilia rode out on the ice and it broke; her brother Prince Erik, came galloping to her aid. John, of East Friesland, was already there, and begged Erik to dismount, as he would, being on horseback, break the ice still more. Erik would not listen to him, and as John saw that there was no time for dispute, he dragged Erik from the horse, sprang into the water himself, and saved Cecilia. Prince Erik was furious with wrath, and no one could appease him. Cecilia lay long in a fever, and during its continuance, her love for him who had saved her life increased. She recovered, and they understood each other, but the day of separation approached. It was on the night previous that John, in his white cloak, ascended from stone to stone, holding by his silk ladder, until he at length entered the window; here they would converse for hours in all modesty and honor, speak about his return and their nuptials the following year; and whilst they sat there the door was hewn down with axes. Prince Erik entered, and raised the murderous weapon to slay the young Lord of East Friesland, when Cecilia threw herself between them. But Erik commanded his menials to seize the lover, whom they put in irons and cast into a low, dark hole, that cold frosty night; and the next day, without even giving him a morsel of bread or a drop of water, he was thrown on a peasant's sledge, and dragged before the King to receive judgment. Erik himself cast his sister's fair name and fame into slander's babbling pool, and high dames and citizen's wives washed unspotted innocence in calumny's impure waters.

It is only when the large wooden shutters of the saloons are opened that the sunbeams stray in here; the dust accumulates in their twisted pillars, and is only just disturbed by the draught of air. In here is a warehouse for corn. Great fat rats make their nests in these halls. The spider spins mourning banners under the beams. This is Wadstena Palace!

We are filled with sad thoughts. We turn our eyes from this place toward the lowly house with the grass turf roof, where the little lamb crops the grass under the cherry-tree, which strews its fragrant leaves over it. Our thoughts descend from the rich cloister, from the proud palace, to the grassy turf, and the sun fades away over the turf, and the old dame goes to sleep under the sod, below which lie the mighty memorials of Wadstena.

IX.

THE PUPPET SHOWMAN.

THERE was an elderly man on the steamboat, with such a contented face that, if it did not lie, he must be the happiest man on earth. That he indeed said he was: I heard it from his own mouth. He was a Dane, consequently my countryman, and was a travelling theatrical manager. He had the whole *corps dramatique* with him; they lay in a large chest — he was a puppet showman. His innate good-humor, said he, had been tried by a polytechnic candidate,[1] and from this experiment on his patience he had become completely happy. I did not understand him at the moment, but he soon laid the whole case clearly before me; and here it is.

"It was in Slagelse," said he, "that I gave a representation at the parsonage, and had a brilliant house and a brilliant company of spectators, all young persons, unconfirmed, except a few old ladies. Then there came a person dressed in black, having the appearance of a student: he sat down amongst the others, laughed quite at the proper time, and applauded quite correctly; that was an unusual spectator!

"I was bent on ascertaining who he was, and then I heard that he was a candidate from the polytechnic school, who had been sent out to instruct people in the provinces. At eight o'clock my representation was over; the children were to go early to bed, and one must think of the convenience of the public.

"At nine o'clock the candidate began his lectures and experiments, and now *I* was one of *his* auditory.

"It was remarkable to hear and look at! The chief part of it went over my head and into the parson's, as one says. Can it be possible, thought I, that we human beings can find

[1] One who has passed his examination at a polytechnic school.

out such things? in that case, we must also be able to hold out longer, before we are put into the earth. It was merely small miracles that he performed, and yet all as easy as an old stocking — quite from nature. In the time of Moses and the prophets, such a polytechnic candidate would have been one of the wise men of the land, and in the Middle Ages he would have been burnt. I could not sleep the whole night, and as I gave a representation the next evening, and the candidate was there again, I got into a real merry humor.

" I have heard of an actor who, when playing the lovers' parts, only thought of one of the spectators; he played for *her* alone, and forgot all the rest of the house; the polytechnic candidate was my *her*, my only spectator, for whom I played. And when the performance was over, all the puppets were called forward, and I was invited by the polytechnic candidate to take a glass of wine with him; and he spoke about my comedy, and I of his science; and I believe we each derived equal pleasure from the other. But yet I had the advantage, for there was so much in his performance that he could not account for: as, for instance, that a piece of iron which falls through a spiral line, becomes magnetic, — well, how is that? The spirit comes over it, but whence does it come from? it is just as with the human beings of this world, I think; our Lord lets them fall through the spiral line of time, and the spirit comes over them — and there stands a Napoleon, a Luther, or a similar person.

" 'All nature is a series of miracles,' said the candidate, 'but we are so accustomed to them that we call them things of every-day life.' And he spoke and he explained, so that it seemed at last as if he lifted my skull, and I honestly confessed, that if I were not an old fellow, I would go directly to the polytechnic school, and learn to examine the world in the summer, although I was one of the happiest of men.

" 'One of the happiest!' said he, and it was just as if he tasted it. 'Are you happy?'—'Yes!' said I, 'I am happy, and I am welcome in all the towns I come to with my company! There is certainly one wish, that comes now and then like a nightmare, which rides on my good-humor, and that is to be a theatrical manager for a living company — a company of real men and women.'

"'You wish to have your puppets animated; you would have them become real actors and actresses,' said he, 'and yourself be the manager? you then think that you would be perfectly happy?'

"Now, he did not think so, but I thought so; and we talked for and against; and we were just as near in our opinions as before. But we clinked our glasses together, and the wine was very good; but there was witchcraft in it, or else the short and the long of the story would be — that I was intoxicated.

"That I was not; my eyes were quite clear; it was as if there was sunshine in the room, and it shone out of the face of the polytechnic candidate, so that I began to think of the old gods in their youth, and when they went about in the world. And I told him so, and then he smiled, and I durst have sworn that he was a disguised god, or one of the family. And he was so — my first wish was to be fulfilled: the puppets became living beings and I the manager of men and women. We drank that it should be so! he put all my puppets in the wooden chest, fastened it on my back, and then let me fall through a spiral line. I can still hear how I came down, slap! I lay on the floor, that is quite sure and certain, and the whole company sprang out of the chest. The spirit had come over us all together; all the puppets had become excellent artists — they said so themselves — and I was the manager. Everything was in order for the first representation; the whole company must speak with me, and the public also. The female dancer said that if she did not stand on one leg the house would be in an uproar: she was master of the whole, and would be treated as such.

"She who played the queen would also be treated as a queen when off the stage, or else she should get out of practice, and he who was employed to come in with a letter made himself as important as the first lover. 'For,' said he, 'the small are of just as much importance as the great, in an artistic whole.' Then the hero demanded that the whole of his part should only be retorts on making his exit, for these the public applauded; the prima donna would only play in a red light, for that suited her best — she would not be blue: they were all like flies in a bottle, and I was also in the bottle — for I was the manager. I lost my breath, my head was quite dizzy I was as miserable as a man can be ; it was a new race of beings I had come amongst ; I wished that I had them altogether again in the chest, that I had never been a manager : I told them that they were in fact only puppets, and so they beat me to death. That was my feeling.

"I lay on the bed in my chamber ; but how I had come there from the polytechnic candidate, he must know best — for I do not. The moon shone in on the floor where the puppet chest lay upset, and all the puppets spread about — great and small, the whole lot. But I was not floored ; I sprang out of bed, and threw them all into the chest, some on their heads, and some on their legs ; I smacked the lid down and sat myself upon it : it was worth painting ; can't you conceive it ? I can ! 'Now you shall be there !' said I, ' and I will never more wish that you may become flesh and blood !' I was so glad ; I was the happiest man alive — the polytechnic candidate had tried me ! I sat in perfect bliss, and fell asleep on the chest ; and in the morning — it was properly speaking, at noon, for I slept so very long that morning — I sat there still, happy and edified — I saw that my previous and only wish had been stupid. I inquired for the polytechnic candidate, but he was gone, like the Greek and Roman gods.

"And from that time I have been the happiest man alive. I am a fortunate manager ; my company does not argue with me, neither does the public ; they are amused to their hearts' content, and I can myself put all my pieces nicely together. I take the best parts out of all sorts of comedies that I choose, and no one troubles himself about it. Pieces that are now despised at the large theatres, but which thirty years ago the public ran to see, and cried over — those pieces I now make use of. I now present them before the young folks ; and the young folks — they cry just as their fathers and mothers used to do. I give 'Johanna Montfakon' and 'Dyveke,' but abbreviated ; for the little folks do not like long, twaddling love stories. They must have it unfortunate — but it must be brief. Now that I have travelled through Denmark, both to the right and left, I know everybody and am known again. Now I have come to Sweden, and if I am successful and gain much money, I will be a Scandinavian, if the humor hold; and this I tell you, as you are my countryman."

And I, as his countryman, naturally tell it again — only for the sake of telling it.

X.

THE SKJÄRGAARDS.

THE canal voyage through Sweden goes at first constantly upward, through elvs and lakes, forests and rocky land. From the heights we look down on vast extents of forest land and large lakes, and by degrees the vessel sinks again down through mountain torrents. At Mem we are again down by the salt fjord: a solitary tower raises its head between the remains of low, thick walls — it is the ruins of Stegeborg. The coast is covered to a great extent with dark, melancholy forests, which inclose small grass-grown valleys. The screaming sea-gulls fly around our vessel ; we are by the Baltic ; we feel the fresh sea-breeze ; it blows as in the times of the ancient heroes, when the sea-kings, sons of high-born fathers, displayed their deeds here. The same sea's surface then appeared to them as now to us, with its numberless isles, which lie strewed about here in the water by thousands along the whole coast. The depth of water between the rocky isles and the solid land is that we call "The Skjärgaards:" their waters flow into each other with varying splendor. We see it in the sunshine, and it is like a large English landscape garden ; but the greensward plain is here the deep sea, the flower-beds in it are rocks and reefs, rich in firs and pines, oaks and bushes. Mark how, when the wind blows from the east, and the sea breaks over sunken rocks and is dashed back again in spray from the cliffs, your limbs feel — even through the ship on which you stand — the power of the sea: you are lifted as if by supernatural hands.

We rush on against wind and sea, as if it were the sea-god's snorting horse that bore us, from Skjärgaard to Skjärgaard. The signal-gun is fired, and the pilot comes from that solitary wooden house. Sometimes we look upon the open sea, sometimes we glide again in between dark, stony islands; they lie like gigantic monsters in the water: one has the form of the tortoise's arched shell, another has the elephant's back and rough gray color. Mouldering, light-gray rocks indicate that the waves for centuries have lashed over them.

We now approach larger rocky islands, and the huge, gray, broken rocks of the main-land, where dwarfish pine woods grow in a continual combat with the blast; the Skjärgaards sometimes become only a narrow canal, sometimes an extensive lake strewed with small islets, all of stone, and often only a mere block of stone, to which a single little fir-tree clings fast: screaming sea-gulls flutter around the landmarks that are set up; and now we see a single farm-house, whose red-painted sides shine forth from the dark background. A group of cows lie basking in the sun on the stony surface, near a little smiling pasture, which appears to have been cultivated here or cut out of a meadow in Scania. How solitary must it not be to live on that little island! Ask the boy who sits there by the cattle, he will be able to tell us. "It is lively and merry here," says he. "The day is so long and light, the seal sits out there on the stone and barks in the early morning hour, and all the steamers from the canal must pass here. I know them all; and when the sun goes down in the evening, it is like a story to look into the clouds over the land; there stand mountains with palaces, in silver and in gold, in red and in blue; sailing dragons with golden crowns, or an old giant with a beard down to his waist — altogether of clouds, and they are always changing.

"The storms come on in the autumn, and then there is often much anxiety when father is out to help ships in distress; but one becomes, as it were, a new being.

"In winter the ice is locked fast and firm, and we drive from island to island and to the main-land; and if the bear or the wolf pays us a visit we take his skin for a winter covering: it is warm in the room there, and they read and tell stories about old times!"

Yes, old Time, how thou dost unfold thyself with remembrances of these very Skjärgaards — old Time which belonged to the grave. These waters, these rocky isles and strands, saw heroes more greatly active than actively good: they swung the axe to give the mortal blow, or, as they called it, "the whining Jetteqvinde."[1]

Here came the Vikings with their ships: on the headland yonder they levied provisions; the grazing cattle were slaughtered and borne away. Ye mouldering cliffs, had ye but a tongue, ye might tell us about the duels with the two-handed sword — about the deeds of the giants. Ye saw the hero hew with the sword, and cast the javelin: his left hand was as cunning as his right. The sword moved so quickly in the air that there seemed to be three. Ye saw him, when he in all his martial array sprang forward and backward, higher than he himself was tall, and if he sprang into the sea he swam like a whale. Ye saw the two combatants: the one darted his javelin, the other caught it in the air, and cast it back again, so that it pierced through shield and man down into the earth. Ye saw warriors with sharp swords and angry hearts; the sword was struck downward so as to cut the knee, but the combatant sprang into the air, and the sword whizzed under his feet. Mighty Sagas from the olden times! Mouldering rocks, could ye but tell us of these things!

Ye, deep waters, bore the Vikings' ships, and when the strong in battle lifted the iron anchor and cast it against the enemy's vessel, so that the planks were rent asunder, ye poured your dark heavy seas into the hold, so that the bark sank. The wild *Berserk*, who with naked breast stood against his enemy's blows, mad as a dog, howling like a bear, tearing his shield asunder, rushing to the bottom of the sea here, and fetching up stones, which ordinary men could not raise — history peoples these waters, these cliffs, for us! A future poet will conjure them to this Scandinavian Archipelago, chisel the true forms out of the old Sagas, the bold, the rude, the greatness and imperfections of the time, in their habits as they lived.

They rise again for us on yonder island, where the wind is whistling through the young fir wood. The house is of beams roofed with bark: the smoke from the fire on the broad stone

---

[1] Giantess.

in the hall, whirls through the air-hole, near which stands the cask of mead; the cushions lie on the bench before the closed bedsteads; deer-skins hang over the log walls, ornamented with shields, helmets, and armor. Effigies of gods, carved on wooden poles, stand before the high seat where the noble Viking sits, a high-born father's youngest son, great in fame, but still greater in deeds; the skjalds (bards) and foster-brothers sit nearest to him. They defended the coasts of their countrymen, and the pious women; they fetched wheat and honey from England; they went to the White Sea for sables and furs — their adventures are related in song. We see the old man ride in rich clothing, with gloves sewn with golden thread, and with a hat brought from Garderike; we see the youth with a golden fillet around his brow: we see him at the *Thing;* we see him in battle and in play, where the best is he that can cut off the other's eyebrows without scratching the skin, or causing a wink with the eyes, on pain of losing his rank. The woman sits in the log-house at her loom, and in the late moonlight nights the spirits of the fallen come and sit down around the fire, where they shake the wet dripping clothes; but the serf sleeps in the ashes, and on the kitchen bench, and dreams that he dips his bread in the fat soup, and licks his fingers.

Thou future poet, thou wilt call forth the vanished forms from the Sagas, thou wilt people these islands, and let us glide past these reminiscences of the olden time with the mind full of them; clearly and truly wilt thou let us glide, as we now with the power of steam fly past that firmly standing scenery, the swelling sea, rocks and reefs, the main-land, and wood-grown islands.

We are already past Braavigen, where numberless ships from the northern kingdoms lay, when Upsala's king, Sigurd Ring, came, challenged by Harald Hildetand, who, old and gray, feared to die on a sick-bed, and would fall in battle; and the main-land thundered like the plains of Marathon beneath the tramp of horses' hoofs during the battle:[1] bards and female warriors surrounded the Danish King. The blind old man raised himself high in his chariot, gave his horse free rein,

---

[1] The battle of Braavalla.

and hewed his way. Odin himself had due reverence paid to Hildetand's bones; and the pile was kindled, and the King laid on it, and Sigurd conjured all to cast gold and weapons, the most valuable they possessed, into the fire; and the bards sang to it, and the female warriors struck the spears on the bright shields. Upsala's lord, Sigurd Ring, became King of Sweden and Denmark: so says the Saga, which sounded over the land and water from these coasts.

The memorials of olden times pass swiftly through our thoughts; we fly past the scene of manly exercises and great deeds — the ship cleaves the mighty waters with its iron paddles, from Skjärgaard to Skjärgaard.

XI.

STOCKHOLM.

WE cast runes[1] here on the paper, and from the white ground the picture of Birger Jarl's six hundred years' old city rises before thee.

The runes roll, you see! Wood-grown rocky isles appear in the light, gray morning mist; numberless flocks of wild birds build their nests in safety here, where the fresh waters of the Mälar rush into the salt sea. The Viking's ship comes; King Agna stands by the prow — he brings as booty the King of Finland's daughter. The oak-tree spreads its branches over their bridal chamber: at daybreak the oak-tree bears King Agna, hanged in his long golden chain: that is the bride's work, and the ship sails away again with her and the rescued Fins.

The clouds drive past — the years too.

Hunters and fishermen erect themselves huts; it is again deserted here, where the sea-birds alone have their homes. What is it that so frightens these numberless flocks? the wild duck and sea-gull fly screaming about, there is a hammering and driving of piles. Oluf Skötkonge has large beams bored down into the ground, and strong iron chains fastened across the stream: "Thou art caught, Oluf Haraldson,[2] — caught with the ships and crews with which thou didst devastate the royal city Sigtuna: thou canst not escape from the closed Mälar Lake!"

It is but the work of one night; the same night when Oluf Hakonson, with iron and with fire, burst his onward way

---

[1] "To cast runes" was, in the olden time, to exercise witchcraft. When the apple, with ciphers cut in it, rolled into the maiden's lap, her heart and mind were infatuated.

[2] Afterward called St. Oluf.

through the stubborn ground; before the day breaks the waters of the Mälar roll there; the Norwegian prince, Oluf, sailed through the royal channel he had cut in the east. The stockades where the iron chains hang must bear the defenses; the citizens from the burnt-down Sigtuna erect themselves a bulwark here, and build their new little town on stock-holms.[1]

The clouds go, and the years go! Do you see how the gables grow. There rise towers and forts. Birger Jarl makes the town of Stockholm a fortress; the warders stand with bow and arrow on the walls, reconnoitering over lake and fjord, over Brunkeberg sand ridge. There where the sand ridge slopes upward from Rörstrand's Lake they build Clara Cloister, and between it and the town a street springs up; several more appear; they form an extensive city, which soon becomes the place of contest for different partisans — where Ladelaas's sons plant the banner, and where the German Albrecht's retainers burn the Swedes alive within its walls. Stockholm is, however, the heart of the kingdom: that the Danes know well; that the Swedes know too, and there is strife and bloody combating. Blood flows by the executioner's hand; Denmark's Christian II., Sweden's executioner, stands in the market-place.

Roll ye runes! see over Brunkeberg sand ridge, where the Swedish people conquered the Danish host, there they raise the May-pole: it is Midsummer Eve — Gustavus Vasa makes his entry into Stockholm.

Around the May-pole there grow fruit and kitchen-gardens, houses and streets; they vanish in flames, they rise again; that gloomy fortress toward the tower is transformed into a palace, and the city stands magnificently, with towers and draw-bridges. There grows a town by itself on the sand ridge, a third springs up on the rock toward the south; the old walls fall at Gustavus Adolphus's command; the three towns are one, large and extensive, picturesquely varied with old stone houses, wooden shops, and grass-roofed huts; the sun shines on the brass balls of the towers, and a forest of masts stands in that secure harbor.

---

[1] Stock signifies bulks, or beams; holms, *i. e.* islets, or river islands; hence Stockholm.

Rays of beauty shoot forth into the world from Versailles' painted divinity; they reach the Mälar's strand, into Tessin's [1] palace, where art and science are invited as guests with the King, Gustavus III., whose effigy, cast in bronze, is raised on the strand before the splendid palace — it is in our times. The acacia shades the palace's high terrace, on whose broad balustrades flowers send forth their perfume from Saxon porcelain; variegated silk curtains hang half-way down before the large glass windows; the floors are polished smooth as a mirror, and under the arch yonder, where the roses grow by the wall, the Endymion of Greece lives eternally in marble. As a guard of honor, here stand Fogelberg's "Odin," and Sergel's "Amor and Psyche."

We now descend the broad, royal staircase, and before it, where, in by-gone times, Oluf Skötkonge stretched the iron chains across the mouth of the Mälar Lake, there is now a splendid bridge, with shops above and the Streamparterre below: there we see the little steamer *Nocken*,[2] steering its way, filled with passengers from Diurgården to the "Strömparterre." And what is the Strömparterre? The Neapolitans would tell us: It is in miniature — quite in miniature — the Stockholmers' "Villa Reale." The Hamburgers would say: It is in miniature — quite in miniature — the Stockholmers' "Jungfernstieg."

It is a very little semicircular island, on which the arches of the bridge rest; a garden full of flowers and trees, which we overlook from the high parapet of the bridge. Ladies and gentlemen promenade there; musicians play, families sit there in groups, and take refreshments in the vaulted halls under the bridge, and look out between the green trees over the open water, to the houses and mansions, and also to the woods and rocks: we forget that we are in the midst of the city.

It is the bridge here that unites Stockholm with Norrmalm, where the greatest part of the fashionable world live, in two long Berlin-like streets; yet amongst all the great houses we will only visit one, and that is the theatre.

We will go on the stage itself — it has an historical signifi-

---

[1] The architect Tessin.
[2] The water-sprite.

cance. Here, by the third side-scene from the stage-lights, to the right, as we look down toward the audience, Gustavus III. was assassinated at a masquerade; and he was borne into that little chamber there, close by the scene, whilst all the outlets were closed, and the motley group of harlequins, punchinellos, wild men, gods and goddesses with unmasked faces, pale and terrified, crept together; the ballet-farce had become a real tragedy.

This theatre is Jenny Lind's childhood's home. Here she has sung in the choruses when a little girl; here she first made her appearance in public, and was cheeringly encouraged when a child; here, poor and sorrowful, she has shed tears, when her voice left her, and sent up pious prayers to her Maker. From hence the world's nightingale flew out over distant lands, and proclaimed the purity and holiness of art.

How beautiful it is to look out from the window up here, to look over the water and the Streamparterre to that great, magnificent palace, to Ladugaards land, with the large barracks; to the Skibsholm and the rocks that rise straight up from the water, with Södermalm's gardens, villas, streets, and church cupolas between the green trees: the ships lie there together, so many and so close, with their waving flags. The beautiful, that a poet's eye sees, the world may also see! Roll, ye runes!

There stretches the whole varied prospect; a rainbow extends its arches like a frame around it. Only see! it is sunset, the sky becomes cloudy over Södermalm, the gray sky becomes darker and darker — a pitch-dark ground — and on it rests a double rainbow. The houses are illumined by so strong a sunlight that the walls seem transparent; the linden-trees in the gardens, which have lately put forth their leaves, appear like fresh young woods; the long, narrow windows in the Gothic buildings on the island shine as if it were a festal illumination, and between the dark firs there falls a lustre from the panes behind them as of a thousand flames, as if the trees were covered with flickering Christmas candles; the colors of the rainbow become stronger and stronger, the background darker and darker, and the white sunlit sea-gulls fly past.

The rainbow has placed one foot high up on Södermalm's

church-yard. Where the rainbow touches the earth, there lie treasures buried, is a popular belief here. The rainbow rests on a grave up there: Stagnalius rests here, Sweden's most gifted singer, so young and so unhappy; and in the same grave lies Nicander, he who sang about King Enzio, and of "Lejonet i Oken;"[1] who sang with a bleeding heart: the fresh vine leaf cooled the wound and killed the singer. Peace be with his dust — may his songs live forever! We go to your grave where the rainbow points. The view from here is splendid. The houses rise terrace-like in the steep, paved streets; the foot-passengers can, however, shorten the way by going through narrow lanes, and up steps made of thick beams, and always with a prospect downward of the water, of the rocks and green trees! It is delightful to dwell here, it is healthy to dwell here, but it is not genteel, as it is by Brunkeberg's sand ridge, yet it will become so: Stockholm's "Strada Balbi" will one day arise on Södermalm's rocky ground.

We stand up here. What other city in the world has a better prospect over the salt fjord, over the fresh lake, over towers, cupolas, heaped-up houses, and a palace, which King Enzio himself might have built, and round about the dark, gloomy forests with oaks, pines, and firs, so Scandinavian, dreaming in the declining sun? It is twilight; the night comes on, the lamps are lighted in the city below, the stars are kindled in the firmament above, and the tower of Ridderholm's church rises aloft toward the starry space. The stars shine through there; it is as if cut in lace, but every thread is of cast-iron and of the thickness of beams.

We go down there, and in there, in the stilly eve. A world of spirits reigns within. See, in the vaulted isles, on carved wooden horses, sits armor that was once borne by Magnus Ladulaas, Christian II., and Charles IX. A thousand flags that once waved to the peal of music and the clang of arms, to the darted javelin and the cannon's roar, moulder away here: they hang in long rags from the staff, and the staves lie cast aside, where the flag has long since become dust. Almost all the Kings of Sweden slumber in silver and copper coffins within these walls. From the altar aisle we look

[1] "The Lion in the desert;" *i. e.* Napoleon.

through the open grated door, in between piled-up drums and hanging flags: here is preserved a bloody tunic, and in the coffin are the remains of Gustavus Adolphus. Who is that dead opposite neighbor in the chapel, across there in the other side-aisle of the church? There, below a glass lid, lies a dress shot through, and on the floor stands a pair of long, thick boots; they belonged to the hero-king, the wanderer, Charles XII., whose realm is now this narrow coffin.

How sacred it is here under this vaulted roof! The mightiest men of centuries are gathered together here, perishable as these moth-eaten flags — mute and yet so eloquent. And without there is life and activity: the world goes on in its old course; generations change in the old houses; the houses change — yet Stockholm is always the heart of Sweden, Birger's city, whose features are continually renewed, continually beautified.

XII.

DIURGÅRDEN.

DIURGÅRDEN is a large piece of land made into a garden by our Lord Himself. Come with us over there. We are still in the city, but before the palace lie the broad hewn stone stairs, leading down to the water, where the Dalkulls — *i. e.*, the Dalecarlian women — stand and ring with metal bells. On board! here are boats enough to choose amongst, all with wheels, which the Dalkulls turn. In coarse white linen, red stockings with green heels, and singularly thick-soled shoes, with the upper-leather right up the shin-bone, stands the Dalkull; she has ornamented the boat, that now shoots away, with green branches. Houses and streets rise and unfold themselves; churches and gardens start forth; they stand on Södermalm high above the tops of the ships' masts. The scenery reminds one of the Bosphorus and Pera: the motley dress of the Dalkulls is quite Oriental — and listen! the wind bears melancholy Skalmeie tones out to us. Two poor Dalecarlians are making music on the quay; they are the same drawn-out, melancholy tones that are played by the Bulgarian musicians in the streets of Pera. We step out, and are in the Diurgården.

What a crowd of equipages pass in rows through the broad avenue! and what a throng of well-dressed pedestrians of all classes! One thinks of the garden of the Villa Borghese, when, at the time of the wine feast, the Roman people and strangers take the air there. We are in the Borghese Garden; we are by the Bosphorus, and yet far in the North. The pine-tree rises large and free; the birch droops its branches, as the weeping-willow alone has power to do — and what magnificently grand oaks! The pine-trees themselves are mighty trees, beautiful to the painter's eye; splendid green grass plains lie stretched before us, and the fjord rolls its green deep waters close past, as if it were a river. Large ships with swelling sails, the one high above the other, steamers and boats, come and go in varied numbers.

Come! let us go to Byström's villa; it lies on the stony cliff up there, where the large oak-trees stand in their stubborn grandeur: we see from here the whole tripartite city, Södermalm, Nordmalm, and the island with that huge palace. It is delightful that it should have been placed here on this rock, and stands built almost entirely of marble, a "Casa santa d'Italia," as if borne through the air here in the North. The walls within are painted in the Pompeiian style, but heavy: there is nothing genial. Round about stand large marble figures by Byström, which have not, however, the soul of antiquity. Madonna is incumbered by her heavy marble drapery; the girl with the flower-garland is an ugly young thing; and on seeing Hero with the weeping Cupid, one thinks of a *posé* arranged by a ballet-master.

Let us, however, see what is pretty. The little Cupid-seller is pretty, and the stone is made as flexible as life in the waists of the bathing-women. One of them, as she steps out, feels the water with her feet, and we feel, with her, a sensation that the water is cold. The coolness of the marble hall realizes this feeling. Let us go out into the sunshine, and up to the neighboring cliff, which rises above the mansions and houses. Here the wild roses shoot forth from the crevices in the rock; the sunbeams fall prettily between the splendid pines and the graceful birches, upon the high grass before the colossal bronze bust of Bellmann. This place was the favorite one of that Scandinavian improvisatore. Here he lay in the grass, composed and sang his anacreontic songs, and here, in the summer-time, his annual festival is held. We will raise his altar here in the red evening sunlight. It is a flaming bowl, raised high on the jolly tun, and it is wreathed with roses. Movits tries his hunting-horn, that which was Oberon's horn, in the inn-parlor, and everything danced, from Ulla to "Mutter paa Tuppen:"[1] they stamped with their feet and clapped their hands, and clinked the pewter lid of the ale-tankard: "Hej

[1] The landlady of an ale-house.

kara Sjæl! fukta din aska!" (Hey! dear soul! moisten your clay).

A Teniers' picture became animated, and still lives in song. Movits blows the horn on Bellmann's place around the flowing bowl, and whole crowds dance in a circle, young and old; the carriages too, horses and wagons, filled bottles and clattering tankards: the Bellmann dithyrambic clangs melodiously; humor and low life, sadness — and amongst others, about

> —— "Hur ögat gret
> Ved de Cypresser, som ströddes."[1]

Painter, seize thy brush and palette and paint the Mænad — but not her who treads the wine-bag whilst her hair flutters in the wind, and she sings ecstatic songs. No, but the Mænad that ascends from Bellmann's steaming bowl is the Punch's Anadyomene — she, with the high heels to the red shoes, with rosettes on her gown and with fluttering veil and mantilla — fluttering, far too fluttering! She plucks the rose of poetry from her breast and sets it in the ale-can's spout; clinks with the lid, sings about the clang of the hunting-horn, about breeches and old shoes, and all manner of stuff. Yet we are sensible that he is a true poet; we see two human eyes shining, that announce to us the human heart's sadness and hope.

[1] How the eyes wept by the cypresses that were strewn around.

XIII.

A STORY.

ALL the apple-trees in the garden had burst forth. They had made haste to get blossoms before they got green leaves ; and all the ducklings were out in the yard — and the cat too ! He was, so to speak, permeated by the sunshine ; he licked it from his own paws ; and if one looked toward the fields, one saw the corn standing so charmingly green ! And there was such a twittering and chirping amongst all the small birds, just as if it were a great feast. And that one might indeed say it was, for it was Sunday. The bells rang, and people in their best clothes went to church, and looked so pleased. Yes, there was something so pleasant in everything : it was indeed so fine and warm a day, that one might well say : " Our Lord is certainly unspeakably good toward us poor mortals ! "

But the clergyman stood in the pulpit in the church, and spoke loud and angrily ! He said that mankind was wicked, and that God would punish them for it, and that when they died, the wicked went down into hell, where they would burn forever ; and he said that their worm would never die, and their fire never be extinguished, nor would they ever get rest and peace !

It was terrible to hear, and he said it so determinedly. He described hell to them as a pestilential hole, where all the filthiness of the world flowed together. There was no air except the hot, sulphureous flames ; there was no bottom ; they sank and sank into everlasting silence ! It was terrible, only to hear about it ; but the clergyman said it right honestly out of his heart, and all the people in the church were quite terrified. But all the little birds outside the church sang pleasantly, and were pleased, and the sun shone so warm : it was as if every little flower said: "God is so wondrous good to us altogether!" Yes, outside it was not at all as the clergyman preached.

In the evening, when it was bed-time, the clergyman saw his wife sit still and thoughtful.

"What ails you?" he said to her.

"What ails me?" she replied; "what ails me is, that I cannot collect my thoughts rightly — that I cannot rightly understand what you said; that there were so many wicked, and that they should burn eternally! — eternally alas how long! I am but a sinful being; but I could not bear the thought in my heart to allow even the worst sinner to burn forever. And how then should our Lord permit it? He who is so wondrously good, and who knows how evil comes both from without and within. No, I cannot believe it, though you say it." . . . .

It was autumn. The leaves fell from the trees; the grave, severe clergyman sat by the bedside of a dying person; a pious believer closed her eyes — it was the clergyman's own wife.

"If any one find peace in the grave, and grace from God, then it is thou," said the clergyman, and he folded her hands, and read a psalm over the dead body.

And she was borne to the grave: two heavy tears trickled down that stern man's cheeks; and it was still and vacant in the parsonage; the sunshine within was extinguished: she was gone.

It was night. A cold wind blew over the clergyman's head; he opened his eyes, and it was just as if the moon shone into his room. But the moon did not shine. It was a figure which stood before his bed — he saw the spirit of his deceased wife. She looked on him singularly afflicted; it seemed as though she would say something.

The man raised himself half erect in bed, and stretched his arms out toward her.

"Not even to thee is granted everlasting peace. Thou dost suffer; thou, the best, the most pious!"

And the dead bent her head in confirmation of his words, and laid her hand on her breast.

"And can I procure you peace in the grave?"

"Yes!" it sounded in his ear.

"And how?"

"Give me a hair, but a single hair, of the head of that sinner whose fire will never be quenched; that sinner whom God will cast down into hell, to everlasting torment."

"Yes; so easily thou canst be liberated, thou pure, thou pious one!" said he.

"Then follow me," said the dead; "thus it is granted us. Thou canst be by my side, wheresoever thy thoughts will. Invisible to mankind, we stand in their most secret places; but thou must point with a sure hand to the one destined to eternal punishment, and ere the cock crow he must be found."

And swift, as if borne on wings of thought, they were in the great city, and the names of the dying sinners shone from the walls of the houses in letters of fire: "Arrogance, Avarice, Drunkenness, Voluptuousness;" in short, sin's whole seven-colored arch.

"Yes, in there, as I thought it, as I knew it," said the clergyman, "are housed those condemned to eternal fire."

And they stood before the splendidly-illumined portico, where the broad stairs were covered with carpets and flowers, and the music of the dance sounded through the festal saloons. The porter stood there in silk and velvet, with a large silver-headed stick.

"*Our* ball can match with the King's," said he, and turned toward the crowd in the street: his magnificent thoughts were visible in his whole person. "Poor devils! who stare in at the portico, you are altogether ragamuffins, compared to me!"

"Arrogance," said the dead; "dost thou see him?"

"Him!" repeated the clergyman; "he is a simpleton — a fool only, and will not be condemned to eternal fire and torment."

"A fool only," sounded through the whole house of Arrogance.

And they flew into the four bare walls of Avarice, where skinny, shivering with cold, hungry and thirsty, the old man clung fast with all his thoughts to his gold. They saw how he, as in a fever, sprang from his wretched pallet, and took a loose stone out of the wall. There lay gold coins in a stocking-foot; he fumbled at his ragged tunic, in which gold coins were sewed fast, and his moist fingers trembled.

"He is ill: it is insanity; encircled by fear and evil dreams."

And they flew away in haste, and stood by the criminals' wooden couch, where they slept side by side in long rows. One of them started up from his sleep like a wild animal, and uttered a hideous scream: he struck his companion with his sharp elbow, and the latter turned sleepily round.

"Hold your tongue, you beast, and sleep! this is your way every night! Every night!" he repeated; "yes, you come every night, howling and choking me! I have done one thing or another in a passion; I was born with a passionate temper, and it has brought me in here a second time; but if I have done wrong, so have I also got my punishment. But one thing I have not confessed. When I last went out from here and passed by my master's farm, one thing and another boiled up in me, and I directly stroked a lucifer against the wall: it came a little too near the thatch, and everything was burnt — hot-headedness came over it, just as it comes over me. I helped to save the cattle and furniture. Nothing living was burnt, except a flock of pigeons, — they flew into the flames, — and the yard dog. I had not thought of the dog. I could hear it howl, and that howl I always hear yet, when I would sleep; and if I do get to sleep, the dog comes also — so large and hairy! He lies down on me, howls, and strangles me! Do but hear what I am telling you. Snore — yes, that you can — snore the whole night through, and I not even a quarter of an hour!"

And the blood shone from the eyes of the fiery one; he fell on his companion, and struck him in the face with his clinched fist.

"Angry Mads has become mad again!" resounded on all sides, and the other rascals seized hold of him, wrestled with him, and bent him double, so that his head was forced between his legs, where they bound it fast, so that the blood was nearly springing out of his eyes, and all the pores.

"You will kill him!" said the clergyman; "poor unfortunate!" and as he stretched his hands out over him, who had already suffered too severely, in order to prevent further mischief, the scene changed.

They flew through rich halls, and through poor chambers; voluptuousness and envy, all mortal sins, strode past them. A recording angel read their sin and their defense; this was assuredly little for God, for God reads the heart; He knows perfectly the evil that comes within it and from without, He, grace, all loving-kindness. The hand of the clergyman trembled: he did not venture to stretch it out, to pluck a hair from the sinner's head. And the tears streamed down from his eyes, like the waters of *grace* and love, which quenched the eternal fire of hell.

The cock then crowed.

"Merciful God! Thou wilt grant her that peace in the grave which I have not been able to redeem."

"That I now have!" said the dead; "it was thy hard words, thy dark, human belief of God and his creatures, which drove me to thee! Learn to know mankind; even in the bad there is a part of God — a part that will conquer and quench the fire of hell."

And a kiss was pressed on the clergyman's lips: it shone around him. God's clear, bright sun shone into the chamber, where his wife, living, mild, and affectionate, awoke him from a dream, sent from God!

XIV.

UPSALA.

IT is commonly said that Memory is a young girl with light-blue eyes. Most poets say so; but we cannot always agree with most poets. To us Memory comes in quite different forms, all according to that land, or that town to which she belongs. Italy sends her as a charming Mignon, with black eyes and a melancholy smile, singing Bellini's soft, touching songs. From Scotland, Memory's sprite appears as a powerful lad with bare knees; the plaid hangs over his shoulder, the thistle-flower is fixed on his cap; Burns's songs then fill the air like the heath-lark's song, and Scotland's wild thistle flowers beautifully fragrant as the fresh rose. But now for Memory's sprite from Sweden, from Upsula. He comes thence in the form of a student — at least, he wears the Upsala student's white cap with the black rim. To us it points out its home, as the Phrygian cap denotes Ganymede.

It was in the year 1843 that the Danish students travelled to Upsala. Young hearts met together; eyes sparkled: they laughed, they sang. Young hearts are the future — the conquering future — in the beautiful, true, and good; it is so good that brothers should know and love each other. Friendship's meeting is still annually remembered in the palace-yard of Upsala, before the monument of Gustavus Vasa — by the hurra! for Denmark, in warm-hearted compliment to me.

Two summers afterward, the visit was returned. The Swedish students came to Copenhagen, and that they might there be known amongst the multitude, the Upsala students wore a white cap with a black rim: this cap is accordingly a memorial, — the sign of friendship's bridge over that river of blood which once flowed between kindred nations. When one meets in heart and spirit, a blissful seed is then sown. Memory's sprite, come to us! we know thee by the cap from Upsala: be thou our guide, and from our more southern home, after years and days, we will make the voyage over again, quicker than if we flew in Doctor Faustus's magic cloak. We are in Stockholm: we stand on the Ridderholm where the steamers lie alongside the docks: one of them sends forth clouds of thick smoke from its chimney; the deck is crowded with passengers, and the white cap with the black rim is not wanting.

We are off to Upsala; the paddles strike the waters of the Mälar, and we shoot away from the picturesque city of Stockholm. The whole voyage, direct to Upsala, is a kaleidoscope on a large scale. It is true, there is nothing of the magical in the scenery, but landscape gives place to landscape, and clouds and sunshine refresh their variegated beauty. The Mälar Lake curves, is compressed, and widens again: it is as if one passed from lake to lake through narrow canals and broad rivers. Sometimes it appears as if the lake ended in small rivulets between dark pines and rocks, when suddenly another large lake, surrounded by corn-fields and meadows, opens itself to view: the light-green linden-trees, which have just unfolded their leaves, shine forth before the dark gray rocks. Again a new lake opens before us, with islets, trees, and red-painted houses, and during the whole voyage there is a lively arrival and departure of passengers, in flat-bottomed boats, which are nearly upset in the billowy wake of the vessel.

It appears most dangerous opposite to Sigtuna, Sweden's old royal city: the lake is broad here; the waves rise as if they were the waters of the ocean; the boats rock — it is fearful to look at! But there must be a calm; and Sigtuna, that little interesting town where the old towers stand in ruins, like outposts along the rocks, reflects itself in the water.

We fly past! and now we are in Tyris rivulet! Part of a meadow is flooded; a herd of horses become shy from the snorting of the steamer's engine; they dash through the water in the meadow, and it spurts up all over them. It glitters there between the trees on the declivity: the Upsala students lie encamped there, and exercise themselves in the use of arms.

The rivulet forms a bay, and the high plain extends itself. We see old Upsala's hills; we see Upsala's city with its church, which, like Notre Dame, raises its stony arms toward heaven. The university rises to the view, in appearance half palace and half barracks, and there aloft, on the greensward-clothed bank, stands the old red-painted huge palace with its towers.

We stop at the bulwark near the arched bridge, and so go on shore. Whither wilt thou conduct us first, thou our guide with the white and black student's cap? Shall we go up to the palace, or to Linnæus's garden! or shall we go to the church-yard where the nettles grow over Geijer's and Törnero's graves? No, but to the young and the living Upsala's life — the students. Thou tellest us about them; we hear the heart's pulsations, and our hearts beat in sympathy!

In the first year of the war between Denmark and the insurgents, many a brave Upsala student left his quiet, comfortable home, and entered the ranks with his Danish brothers. The Upsala students gave up their most joyous festival — the May-day festival — and the money they at other times used to contribute annually toward the celebration thereof, they sent to the Danes, after the sum had been increased by concerts which were given in Stockholm and Westerås. That circumstance will not be forgotten in Denmark.

Upsala student, thou art dear to us by thy disposition! thou art dear to us from thy lively jests! We will mention a trait thereof. In Upsala, it had become the fashion to be Hegelianers — that is to say, always to interweave Hegel's philosophical terms in conversation. In order to put down this practice, a few clever fellows took upon themselves the task of hammering some of the most difficult technical words into the memory of a humorous and commonly drunken country innkeeper, at whose house many a *Sexa* was often held; and the man spoke Hegelianic in his mellow hours, and the effect was so absurd, that the employment of philosophical scraps in his speech was ridiculed, understood, and the nuisance abated.

Beautiful songs resound as we approach: we hear Swedish, Norwegian, and Danish. The melody's varied beacon makes known to us where Upsala's students are assembled. The song proceeds from the assembly-room — from the tavern saloon, and like serenades in the silent evening, when a young friend departs, or a dear guest is honored. Glorious melodies! ye enthrall, so that we forget that the sun goes down, and the moon rises.

> "Herre min Gud hvad din Månen lyser
> Se, hvilken Glands ut ofver Land och Stad!"

is now sung, and we see, —

> "Högt opp i Slottet hvarenda ruta
> Blixtrar some vore den en ädelsten."[1]

Up thither, then, is our way! Lead us, Memory's sprite, into the palace, the courteous governor of Upland's dwelling. Mild glances greet us; we see dear beings in a happy circle, and all the leading characters of Upsala. We again see him whose cunning quickened our perceptions as to the mysteries of vegetable life, so that even the toad-stool is unveiled to us as a building more artfully constructed than the labyrinths of the olden time. We see "The Flowers'" singer, he who led us to "The Island of Bliss;" we meet with him whose popular lays are borne on melodies into the world; his wife by his side. That quiet, gentle woman with those faithful eyes is the daughter of Frithiof's bard; we see noble men and women, ladies of the high nobility, with sounding and significant family names with *silver* and *lilies*, — *stars* and *swords*.

Hark! listen to that lively song. Gunnar Wennerberg, Gluntarna's poet and composer, sings his songs with Boronees,[2] and they acquire a dramatic life and reality.

How spiritual and enjoyable! one becomes happy here, one feels proud of the age one lives in, happy in being distant from the horrible tragedies that history speaks of within these walls.

We can hear about them when the song is silent, when those friendly forms disappear, and the festal lights are extinguished: from the pages of history that tale resounds with a clang of horror. It was in those times which the many still call poetic — the romantic Middle Ages — that bards sang of its most

---

[1] Lord, my God, how Thy moon shines! See what lustre over land and city! High up in the palace every pane glistens as if it were a gem.

[2] Gluntarna duets, by Gunnar Wennerberg.

brilliant periods, and covered with the radiance of their genius the sanguinary gulf of brutality and superstition. Terror seizes us in Upsala's palace: we stand in the vaulted hall, the wax-tapers burn from the walls, and King Erik XIV. sits with Saul's dark despondency, with Cain's wild looks. Niels Sture occupies his thoughts, the recollection of injustice exercised against him lashes his conscience with scourges and scorpions, as deadly terrible as they are revealed to us in the page of history.

King Erik XIV. whose gloomy distrust often amounted to insanity, thought that the nobility aimed at his life. His favorite, Goran Persson, found it to his advantage to strengthen him in this belief. He hated most the popularly favored race of the Stures, and of them, the light-haired Niels Sture in particular; for Erik thought that he had read in the stars that a man with light hair should hurl him from the throne; and as the Swedish General, after the lost battle of Svarteaa, laid the blame on Niels Sture, Erik directly believed it, yet dared not to act as he desired, but even gave Niels Sture royal presents. Yet because he was again accused by one single person of having checked the advance of the Swedish army at Båhus, Erik invited him to his palace at Svartsjö, gave him an honorable place at his royal table, and let him depart in apparent good faith for Stockholm, where, on his arrival, the heralds were ordered to proclaim in the streets: "Niels Sture is a traitor to his country!"

There Gorau Persson and the German retainers seized him and sat him by force on the executioner's most miserable hack; struck him in the face so that the blood streamed down, placed a tarred straw crown on his head, and fastened a paper with derisive words, on the saddle before him. They then let a row of hired beggar-boys and old fishwives go in couples before, and to the tail of the horse they bound two fir-trees, the roots of which dragged on the ground and swept the street after the traitor. Niels Sture exclaimed that he had not deserved this treatment from his King, and he begged the groom, who went by his side, and had served him in the field of battle, to attest the truth like an honest man; when they all shouted aloud that he suffered innocently, and had acted like a true Swede. But the procession was driven forward through the streets without stopping, and at night Niels Sture was conducted to prison.

King Erik sits in his royal palace: he orders the torches and candles to be lighted, but they are of no avail — his thoughts' scorpions sting his soul.

"I have again liberated Neils Sture," he mutters; "I have had placards put up at every street-corner, and made the heralds proclaim that no one shall dare to speak otherwise than well of Niels Sture! I have sent him on an honorable mission to a foreign court, in order to sue for me in marriage! He has had reparation enough made to him; but never will he, nor his mighty race, forget the derision and shame I have made him suffer. They will all betray me — kill me!"

And King Erik commands that all Sture's kindred shall be made prisoners.

King Erik sits in his royal palace; the sun shines, but not into the King's heart. Niels Sture enters the chamber with an answer of consent from the royal bride, and the King shakes him by the hand, making fair promises — and the following evening Niels Sture is a prisoner in Upsala Palace.

King Erik's gloomy mind is disturbed; he has no rest; he has no peace, between fear and distrust. He hurries away to Upsala Palace; he will make all straight and just again by marrying Niels Sture's sister. Kneeling, he begs her imprisoned father's consent, and obtains it; but in the very moment, the spirit of distrust is again upon him, and he cries in his insanity, —

"But you will not forgive me the shame I brought on Niels!"

At the same time, Goran Persson announced that King Erik's brother, John, had escaped from his prison, and that a revolt was breaking out. And Erik ran, with a sharp dagger, into Niels Sture's prison.

"Art thou there, traitor to thy country!" he shouted, and thrust the dagger into Sture's arm; and Sture drew it out again, wiped off the blood, kissed the hilt, and returned the weapon to the King, saying, —

"Be lenient with me, Sire; I have not deserved your disfavor."

Erik laughed aloud.

"Ho, ho! do but hear the villain! how he can pray for himself!"

And the King's halberdier stuck his lance through Niels Sture's eye, and thus gave him his death. Sture's blood cleaves to Upsala Palace — to King Erik always and everlastingly. No church masses can absolve his soul from that base crime.

Let us now go to the church.

A little flight of stairs in the side-aisle leads us up to a vaulted chamber, where kings' crowns and sceptres, taken from the coffins of the dead, are deposited in wooden closets. Here, in the corner, hangs Niels Sture's blood-covered clothes and knight's hat, on the outside of which a small silk glove is fastened. It was his betrothed one's dainty glove — that which he, knight-like, always bore.

O, barbarous era! highly vaunted as you are in song, retreat, like the storm-cloud, and be poetically beautiful to all who do not see thee in thy true light.

We descend from the little chamber, from the gold and silver of the dead, and wander in the church's aisles. The cold marble tombs, with shields of arms and names, awaken other, milder thoughts.

The walls shine brightly, and with varied hues, in the great chapel behind the high altar. The fresco paintings present to us the most eventful circumstances of Gustavus Vasa's life. Here his clay moulders, with that of his three consorts. Yonder, a work in marble, by Sargel, solicits our attention: it adorns the burial chapel of the De Geers; and here, in the centre aisle, under that flat stone, rests Linnæus. In the side chapel is his monument, erected by *amici* and *discipuli*: a sufficient sum was quickly raised for its erection, and the King, Gustavus III., himself brought his royal gift. The projector of the subscription then explained to him that the purposed inscription was, that the monument was erected only by friends and disciples, and King Gustavus answered: "And am not I also one of Linnæus's disciples?"

The monument was raised, and a hall built in the botanical garden, under splendid trees. There stands his bust; but the remembrance of himself, his home, his own little garden — where is it most vivid? Lead us thither.

On yonder side of Fyri's rivulet, where the street climbs a declivity, and red-painted wooden houses boast their living grass roofs, as fresh as if they were planted terraces, lies Linnæus's garden. We stand within it. How solitary! how overgrown! Tall nettles shoot up between the old, untrimmed, rank hedges. No water-plants appear more in that little, dried-up basin; the hedges that were formerly clipped, put forth fresh leaves without being checked by the gardener's shears.

It was between these hedges that Linnæus at times saw his own double — that optical illusion which presents the express image of a second self — from the hat to the boots.

Where a great man has lived and worked, the place itself becomes, as it were, a part and parcel of him: the whole, as well as a part, has mirrored itself in his eye; it has entered into his soul, and become linked with it and the whole world.

We enter the orangeries: they are now transformed into assembly rooms; the blooming winter-garden has disappeared; but the walls yet show a sort of herbarium. They are hung round with the portraits of learned Swedes — a herbarium from the garden of science and knowledge. Unknown faces — and, to the stranger, the greatest part are unknown names — meet us here.

One portrait amongst the many attracts our attention: it looks singular; it is the half-length figure of an old man in a shirt, lying in his bed. It is that of the learned theologian, Ödmann, who, after he had been compelled to keep his bed by a fever, found himself so comfortable in it, that he continued to lie there during the remainder of his long life, and was not to be induced to get up. Even when the next house was burning, they were obliged to carry him out in his bed into the street. Death and cold were his two bugbears. The cold would kill him, was his opinion; and so, when the students came with their essays and treatises, the manuscripts were warmed at the stove before he read them. The windows of his room were never opened, so that there was a suffocating and impure air in his dwelling. He had a writing-desk on the bed; books and manuscripts lay in confusion round about; dishes, plates, and pots stood here or there, as the convenience of the moment dictated, and his only companion was a deaf and dumb daughter.

She sat still in a corner by the window, wrapped up in herself, and staring before her, as if she were a figure that had flown out of the frame around the dark, mouldy canvas, which had once shown a picture on the wall.

Here, in the room, in this impure atmosphere, the old man lived happily, and reached his seventieth year, occupied with the translation of travels in Africa. This tainted atmosphere, in which he lay, became, to his conceit, the dromedary's high back, which lifted him aloft in the burning sun; the long, hanging-down cobwebs were the palm-trees' waving banners, and the caravan went over rivers to the wild bushmen. Old Ödmann was with the hunters, chasing the elephants in the midst of the thick reeds; the agile tiger-cat sprang past, and the serpents shone like garlands around the boughs of the trees: there was excitement, there was danger — and yet he lay so comfortably in his good and beloved bed in Upsala.

One winter's day, it happened that a Dalecarlian peasant mistook the house, and came into Ödmann's chamber in his snow-covered skin cloak, and with his beard full of ice. Ödmann shouted to him to go his way, but the peasant was deaf, and therefore stepped quite close up to the bed. He was the personification of Winter himself, and Ödmann fell ill from this visit: it was his only sickness during the many years he lay here as a polypus, grown fast, and where he was painted, as we see his portrait in the assembly room.

From the hall of learning we will go to its burial place — that is to say, its open burial place — the great library. We wander from hall to hall, up stairs and down stairs. Along the shelves, behind them and round about, stand books, those petrifactions of the mind, which might again be vivified by spirit. Here lives a kind-hearted and mild old man, the librarian, Professor Schröder. He smiles and nods as he hears how Memory's sprite takes his place here as guide, and tells of and shows, as we see, Tegnér's copy and translation of Oehlenschläger's "Hakon Jarl" and "Palnatoke." We see

Wadstena cloister's library, in thick hog's leather bindings, and think of the fair hands of the nuns that have borne them, — the pious, mild eyes that conjured the spirit out of the dead letters. Here is the celebrated Codex Argenteus, the translation of the " Four Evangelists." [1] Gold and silver letters glisten from the red parchment leaves. We see ancient Icelandic manuscripts, from De la Gardie's refined French saloon, and Thunberg's Japanese manuscripts. By merely looking at these books, their bindings and names, one at last becomes, as it were, quite worm-eaten in spirit, and longs to be out in the free air — and we are there, by Upsala's ancient hills. Thither do thou lead us, Remembrance's elf, out of the city, out on the far extended plain, where Denmark's church stands — the church that was erected from the booty which the Swedes gained in the war against the Danes. We follow the broad high-road; it leads us close past Upsala's old hills — Odin's, Thor's, and Freia's graves, as they are called.

There once stood ancient Upsala; here now are but a few peasants' farms. The low church, built of granite blocks, dates from a very remote age; it stands on the remains of a heathen temple. Each of the hills is a little mountain, yet each was raised by human hands. Letters an ell long, and whole names, are cut deep in the thin greensward, which the new sprouting grass gradually fills up. The old housewife, from the peasant's cot close by the hill, brings the silver-bound horn, a gift of Charles John XIV., filled with mead. The wanderer empties the horn to the memory of the olden time, for Sweden, and for the heart's constant thoughts — young love!

Yes, thy toast is drunk here, and many a beauteous rose has been remembered here with a heartfelt hurra; and years after, when the same wanderer again stood here, she, the blooming rose, had been laid in the earth; the spring roses had strewn their leaves over her coffined clay; the sweet music of her lips sounded but in memory; the smile in her eyes and around he mouth was gone, like the sunbeams which then shone on Upsala's hills. Her name in the greensward is grown over; she herself is in the earth, and it is closed above her; but the hill here, closed for a thousand years, is open.

[1] A Gothic translation of the Four Evangelists, and ascribed to the Mœsogothic Archbishop Ulphilas.

Through the passage which is dug deep into the hills, we come to the funereal urns which contain the bones of youthful kindred; the dust of kings, the gods of the earth.

The old housewife, from the peasant's cot, has lighted half a hundred wax-candles and placed them in rows in the otherwise pitchy-dark, stone-paved passage. It shines so festally in here over the bones of the olden time's mighty ones,— bones that are now charred and burnt to ashes. And whose were they? Thou world's power and glory, thou world's posthumous fame — dust, dust like beauty's rose, laid in the dark earth, where no light shines; thy memorials are but a name, the name but a sound. Away hence, and up on the hill where the wind blows, the sun shines, and the eye looks over the green plain, to the sunlit, dear Upsala, the students' city.

XV.

SALA.

SWEDEN'S great King, Germany's preserver, Gustavus Adolphus, founded Sala. The little forest close by still preserves legends of the heroic King's youthful love — of his meeting here with Ebba Brahe.

Sala's silver mines are the largest, the deepest, and oldest in Sweden: they reach to the depth of one hundred and seventy fathoms, consequently they are almost as deep as the Baltic. This of itself is enough to awaken an interest for a little town; but what is its appearance? "Sala," says the guide-book, "lies in a valley, in a flat, and not very pleasant district." And so truly it is: it was not very attractive approaching it our way, and the high-road led directly into the town, which is without any distinctive character. It consists of a long street, with what we may term a nucleus and a few fibres. The nucleus is the market-place, and the fibres are the few lanes diverging from it. The long street — that is to say, long in a little town — is quite without passengers; no one comes out from the doors, no one is to be seen at the windows.

It was therefore with pleased surprise that I at length descried a human being; it was at an ironmonger's, where there hung a paper of pins, a handkerchief, and two tea-pots in the window. There I saw a solitary shop-boy, standing quite still, but leaning over the counter and looking out of the open door. He certainly wrote in his journal, if he had one, in the evening: "To-day a traveller drove through the town: who he was, God knows, for I don't!" — yes, that was what the shop-boy's face said, and an honest face it was.

In the inn at which I arrived, there was the same gravelike stillness as in the street. The gate was certainly closed, but all the inner doors were wide open; the farm-yard cock stood on tiptoe in the middle of the travellers' room and crowed, in order to show that there was somebody at home. The house, however, was quite picturesque: it had an open balcony, from which one might look out upon the yard, for it would have been far too lively had it been facing the street. There hung the old sign and creaked in the wind, as if to show that it at least was alive. I saw it from my window; I saw also how the grass in the street had got the mastery over the pavement. The sun shone brightly, but shone as into a bachelor's solitary room, and on the old maid's balsams in the flower-pots. It was as still as a Scotch Sunday — and yet it was a Tuesday. One was disposed for Young's "Night Thoughts."

I looked out from the balcony into the neighboring yard; there was not a soul to be seen, but children had been playing there. There was a little garden made of dry sticks; they were stuck down in the soft soil, and had been watered; a broken pan, which had certainly served by way of watering pot, lay there still. The sticks signified roses and geraniums.

It had been a delightful garden — alas, yes! We great, grown-up men — we play just so: we make ourselves a garden with what we call love's roses and friendship's geraniums; we water them with our tears and with our heart's blood; and yet they are, and remain, dry sticks without root. It was a gloomy thought; I felt it, and in order to get the dry sticks in my thoughts to blossom, I went out. I wandered in the fibres and in the long threads — that is to say, in the small lanes — and in the great street; and here was more life than I dared to expect. I met a herd of cattle returning or going — which I knew not — for they were without a herdsman. The shop-boy stood still behind the counter, leaned over it, and greeted me; the stranger took off his hat in return — that was my day's employment in Sala.

Pardon me, thou silent town, which Gustavus Adolphus built, where his young heart felt the first emotions of love, and where the silver lies in the deep shafts — that is to say, outside the town, " in a flat, and not very pleasant district."

I knew no one in the town; I had no one to be my guide,

so I accompanied the cows, and came to the church-yard. The cows went past, but I stepped over the stile, and stood amongst the graves, where the grass grew high, and almost all the tombstones lay with worn-out inscriptions. On a few only the date of the year was legible. "Anno"—yes, what then? And who rested here? Everything on the stone was erased —blotted out like the earthly life of those mortals that here were earth in earth. What life's dream have ye dead played here in silent Sala?

The setting sun shone over the graves; not a leaf moved on the trees; all was still — still as death — in the city of the silver-mines, of which this traveller's reminiscence is but a frame around the shop-boy who leaned over the counter.

XVI.

THE MUTE BOOK.

BY the high-road into the forest there stood a solitary farm-house. Our way lay right through the farm-yard; the sun shone; all the windows were open; there was life and bustle within, but in the yard, in an arbor of flowering lilacs, there stood an open coffin. The corpse had been placed out here, and it was to be buried that forenoon. No one stood by and wept over that dead man; no one hung sorrowfully over him; his face was covered with a white cloth, and under his head there lay a large thick book, every leaf of which was a whole sheet of gray paper, and between each lay withered flowers, deposited and forgotten — a whole herbarium, gathered in different places. He himself had requested that it should be laid in the grave with him. A chapter of his life was blended with every flower.

"Who is that dead man?" we asked, and the answer was: "The old student from Upsala. They say he was once very clever; he knew the learned languages, could sing and write verses too; but then there was something that went wrong, and so he gave both his thoughts and himself up to drinking spirits, and as his health suffered by it, he came out here into the country, where they paid for his board and lodging.

"He was as gentle as a child, when the dark humor did not come over him, for then he was strong, and ran about in the forest like a hunted deer; but when we got him home, we persuaded him to look into the book with the dry plants. Then he would sit the whole day and look at one plant, and then at another, and many a time the tears ran down his cheeks. God knows what he then thought! But he begged that he might have the book with him in his coffin; and now it lies there, and the lid will soon be fastened down, and then he will take his peaceful rest in the grave!"

They raised the winding-sheet. There was peace in the face of the dead: a sunbeam fell on it; a swallow in its arrowy flight, darted into the new-made arbor, and in its flight circled twittering over the dead man's head.

How strange it is! — we all assuredly know it — to take out old letters from the days of our youth and read them: a whole life, as it were, then rises up with all its hopes, and all its troubles. How many of those with whom we, in their time, lived so devotedly, are now even as the dead to us, and yet they still live! But we have not thought of them for many years — those whom we once thought we should always cling to, and share our mutual joys and sorrows with.

The withered oak leaf in the book here is a memorial of the friend — the friend of his school-days — the friend for life. He fixed this leaf on the student's cap in the green wood, when the vow of friendship was concluded for the whole of life. Where does he now live? The leaf is preserved; friendship forgotten. Here is a foreign conservatory-plant, too fine for the gardens of the North — it looks as if there still were fragance in these leaves! — *she* gave it to him — she, the young lady of that noble garden.

Here is the marsh-lotus which he himself has plucked and watered with salt tears — the marsh-lotus from the fresh waters. And here is a nettle: what does its leaf say? What did he think on plucking it — on preserving it? Here are lilies of the valley from the woodland solitudes; here are honeysuckle leaves from the village ale-house flower-pot; and here the bare, sharp blade of grass.

The flowering lilac bends its fresh, fragrant clusters over the dead man's head; the swallow again flies past: "Quivit! quivit!" Now the men come with nails and hammer; the lid is placed over the corpse, whose head rests on the Mute Book — preserved — forgotten!

XVII.

THE SÄTHER DALE.

EVERYTHING was in order, the carriage examined, even a whip with a good lash was not forgotten. "Two whips would be best," said the ironmonger, who sold it, and the ironmonger was a man of experience, which travellers often are not. A whole bag full of "slanter"—that is, copper coins of small value—stood before us for bridge-money, for beggars, for shepherds' boys, or whoever might open the many field-gates for us that obstructed our progress. But we had to do this ourselves, for the rain pattered down and lashed the ground; no one had any desire to come out in such weather. The rushes in the marsh bent and waved; it was a real rain feast for them, and it whistled from the tops of the rushes: "We drink with our feet, we drink with our heads, we drink with the whole body, and yet we stand on one leg; hurra! We drink with the bending willow, with the dripping flowers on the bank; their cups run over—the marsh-marigold, that fine lady, can bear it better! Hurra! it is a feast! it pours, it pours; we whistle and we sing; it is our own song. To-morrow the frogs will croak the same after us and say, "It is quite new!"

And the rushes waved, and the rain pattered down with a splashing noise—it was fine weather to travel in to Säther Dale, and to see its far-famed beauties. The whip-lash now came off the whip; it was fastened on again, and again, and every time it was shorter, so that at last there was not a lash, nor was there any handle, for the handle went after the lash—or sailed after it—as the road was quite navigable, and gave one a vivid idea of the beginning of the Deluge.

One poor jade now drew too much, the other drew too little, and one of the splinter bars broke; well, by all that is vexatious, that was a fine drive! The leather apron in front had a deep pond in its folds with an outlet into one's lap. Now one of the linch-pins came out; now the twisting of the rope harness became loose, and the cross-strap was tired of holding any longer. Glorious inn in Säther, how I long more for thee than thy far-famed dale. And the horses went slower, and the rain fell faster, and so — yes, so we were not yet in Säther.

Patience, thou lank spider, that in the antechamber quietly dost spin thy web over the expectant's foot, spin my eyelids close in a sleep as still as the horse's pace! Patience? no, she was not with us in the carriage to Säther. But to the inn, by the road-side, close to the far-famed valley, I got at length, toward evening.

And everything was flowing in the yard, chaotically mingled; manure and farming implements, staves and straw. The poultry sat there washed to shadows, or at least like stuck-up hens' skins with feathers on, and even the ducks crept close up to the wet wall sated with the wet. The stable-man was cross, the girl still more so; it was difficult to get them to bestir themselves: the steps were crooked, the floor sloping and but just washed, sand strewn thickly on it, and the air was damp and cold. But without, scarcely twenty paces from the inn, on the other side of the road, lay the celebrated valley, a garden made by Nature herself, and whose charm consists of trees and bushes, wells and purling brooks.

It was a long hollow; I saw the tops of the trees looming up, and the rain drew its thick veil over it. The whole of that long evening did I sit and look upon it during that shower of showers. It was as if the Wenern, the Wettern, and a few more lakes ran through an immense sieve from the clouds. I had ordered something to eat and drink, but I got nothing. They ran up and they ran down; there was a hissing sound of roasting by the hearth; the girls chattered, the men drank "sup;"[1] strangers came, were shown to their rooms, and got both roast and boiled. Several hours had passed, when I made a forcible appeal to the girl, and she answered phlegmatically: "Why, sir, you sit there and write without stopping, so you cannot have time to eat."

[1] Swedish, *sup;* Danish, *snaps;* German, *schnaps:* English, *drams.*

It was a long evening, "but the evening passed!" It had become quite still in the inn; all the travellers, except myself, had again departed, certainly in order to find better quarters for the night at Hedemora or Brunbäck. I had seen, through the half open door into the dirty tap-room, a couple of fellows playing with greasy cards; a huge dog lay under the table and glared with its large red eyes; the kitchen was deserted; the rooms too; the floor was wet, the storm rattled, the rain beat against the windows — "and now to bed!" said I.

I slept an hour, perhaps two, and was awakened by a loud calling from the high-road. I started up: it was twilight, — the night at that period is not darker, — it was about one o'clock. I heard the door shaken roughly; a deep manly voice shouted aloud, and there was a hammering with a cudgel against the planks of the yard-gate. Was it an intoxicated or a mad man that was to be let in? The door was now opened, but many words were not exchanged. I heard a woman scream at the top of her voice from terror. There was now a great bustling about; they ran across the yard in wooden shoes; the bellowing of cattle and the rough voices of men were mingled together. I sat on the edge of the bed. Out or in! what was to be done? I looked from the window; in the road there was nothing to be seen, and it still rained. All at once some one came up stairs with heavy footsteps: he opened the door of the room adjoining mine — now he stood still! I listened — a large iron bolt fastened my door. The stranger now walked across the floor, now he shook my door, and then kicked against it with a heavy foot, and whilst all this was passing, the rain beat against the windows, and the blast made them rattle.

"Are there any travellers here?" shouted a voice; "the house is on fire!"

I now dressed myself and hastened out of the room and down the stairs. There was no smoke to be seen, but when I reached the yard, I saw that the whole building — a long and extensive one of wood — was enveloped in flames and clouds of smoke. The fire had originated in the baking oven, which no one had looked to; a traveller, who accidentally came past, saw it, called out, and hammered at the door: and the women screamed, and the cattle bellowed, when the fire stuck its red tongue into them.

Now came the fire-engine and the flames were extinguished. By this time it was morning. I stood in the road, scarcely a hundred steps from the far-famed dale. "One may as well spring into it as walk into it!" and I sprang into it; and the rain poured down, and the water flowed — the whole dale was a well.

The trees turned their leaves the wrong side out, purely because of the pouring rain, and they said, as the rushes did the day before: "We drink with our heads, we drink with our feet, and we drink with the whole body, and yet stand on our legs: hurra! it rains, and it pours; we whistle and we sing; it is our own song — and it is quite new!"

Yes, that the rushes also sang yesterday — but it was the same, ever the same. I looked and looked, and all I know of the beauty of Säther Dale is, that she had washed herself!

XVIII.

THE MIDSUMMER FESTIVAL IN LEKSAND.

LEKSAND lay on the other side of the dale-elv, which the road now led us over for the third or fourth time. The picturesque bell-tower of red painted beams, erected at a distance from the church, rose above the tall trees on the clayey declivity: old willows hung gracefully over the rapid stream. The floating bridge rocked under us — nay, it even sank a little, so that the water splashed under the horses' hoofs; but these bridges have such qualities! The iron chains that held it rattled, the planks creaked, the boards splashed, the water rose and murmured and roared, and so we got over where the road slants upward toward the town. Close opposite here the last year's May-pole still stood with withered flowers. How many of the hands that bound these flowers are now withered in the grave?

It is far prettier to go up on the sloping bank along the elv, than to follow the straight high-road into the town. The path leads us, between pasture fields and leaf trees, up to the parsonage, where we passed the evening with the friendly family. The clergyman himself was but lately dead, and his relatives were all in mourning. There was something about the young daughter — I knew not myself what it was — but I was led to think of the delicate flax-flower, too delicate for the short northern summer.

They spoke about the Midsummer Festival the next day, and of the winter season here, when the swans, often more than thirty at a time, sit (motionless themselves) on the elv, and utter strange, mournful tones. They always come in pairs, they said, two and two, and thus they also fly away again. If one of them dies, its partner always remains a long time after all the others are gone; lingers, laments, and then flies away alone and solitary.

When I left the parsonage in the evening, the moon, in its first quarter, was up. The May-pole was raised; the little steamer *Prince August*, with several small vessels in tow, came over the Siljan Lake and into the elv; a musician sprang on shore, and began to play dances under the tall wreathed May-pole. And there was soon a merry circle around it — all so happy, as if the whole of life were but a delightful summer night.

Next morning was the Midsummer Festival. It was Sunday, the 24th of June, and a beautiful sunshiny day it was. The most picturesque sight at the festival is to see the people from the different parishes coming in crowds, in large boats over Siljan's lake, and landing on its shores. We drove out to the landing-place, Barkedale, and before we got out of the town, we met whole troops coming from there, as well as from the mountains.

Close by the town of Leksand there is a row of low wooden shops on both sides of the way, which only get their interior light through the doorway. They form a whole street, and serve as stables for the parishioners, but also — and it was particularly the case that morning — to go into and arrange their finery. Almost all the shops or sheds were filled with peasant women, who were anxiously busy about their dresses, careful to get them into the right folds, and in the mean time peeped continually out of the door to see who came past. The number of arriving church-goers increased; men, women, and children, old and young, even infants; for at the Midsummer Festival no one stays at home to take care of them, and so of course they must come too — all must go to church.

What a dazzling array of colors! Fiery red and grass green aprons meet our gaze. The dress of the women is a black skirt, red bodice, and white sleeves: all of them had a psalm-book wrapped in the folded silk pocket handkerchief. The little girls were entirely in yellow, and with red aprons; the very least were in Turkish-yellow clothes. The men were dressed in black coats, like our paletôts, embroidered with red woolen cord; a red band with a tassel hung down from the large black hat; with dark knee-breeches, and blue stockings, with red leather gaiters — in, short, there was a dazzling richness of color, and that, too, on a bright sunny morning in the forest road.

This road led down a steep to the lake, which was smooth and blue. Twelve or fourteen long boats, in form like gondolas, were already drawn up on the flat strand, which here is covered with large stones. These stones served the persons who landed, as bridges; the boats were laid alongside them, and the people clambered up, and went and bore each other on land. There certainly were at least a thousand persons on the strand; and far out on the lake, one could see ten or twelve boats more coming, some with sixteen oars, others with twenty nay, even with four-and-twenty, rowed by men and women, and every boat decked out with green branches. These and the varied clothes gave to the whole an appearance of something so festal, so fantastically rich, as one would hardly think the North possessed. The boats came nearer, all crammed full of living freight; but they came silently, without noise or talking, and rowed up to the steep forest side.

The boats were drawn up on the sand: it was a fine subject for a painter, particularly one point — the way up the slope, where the whole mass moved on between the trees and bushes. The most prominent figures there were two ragged urchins, clothed entirely in bright yellow, each with a skin bundle on his shoulders. They were from Gagne, the poorest parish in Dalecarlia. There was also a lame man with his blind wife; I thought of the fable of my childhood, of the lame and the blind man: the lame man lent his eyes, and the blind his legs, and so they reached the town.

And we also reached the town and the church, and thither they all thronged: they said there were above five thousand persons assembled there. The church-service began at five o'clock. The pulpit and organ were ornamented with flowering lilacs; children sat with lilac-flowers and branches of birch; the little ones had each a piece of oat-cake, which they enjoyed. There was the sacrament for the young persons who had been confirmed; there was organ-playing and psalm-singing; but there was a terrible screaming of children, and the sound of heavy footsteps; the clumsy, iron-shod Dal shoes tramped loudly upon the stone floor. All the church pews, the gallery pews, and the centre aisle were quite filled with people. In the side-aisle one saw various groups — playing children and pious old folks; by the sacristy there sat a young mother giving suck to her child — she was a living image of the Madonna herself.

The first impression of the whole was striking, but only the first — there was too much disturbance. The screaming of children, and the noise of persons walking were heard above the singing, and, besides that, there was an insupportable smell of garlic; almost all the congregation had small bunches of garlic with them, of which they ate as they sat. I could not bear it, and went out into the church-yard: here — as it always is in nature — it was affecting, it was holy. The church door stood open; the tones of the organ and the voices of the psalm-singers were wafted out here in the bright sunlight, by the open lake: the many who could not find a place in the church stood outside, and sang with the congregation from the psalm-book: round about on the monuments, which are almost all of cast-iron, there sat mothers suckling their infants — the fountain of life flowed over death and the grave. A young peasant stood and read the inscription on a grave: —

"Ach hur södt att hafve lefvet,
Ach hur skjönt att kunne döe!"[1]

Beautiful Christian, scriptural language, verses certainly taken from the psalm-book, were read on the grave-stones; they were all read, for the service lasted several hours. This, however, by the bye, can never be good for devotion.

The crowd at length streamed from the church; the fiery-red and grass-green aprons glittered; but the mass of human beings became thicker and closer, and pressed forward. The white head-dresses, the white band over the forehead, and the white sleeves, were the prevailing colors — it looked like a long procession in Catholic countries. There was again life and motion on the road; the over-filled boats again rowed away; one wagon drove off after the other; but yet there were people left behind. Married and unmarried men stood

[1] "How sweet to have lived — how beautiful that one can die!"

in groups in the broad street of Leksand, from the church up to the inn. I was staying there, and I must acknowledge that my Danish tongue sounded quite foreign to them all. I then tried the Swedish, and the girl at the inn assured me that she understood me better than she had understood the Frenchman who the year before had spoken French to her.

As I sit in my room, my hostess's granddaughter, a nice little child, comes in, and is pleased to see my parti-colored carpet-bag, my Scotch plaid, and the red leather lining of the portmanteau. I directly cut out for her, from a sheet of white paper, a Turkish mosque, with minarets and open windows, and away she runs with it — so happy, so happy!

Shortly after, I heard much loud talking in the yard, and I had a presentiment that it was concerning what I had cut out; I therefore stepped softly out into the balcony, and saw the grandmother standing below, and with beaming face, holding my clipped-out paper at arm's length. A whole crowd of Dalecarlians, men and women, stood around, all in artistic ecstasy over my work; but the little girl — the sweet little child — screamed, and stretched out her hands after her lawful property, which she was not permitted to keep, as it was too fine.

I came in again quietly, yet, of course, highly flattered and cheered; but a moment after there was a knocking at my door; it was the grandmother, my hostess, who came with a whole plate full of spice-nuts.

"I bake the best in all Dalecarlia," said she; "but they are of the old fashion, from my grandmother's time. You cut out so well, sir, should you not be able to cut me out some new fashions?"

And I sat the whole of Midsummer Night, and clipped fashions for spice-nuts. Nut-crackers with knight's boots; windmills which were both mill and miller — but in slippers, and with the door in the stomach; and ballet-dancers that pointed with one leg toward the seven stars. Grandmother got them, but she turned the ballet-dancers up and down; the legs went too high for her; she thought that they had one leg and three arms.

"They will be new fashions," said she; "but they are difficult."

XIX.

AT THE LAKE OF SILJAN.

WE are far up in Dalarne, at the Lake of Siljan, — "Dalarne's eye," where the island of Soller, with the shining white church, forms the eye-stone. At midsummer time it is delightful to be up here. The distant mountains appear of a clear blue hue; the sunlight pours out over the bright, shining surface of water, where now and then the desert fairy, the witch of the Mediterranean Sea, Fata Morgana, comes and builds her airy castle. The Dal-peasant will tell you of the merman swimming across the Lake of Siljan, like the river-horse, with his mane of green rushes. Look out over the water, where boats are coming with bride and bridegroom and their attendants, singing and playing; look up at the neighboring woody slopes, where the red-painted wooden houses glitter in the sunshine, where the goat-bells tinkle, and songs resound full and mighty, as if resounded through the shepherd's "luur," "hoa! hoa!" It is charming here on a summer day, charming, also, in winter time, although the mercury freezes in the severe cold. The skies then seem to be higher and bluer; the pine-woods stand green in the white snow. The coal-burners' fires shine through it; the swift hunter chases the wolf and the bear, and hundreds of sleighs are gliding over Siljans' deep waters, upon its mirror of ice; the driver's furs, his cap, and beard are covered with rime. Come and see it by the full moon's light, by the red and green flashes of the aurora borealis. Enter the room when the fire sparkles in the stove and the family sit around it. There is a home feeling about it all. Ask the Dal-people! wherever they go in the world and however well they succeed, they always have a longing for their lowly home: "We live so affectionately together at home," they say.

Health, a love of work, and good-humor are the Dal-peasant's riches; he has the feeling, besides, of an ancient line, that he is nobly born, and that he is master of the house, and its squire; even the king he says "thou" to. Once when one of the grandsons of King Carl Johan was in Dalarne, an old peasant came up to him, pressed his hand, and said, "Please greet thy old grandfather for me at Stockholm!"

The Dal-people are fond of singing and dancing. They have the harp and the buckhorn, the bagpipe and the violin. They are a people endowed with a poetic heart, and the poetic heart loves its king. The Dal-people endured a long while the violence and evils which avaricious and wicked officers of justice (Fogder) practiced in the King's name. That was under the Danish government. The Danes in old time acted very harshly in the Swedish country; the Swedish soldier bore it in mind when, in the reign of Charles X., he was so severe upon the peasantry in Denmark.

Blessed be the harps that sounded, the voices that sung of reconciliation! Blessed be the modern time! Let us already in this world understand and love each other! There is such happiness when neighbors and brothers live together in unity and friendship. May the sunlight of peace in God shine over these countries!

The historical traditions from Dalarne turn our thoughts to those bloody days; it was in Dalarne that Sweden's star of unity rose.

The Scandinavian Queen Margareta was not a kind mother to her Swedish country. King Eric of Pomerania, whom some coming poet may place before the tribunal of nations, was still harsher toward it; his name resounded with maledictions under the cruelties of rough "Fogder." "Swenska Folkets Sago-Haefder" ("Traditions of the Swedish People") tells us of the "prison-stone" by the open sea, on which the peasant was placed naked in frost and cold; tells us how heroes were hung up in smoke, and often stifled by it. That was according to justice, they said, when he could not or would not pay. If the peasant's last jade died, they put him to the plough and his wife to the hay-cart. A Danish "Foged," Jösse Ericson, as cruel as the Swiss Gessler, did all that was cruel and evil toward the brave Dal-people; the bitter cup at last ran over its edges, and the Dal-men drove him away and bade him take care not to show himself among them again. The arrows were sharpened, the steel bows, taken out, and Engelbrecht Engelbrechtsson chosen their leader. He lived at "Kopparberget" (the copper mountain), where now Fahlun is situated; he was in the flower of his manhood, free-born and noble; he had served in foreign countries, and was skillful in the use of weapons and chivalric customs. To rebel against the "Foged," said he, was to rebel against the King, and he bade them restrain themselves until he had made the long journey to Copenhagen and spoken with the King. The little square built Dalcarl, with his bright eyes, his proud forehead, and the hair hanging down over his temples, entered the hall of King Eric, and uttered with clear and loud voice his people's complaints. Good promises were given him, but they were not kept, and Engelbrecht went the second time to the King but that time he was not admitted. So the Dal-people rose under the lead of Engelbrecht, drove away the wicked "Fogder," and destroyed their houses: the Dal-axe cut off the tie between King Eric and the Swedish kingdom.

History throws a gleam over Dalarne, and its pages utter stirring sounds when you visit this country. It was at the Lake of Siljan, where Rättvik and Mora's church steeples are mirrored in its surface, and in the dark forests here, that Gustavus Vasa, abandoned and pursued, strolled about in the bitter days of his youth, — the proud subject of picture and song. Christjern had decreed that the best members of the noble family of Sture, and among them the young Gustavus Ericson Vasa, should be carried as hostages to Copenhagen, and there be confined in "the blue tower." Soon after, however, Gustavus was transferred to a milder prison, to that of Kalö Castle in Jutland. His youth and beauty captivated all; he was allowed to go about surrounded only by a few guards. He was often seen sitting half dreaming, and with his large blue eyes sadly looking out over the Kattegat, toward the Swedish shores. They thought him safe, and, taking advantage of this security, he escaped, ran through woods and over heaths, and did not stop until he was twelve miles from his prison. Jutland cattle were then driven to Germany, and Gustavus Vasa became a cattle-drover. In that disguise he reached Lubeck, where he pleaded his cause so well before the burgomaster and council, that they gave him protection, and sent him on board a ship bound for Sweden. He landed at Steenso Cape, near Calmar, where he went ashore, and as most of the people here still depended on King Christjern's promises of mildness and grace, Gustavus was obliged to slink away during the night through the dense forests of his country; the best men of the family of Sture gathered here like outlaws, and the Danish "Fogder" searched for them, but most of all for Gustavus. The soldiers marched up to Stockholm, where the massacre took place. At the report of this, Gustavus fled to Dalarne. Dressed as a Dal-peasant, with an axe on his shoulder, he came to "Rankhyttan," two miles from Fahlun, and here, in the house of his former school companion, the rich miner Anders Pehrson, he entered his service and threshed grain for wages. It happened that the servant-girl saw the collar embroidered with gold-thread, which he had under his coarse dress, and told it to her master, who then privately called Gustavus before him: he heard now from him of the massacre in Stockholm, of Gustavus' mother who was imprisoned in Copenhagen, of all the hardships Sweden was suffering, and the life and blood that were sacrificed; but they were lost words, and Gustavus was obliged to run away from "Rankhyttan" and to seek refuge in the forests. It was winter time; the ice on "Lille Aaen" (the little river) broke under his weight; he dried his wet clothes at the fire in Glottorps' ferry-cottage, and then wandered to Orness, where Arendt Pehrson lived: but he was a false friend to him, and betrayed him, and sent for the "Foged," who came with seven of his men. They were already in the yard, but Arendt's wife, the kind Barbro Stigsdotter, had warned Gustavus, who, before they entered the room, swung himself down from the opening in the roof to the boy, who by Barbro's orders was on hand with a sleigh and horse, and they drove away to Korsness, to the Sandwicks cottages, and to the lake of Swartsjö (the black lake), all the time chased and startled by spies and persecutors. He was well received by the parson, Mr. Jonn, his school-boy friend. During the eight days he remained here, they talked quietly and heartily together about Sweden. But Arendt from Orness, and the "Foged," constantly sending out spies in search of him, Gustavus was again obliged to flee, and scarcely had he entered the hospitable room of Mr. Swen in Isala, when the people of the "Foged" arrived; but Swen's wife ingeniously rushed upon Gustavus, gave him a blow on the back, and scolded at him with an angry voice: "Why do you stand gaping there at the strangers, as if you had never seen people before; hurry out in the barn and thresh!" Gustavus feigned stupidity, and went out to thresh. The "Foged's" people did not think that the beaten chap was the one they were sent to catch. All the roads in Dalarne swarmed with spies and armed people; they were in search of the outlaws, but especially of Gustavus Ericson Vasa.

The Dal-people knew that he was up there, they knew that he had given himself up to them, and every one of them swore in their hearts that he, as a guest, should be safe among them, and none would betray him, like Arendt of Orness. Swen in Isala thought that Gustavus was not safe in his house, and wished to have him further up in the forest near the town of Marness. Here lived two honest men, the brothers Maths and Pehr Olofsson; but on all the roads thither, at every gate and at each bridge, stood men watching; therefore Gustavus was hidden in a cart-load of straw, driven by Swen himself, and that, too, amongst the messengers of the "Fogder." One of them thrust his long spear into the straw and pierced Gustavus in his leg. It made but a slight wound, still the blood dripped from the straw, and Swen, perceiving it, secretly cut his horse's foot so that it bled, and nobody had any suspicion of the wound. In the forests of Leksand, at the river of Liüngsoe, under a large fallen tree, whose wide-spreading branches covered a large space, the brothers hid the fugitive during three nights and days, and supplied him with food. One night, besides, he had his shelter here under the branches of a large overhanging birch-tree. Here the resolution sprang up within him to speak to the assembled people, and he ventured to go to Rättvik. In the church-yard he spoke to the parishioners of the massacre in Stockholm, and of all the evils the Swedish people were suffering. The multitude became enraged, and swore to take vengeance, but were cautious enough first to hear what the neighboring parishes would say about these things.

Gustavus went by Mora to the town of Ulmeland, where Maths Larssen's wife hid him in her cellar, and placed a large beer-tub over the trap-door, so that the Foged people might not find him when they came. He was hidden here till Christmas-time, and on one of the holy days he ascended a hill at Mora, and spoke with high and sonorous voice to the Dalmen, as they came from church. He put them in mind of their forefathers' love of liberty and father-land, how they had fought under Engelbrecht and the Stures; he spoke of the massacre in Stockholm, and of Christjern's cruelties toward Sture's widow and children. The whole assemblage was touched, some of them wept, others cried out that they would fly to arms, but soon many others came forward and spoke against Gustavus. They said that Christjern's bloodshed concerned only the nobles and not the peasants; and they might well believe it, because Christjern, so tyrannical to the nobility, was the poor man's friend. His humane laws protecting the cruelly treated peasants are witnesses in his favor in the present time. The Mora fellows wavered in their intentions, and most of them advised Gustavus to go further away, across the Norwegian frontiers, and he went away disheartened, despairing of his country.

The Norway mountains were already in sight; with dejected mind he made a halt, hungry and thirsty. The bells chimed from Lima church; he went in there to pray. His despondent heart was raised in ardent prayer to his God, and that gave him courage, fire, and strength once more to speak to the peasants. They heard him, they understood him, but dared not do anything, and he went away again and came to the town of Saelen, the last Swedish town on the frontier of Norway. Once more, last of all, he turned his eyes toward the Dal-country, and threw his glance over its pine-woods, its ice and snow. Then came with the swiftness of steam two men on skates, hurrying over ice and crusty snow; they were fleet runners dispatched from the people in Mora to look for Gustavus and call him back to be their chieftain. Our Lord ordered that just as Gustavus departed from Mora, the renowned warrior, Lars

Olafsson, arrived, an outlaw. He told them of the massacre, and that Christjern was erecting gallows all about in the country, and that he would soon do the same in Dalarne; that taxes and burdens were to be laid on them for their faithfulness to the Stures; and they repented of letting Gustavus go. Then arose an old man and said, that every time Gustavus spoke here a fresh north wind had blown: they remembered this, and as it is an old superstition here that every enterprise undertaken when the north wind blows will succeed, they all rose at once, and vowed they would sacrifice life and property for father-land and for Gustavus Ericson Vasa.

He was received with a great welcome in Mora, and marched with one thousand men to "the great copper mountain," and took as prisoners the bailiff of the mines and others of Christjern's men. The outlaws sought him wherever he came; everybody joined him, and his army had increased to fifteen thousand men when at Brunbaeck ferry he met his armed enemies.

"And more Dal-arrows swam in the air,
Than hail rains down from the sky,"

says an old song. Dal-arrows whistled over Dal-Elven's stream.

"A people that eat bark and drink nothing but water, the devil himself cannot master!" said the Danish bishop Beldenack, who went there to advise his countrymen to come away. But the Dal-men rushed on, corpses lay side by side, pierced by steel arrows that entered the breast and came out at the back. The Danes lost heavily, and the Dal-people still sing, —

"From broad and deep Brunbäcka's bank
The Jutes were hurled and heavily sank;
So Danes were driven from Sweden."

And Gustavus with his Dal-men advanced to Upsala, gave battle at Brunkeberg, and made his triumphal entrance into Stockholm, where he could then say to his Dal-men, as an old lay sings, —

"You have stood by my side like faithful Swedish men,
And if God will grant me life, I will recompense you again."

And now to Dalarne, where Gustavus wandered forlorn and persecuted; to Dalarne, where the people are frugal and contented, where the old steel bows and arrows are hanging over the chimney; where dancing goes on round the May-poles at midsummer time,— there we will go, painter and poet! We are a little of both together, otherwise we should not understand them.

The coach is ready, the coachman waits. From Leksand we drive along the lake to Rättvik and Mora. The driver will tell you of King Gustavus, every child knows of him; and if you are a Dane, and the peasant perceives it, he will with a friendly smile talk with you of the old hostile times, and of the harmony that now exists. "We know each other, and we are so much alike. Danes visit us, and Swedes visit the Danes; the Swedish soldiers wrote home and told how well they were received in the country of the Danes." He will tell you how well they understood each other, how closely they resembled each other, in customs and manners, in belief and ways of thinking. He will also tell you how abundantly corn grows in Sweden, and even up in Dalarne. Not many years ago the famine was so great that the peasant went to the dean to buy a bunch of straw, which was cut fine and mixed with the bark-bread and eaten. "Now these are good days!" he says; and he shows you his black, hard "Knukke-bröd,"[1] which he breaks with his white, strong teeth. The sun shines bright over the dark, woody mountains and over the quiet surface of the lake.

From the road at Bergsäng, the view stretches over Siljan Lake; from here you will see the copper steeple of Mora church, and behind it the blue mountains in double rank. The traveller does not go farther than to Bergsäng; here he turns back; he has now seen the most beautiful parts of Dalarne, but he has not seen the country in all its variety. Below us, but near by, lies Rättvik church, shining white like a swan on the green lake; we are going to a friendly home, to the parsonage, to happy, good-natured people. The wood is fragrant, wild currant bushes grow round about, the midsummer flower, *Primula farinosa*, blooms with its red leaves.

"You are very welcome!" and you are ushered into the large garden-parlor of the parsonage. It is as cold here as in winter, although it is midsummer, but it soon becomes comfortable; large pieces of wood are placed on end in both chim-

[1] Crack-bread; a sort of hard, dried bread of oatmeal.

neys, the fire sparkles and lifts its flames on high. Familiar neighbors, the minister, the doctor, friends from surrounding farms are gathered, the punch-bowl steams, and the conversation becomes animated, fresh, and hearty, like nature up here.

After supper we take a walk down to the church; the strong sunlight shines upon the illuminated statues. Out of the church door stands the poor-box, called Lazarus, — a very strange wooden image representing a beggar. Now come men, women, and children; a corpse is followed to the grave; men lift their hats for the dead one, the same custom which Catholic countries have. We walk through the wood, passing a little cornfield. One of our company said to us, " Passing here last summer I saw a person in the midst of the field who I thought was the minister, and was going to bid him good-day; but I saw in a moment that it was "Nalle," as we call him, a large bear, walking on his hind legs in very good humor, gnawing at an ear of corn and growling a little. I did not wish him good-day; I took care of myself, and he did the same."

From the wood we came out on the highway, from which the church of Rättvik, the lake, and the distant mountains, formed a beautiful view; we came to the new bath-house; it is comfortable and well arranged, with pleasant rooms, a reading-room, and bathing-rooms. There you may see Dal-mummies, — living, fresh-blooming, red-cheeked men, wrapped up in blankets, with the head only free; they are the bath-guests, just coming up from the cold bath. The water-cure is precisely the same as that in Graefenberg in Silesia. Books and newspapers lie on the table in the reading-room. By these you touch again the threads of the living, turbulent world; you feel through the electro-magnetic current of printed words what stirs and happens abroad; and again you spring into the open air and rejoice in the sunlight, in the exhalations of the birch-trees, by the open Siljan Lake.

We walk to the minister's house under the lofty trees and with a view over the lake. It is so pleasant and pretty in these small rooms; well-known names speak to us from the large book-shelves; all the modern literature of Scandinavia is waiting for the winter to open its enchanted garden, when ice and snow cover the earth, and Dalarne is shut out from

Europe. Poetry and science flow from eternal sources, while nature must slumber its winter sleep.

From Rättvik we drove to Mora, where Gustavus spoke to the folk ; we went up to the porphyry, factory where fine vases are fashioned ; we went on horseback on the lonely, narrow wood path up to the cottages of the Finns. It is lonely and sacred, full of grandeur and variety in Dalarne, but most beautiful of all at Siljan.

Painter, take your sketch book and colors, go up to Dalarne, and one picture after another will reveal itself to you. Come hither in the spring-time, when the young fellows are going into camp to drill ; take your place on the route near the gate as the whole crowd comes with the fiddler at their head. Children and old folks are standing upon the hill, under the drooping birch, bidding them farewell.

Enter the cloth room : no Turk's room can show such a richness of colors as here. The cloth room is usually an isolated wooden house, and is the family's wardrobe ; it is built upon high poles to hinder rats and other animals from entering ; a ladder is placed at the door that you may enter. Under the ceiling and on the walls are women's skirts and dresses of all colors, suspended on hoops, to an incredible number ; every person of the family possesses often seventeen or eighteen pieces. Here you will see aprons and bodices, the men's coats, vests, and breeches ; there are such a quantity of hose and stockings that it seems as if they were growing out of the earth. The linen seems to have its distinct place, both that with sleeves and without. The floor is covered with shoes, so clumsy, ingenious, and hump-backed that it seems to me a real invention to make such a pair. The prayer-books are placed in a row on the flower-painted shelf ; the wall itself, if you may see it for clothes, is also painted. There for instance you will see the prophet Elias hovering in his fiery chariot, drawn by sun-horses, which in the painting very much resemble hogs ; also Jacob in his wrestle with the angel. The angel is dressed in dress-coat, leather breeches, and cavalry-boots. On the windows are painted scriptural sentences and names ; tulips and roses are blooming here which you would never have seen in nature. Give us a picture of the clothing room when the young girls come for their dresses, or are hanging them up again. You will perhaps say: "That is nothing to paint;" well, be that so, but there is something to see, and therefore come.

Painter and poet, shake hands and go up to Dalarne; that poor country is rich in beauty and poetry, and richest at Siljan Lake.

XX.

FAITH AND KNOWLEDGE.

TRUTH can never be at variance with truth, science can never militate against faith: we naturally speak of them both in their purity: they respond to and they strengthen man's most glorious thought: *immortality*. And yet you may say, "I was more peaceful, I was safer when, as a child, I closed my eyes on my mother's breast and slept without thought or care, wrapping myself up simply in faith." This prescience, this compound of understanding in everything, this entering of the one link into the other from eternity to eternity, tears away from me a support — my confidence in prayer; that which is, as it were, the wings wherewith to fly to my God! If it be loosened, then I fall powerless in the dust, without consolation or hope.

I bend my energies, it is true, toward attaining the great and glorious light of knowledge, but it appears to me that therein is human arrogance: it is, as if one should say, "I will be as wise as God." "That you shall be!" said the serpent to our first parents when it would seduce them to eat of the tree of knowledge. Through my understanding I must acknowledge the truth of what the astronomer teaches and proves. I see the wonderful, eternal omniscience of God in the whole creation of the world — in the great and in the small, where the one attaches itself to the other, is joined with the other, in an endless harmonious entireness; and I tremble in my greatest need and sorrow. What can my prayer change, where everything is law, from eternity to eternity?

You tremble as you see the Almighty, who reveals Himself in all loving-kindness — that Creator, according to man's expression, whose understanding and heart are one; you tremble when you know that He has elected you to immortality

I know it in the faith, in the holy, eternal words of the Bible. Knowledge lays itself like a stone over my grave, but my faith is that which breaks it.

Now, thus it is! The smallest flower preaches from its green stalk, in the name of knowledge — *immortality*. Hear it! the beautiful also bears proofs of immortality, and with the conviction of faith and knowledge, the immortal will not tremble in his greatest need; the wings of prayer will not droop; you will believe in the eternal laws of love, as you believe in the laws of sense.

When the child gathers flowers in the fields and brings us the whole handful, where one is erect and the other hangs the head, thrown as it were among one another, then it is that we see the beauty in every one by itself — that harmony in color and in form which pleases our eye so well. We arrange them instinctively, and every single beauty is blended together in one entire beauteous group. We do not look at the flower, but on the whole bouquet. The beauty of harmony is an instinct in us; it lies in our eyes and in our ears, those bridges between our soul and the creation around us — in all our senses there is such a divine, such an entire and perfect stream in our whole being, a striving after the harmonious, as it shows itself in all created things, even in the pulsations of the air, made visible in Chladni's figures.

In the Bible we find the expression: "God in spirit and in truth," — and hence we most significantly find an expression for the admission of what we call a feeling of the beautiful; for what else is this revelation of God but spirit and truth? And just as our own soul shines out of the eye and the fine movement around the mouth, so does the created image shine forth from God in spirit and truth. There is harmonious beauty from the smallest leaf and flower to the large, swelling bouquet; from our earth itself to the numberless globes in the firmamental space — as far as the eye sees, as far as science ventures, all, small and great, is beauty and harmony.

But if we turn to mankind, for whom we have the highest, the holiest expression, "created in God's image," — man, who is able to comprehend and admit in himself all God's creation, the harmony in the harmony then seems to be defective, for at our birth we are all equal! as creatures we have equally "no right to demand;" yet how differently God has granted us abilities! some few so immensely great, others so mean! At our birth God places us in our homes and positions; and to how many of us are allotted the hardest struggles! We are placed *there*, introduced *there* — how many may not justly say: "It were better for me that I had never been born!"

Human life, consequently, — the highest here on the earth, — does not come under the laws of harmonious beauty: it is inconceivable, it is an injustice, and thus cannot take place.

The defect of harmony in life lies in this, — that we only see a small part thereof, namely, existence here on the earth: there must be a life to come — an immortality.

That, the smallest flower preaches to us, as does all that is created in beauty and harmony.

If our existence ceased with death here, then the most perfect work of God was not perfect; God was not justice and love, as everything in nature and revelation affirms; and if we be referred to the whole of mankind, as that wherein harmony will reveal itself, then our whole actions and endeavors are but as the labors of the coral insect: mankind becomes but a monument of greatness to the Creator: He would then only have raised His *glory*, not shown His greatest *love*. Loving-kindness is not self-love.

We are immortal! In this rich consciousness we are raised toward God, fundamentally sure that whatever happens to us is for our good. Our earthly eye is only able to reach to a certain boundary in space; our soul's eye also has but a limited scope; but beyond *that*, the same laws of loving-kindness must reign, as here. The prescience of eternal omniscience cannot alarm us; we human beings can apprehend the notion thereof in ourselves. We know perfectly what development must take place in the different seasons of the year; the time for flowers and for fruits; what kinds will come forth and thrive; the time of maturity, when the storms must prevail, and when it is the rainy season. Thus must God, in an infinitely greater degree, have the same knowledge of the whole created globes of His universe, as of our earth and the human race here. He must know when that development, that flowering in the human race ordained by Himself, shall come to pass; when the powers of intellect, of full development, are to reign; and under these characters, come to a maturity of development, men will become mighty, driving-wheels — every one be the eternal God's likeness indeed.

History shows us these things: joint enters into joint, in the world of spirits, as well as in the materially created world; the eye of wisdom — the all-seeing eye — encompasses the whole! And should we then not be able, in our heart's distress, to pray to this Father with confidence — to pray as the Saviour prayed: "If it be possible, let this cup pass from me; nevertheless, not as I will, but as Thou wilt."

These last words we do not forget! and our prayer will be granted, if it be for our good; or if it be not, then let us, as the child here, that in its trouble comes to its earthly father, and does not get its wish fulfilled, but is refreshed by mild words, and the affectionate language of reason, so that the eye weeps, which thereby mitigates sorrow, and the child's pain is soothed. This will prayer also grant us: the eye will be filled with tears, but the heart will be full of consolation! And who has penetrated so deeply into the ways of the soul, that he dare deny that prayer is the wings that bear thee to that sphere of inspiration whence God will extend to thee the olive-branch of help and grace?

By walking with open eyes in the path of knowledge, we see the glory of the Annunciation. The wisdom of generations is but a span on the high pillar of revelation, above which sits the Almighty; but this short span will grow through eternity, in faith and with faith. Knowledge is like a chemical test that pronounces the gold pure!

XXI.

IN THE FOREST.

WE are a long way over the Elv. We have left the corn-fields behind, and have just come into the forest, where we halt at that small inn, which is ornamented over the doors and windows with green branches for the Midsummer Festival. The whole kitchen is hung round with branches of birch and the berries of the mountain-ash: the oat-cakes hang on long poles under the ceiling; the berries are suspended above the head of the old woman who is just scouring her brass kettle bright.

The tap-room, where the peasants sit and carouse, is just as finely hung round with green. Midsummer raises its leafy arbor everywhere, yet it is most flush in the forest — it extends for miles around. Our road goes for miles through that forest, without seeing a house, or the possibility of meeting travellers, driving, riding, or walking. Come! The ostler puts fresh horses to the carriage: come with us into the large woody tract: we have a regular trodden way to travel, the air is clear; here is summer's warmth and the fragrance of birch and linden. It is an up and down hill road, always bending, and so ever changing, but yet always forest scenery — the close, thick forest. We pass small lakes, which lie as still and deep as if they concealed night and sleep under their dark, glassy surfaces.

We are now on a forest plain, where only charred stumps of trees are to be seen; this long tract is black, burnt, and deserted — not a bird flies over it. Tall, hanging birches now greet us again; a squirrel springs playfully across the road, and up into the tree; we cast our eye searchingly over the wood-grown mountain-side, which slopes far, far forward, but not a trace of a house is to be seen: nowhere does that bluish smoke-cloud rise that shows us here are fellow-men.

The sun shines warm; the flies dance around the horses, settle on them, fly off again, and dance, as though it were to qualify themselves for resting and being still. They perhaps think: "Nothing is going on without us: there is no life while we are doing nothing." They think, as many persons think, and do not remember that Time's horses always fly onward with us!

How solitary it is here! — so delightfully solitary! one is so entirely alone with God and one's self. As the sunlight streams forth over the earth, and over the extensive solitary forests, so does God's spirit stream over and into mankind; ideas and thoughts unfold themselves — endless, inexhaustible, as He is — as the magnet which apportions its powers to the steel, and itself loses nothing thereby. As happens on our journey through the forest scenery here along the extended, solitary road, so, travelling on the great high-road of thought, ideas pass through our head. Strange, rich caravans pass by from the works of the poets, from the home of memory — strange and novel for capricious fancy gives birth to them at the moment. There comes a procession of pious children with waving flags and joyous songs; there come dancing Mænads, the blood's wild Bacchantes. The sun pours down hot in the open forest: it is as if the southern summer had laid itself up here to rest in Scandinavian forest solitude, and sought itself out a glade where it might lie in the sun's hot beams and sleep: hence this stillness, as if it were night. Not a bird is heard to twitter, not a pine-tree moves: of what does the southern summer dream here in the North, amongst pines and fragrant birches?

In the writings of the olden time, from the classic soil of the South, are *sagas* of mighty fairies who, in the skins of swans, flew toward the North, to the Hyperborean land, to the east of the north wind; up there, in the deep, still lakes, they bathed themselves, and acquired a renewed form. We are in the forest by these deep lakes; we see swans in flocks fly over us, and swim upon the rapid Elv and on the still waters. The forests, we perceive, continue to extend further toward the west and the north, and are more dense as we proceed: the carriage-roads cease, and one can only pursue one's way along the outskirts by the solitary path, and on horseback.

The saga, from the time of the plague (A. D. 1350), here impresses itself on the mind, when the pestilence passed through the land, and transformed cultivated fields and towns — nay, whole parishes — into barren fields and wild forests. Deserted and forgotten, overgrown with moss, grass, and bushes, churches stood for years far in the forest; no one knew of their existence, until, in a later century, a huntsman lost himself here: his arrow rebounded from the green wall, the moss of which he loosened, and the church was found. The wood-cutter felled the trees for fuel; his axe struck against the overgrown wall, and it gave way to the blow; the fir-planks fell, and the church from the time of the pestilence was discovered; the sun again shone bright through the openings of the doors and windows, on the brass candelabra and the altar, where the communion-cup still stood. The cuckoo came, sat there, and sang: "Many, many years shalt thou live!"

Woodland solitude! what images dost thou not present to our thoughts! Woodland solitude! through thy vaulted halls people now pass in the summer time with cattle and domestic utensils; children and old men go to the solitary pasture where echo dwells, where the national song springs forth with the wild mountain flower! Dost thou see the procession? paint it if thou canst! The broad wooden cart laden high with chests and barrels, with jars and with crockery. The bright copper kettle and the tin dish shine in the sun. The old grandmother sits at the top of the load and holds her spinning-wheel, which completes the pyramid. The father drives the horse, the mother carries the youngest child on her back, sewed up in a skin, and the procession moves on step by step. The cattle are driven by the half-grown children: they have stuck a birch branch between one of the cow's horns, but she does not appear to be proud of her finery, — she goes the same quiet pace as the others and lashes the saucy flies with her tail. If the night becomes cold on this solitary pasture, there is fuel enough here — the tree falls of itself from old age, and lies and rots.

But take especial care of the fire: fear the fire-spirit in the forest desert! He comes from the unextinguishable pile: he comes from the thunder-cloud, riding on the blue lightning's flame, which kindles the thick dry moss of the earth: trees and bushes are kindled, the flames run from tree to tree — it is like a snow-storm of fire! the flame leaps to the tops of the trees — what a crackling and roaring, as if it were the ocean in its course! The birds fly upward in flocks, and fall down suffocated by the smoke; the animals flee, or, encircled by the fire, are consumed in it! Hear their cries and roars of agony! The howling of the wolf and the bear, — dost thou know it? A calm, rainy day, and the forest-plains themselves alone are able to confine the fiery sea, and the burnt forest stands charred, with black trunks and black stumps of trees, as we saw them here in the forest by the broad high-road. On this road we continue to travel, but it becomes worse and worse; it is, properly speaking, no road at all, but it is about to become one. Large stones lie half dug up, and we drive past them; large trees are cast down, and obstruct our way, and therefore we must descend from the carriage. The horses are taken out, and the peasants help to lift and push the carriage forward over ditches and opened paths.

The sun now ceases to shine; some few rain-drops fall, and now it is a steady rain. But how it causes the birch to shed its fragrance! At a distance there are huts erected, of loose trunks of trees and fresh green boughs, and in each there is a large fire burning. See where the blue smoke curls through the green leafy roof; peasants are within at work, hammering and forging; here they have their meals. They are now laying a mine in order to blast a rock, and the rain falls faster and faster, and the pine and birch emit a finer fragrance. It is delightful in the forest.

XXII.

FAHLUN.

WE made our way at length out of the forest, and saw a town before us enveloped in thick smoke, having a similar appearance to most of the English manufacturing towns, save that the smoke was greenish — it was the town Fahlun.

The road now went downward between large banks, formed by the dross deposited here from the smelting furnaces, and which looks like burnt-out hardened lava. No sprout or shrub was to be seen, not a blade of grass peeped forth by the wayside, not a bird flew past, but a strong sulphureous smell, as from among the craters in Solfatara, filled the air. The copper roof of the church shone with corrosive green.

Long straight streets now appeared in view. It was as deathly still here as if sickness and disease had lain within these dark wooden houses, and frightened the inhabitants from coming abroad; yet sickness and disease come but to few here, for when the plague raged in Sweden, the rich and powerful of the land hastened to Fahlun, whose sulphureous air was the most healthy. An ochre-yellow water runs through the brook, between the houses: the smoke from the mines and smelting furnaces has imparted its tinge to them; it has even penetrated into the church, whose slender pillars are dark from the fumes of the copper. There chanced to come on a thunder-storm when we arrived, but its roaring and the lightning's flashes harmonized well with this town, which appears as if it were built on the edge of a crater.

We went to see the copper mine which gives the whole district the name of "Stora-Kopparberget" (the great copper mountain). According to the legend, its riches were discovered by two goats which were fighting — they struck the ground with their horns and some copper ore adhered to them.

From the solitary red-ochre street we wandered over the great heaps of burnt-out dross and fragments of stone, accumulated to whole ramparts and hills. The fire shone from the smelting furnaces with green, yellow, and red tongues of flame under a blue-green smoke; half-naked, black-smeared fellows threw out large glowing masses of fire, so that the sparks flew around and about: one was reminded of Schiller's "Fridolin."

The thick sulphureous smoke poured forth from the heaps of cleansed ore, under which the fire was in full activity, and the wind drove it across the road which we must pass. In smoke, and impregnated with smoke, stood building after building: three buildings had been strangely thrown, as it were, by one another: earth and stone-heaps, as if they were unfinished works of defense, extended around. Scaffolding, and long wooden bridges, had been erected there; large wheels turned round; long and heavy iron chains were in continual motion.

We stood before an immense gulf, called "Stora Stöten" (the great mine). It had formely three entrances, but they fell in and now there is but one. This immense sunken gulf now appears like a vast valley: the many openings below, to the shafts of the mine, look, from above, like the sand-martin's dark nestholes in the declivities of the shore: there were a few wooden huts down there. Some strangers in miners' dresses, with their guide, each carrying a lighted fir-torch, appeared at the bottom, and disappeared again in one of the dark holes. From within the dark wooden houses, in which great water-wheels turned, issued some of the workmen. They came from the dizzying gulf — from narrow, deep wells: they stood in their wooden shoes two and two, on the edge of the tun which, attached to heavy chains, is hoisted up, singing, and swinging the tun on all sides: they came up merry enough. Habit makes one daring.

They told us that, during the passage upward, it often happened that one or another, from pure wantonness, stepped quite out of the tun, and sat himself between the loose stones on the projecting piece of rock, whilst they fired and blasted the rock below so that it shook again, and the stones about him thundered down. Should one expostulate with him on his foolhardiness, he would answer with the usual witticism here : " I have never before killed myself."

One descends into some of the shafts by a sort of machinery, which looks as if they had placed two iron ladders against each other, each having a rocking movement, so that by treading on the ascending-step on the one side and then on the other, which goes upward, one gradually ascends, and by going on the downward sinking-step one gets by degrees to the bottom. They said it was very easy, only one must step boldly, so that the foot should not come between and get crushed; and then one must remember that there is no railing or balustrade here, and directly outside these stairs there is the deep abyss into which one may fall headlong. The deepest shaft has a perpendicular depth of more than a hundred and ninety fathoms; but for this there is no danger, they say, only one must not be dizzy, nor get alarmed. One of the workmen, who had come up, descended with a lighted pine-branch as a torch: the flame illumined the dark rocky wall, and by degrees became only a faint streak of light which soon vanished.

We were told that a few days before, five or six school-boys had, unobserved, stolen in here, and amused themselves by going from step to step on these machine-like rocking stairs, in pitchy darkness, but at last they knew not rightly which way to go, up or down, and they began to shout and scream lustily. They escaped luckily that bout.

By one of the large openings called " Fat Mads," there are rich copper mines, but which have not yet been worked. A building stands above it : it was at the bottom of this that they found, in the year 1719, the corpse of a young miner. It appeared as if he had fallen down that very day, so unchanged did the body seem — but no one knew him. An old woman then stepped forward and burst into tears; the deceased was her bridegroom, who had disappeared forty-nine years ago. She stood there old and wrinkled; he looked as young as when they had met for the last time nearly half a century before.[1]

---

[1] In another mine they found, in the year 1635, a corpse perfectly fresh, and almost with the appearance of one asleep; but his clothes, and the

We went to "The Plant House," as it is called, where the vitriolated liquid is crystallized to sulphate of copper. It grew like long sticks placed upright in the boiling water, resembling long pieces of grass-green sugar. The steam was pungent, and the air in here flavored our tongues — it was just as if one had a corroded spoon in one's mouth. It was really a luxury to come out again, even into the rarefied copper smoke, under the open sky.

Steaming, burnt-out, and herbless as the district is on this side of the town, it is just as refreshing, green, and fertile on the opposite side of Fahlun. Tall leafy trees grow close to the farthest houses. One is directly in the fresh pine and birch forests, thence to the lake and to the distant bluish mountain sides near Säther.

The people here can tell you and show you memorials of Engelbrekt and his Dalecarlians' deeds, and of Gustavus Vasa's adventurous wanderings. But we will remain here in this smoke-enveloped town, with the silent street's dark houses. It was almost midnight when we went out and came to the market-place. There was a wedding in one of the houses, and a great crowd of persons stood outside, the women nearest the house, the men a little further back. According to an old Swedish custom, they called for the bride and bridegroom to come forward, and they did so — they durst not do otherwise. Peasant girls, with candles in their hands, stood, on each side; it was a perfect tableau: the bride with downcast eyes, the bridegroom smiling, and the young bridesmaids each with a laughing face. And the people shouted: "Now turn yourselves a little! now the back! now the face! the bridegroom quite round, the bride a little nearer!" And the bridal pair turned and turned — nor was criticism wanting. In this instance, however, it was to their praise and honor, but that is not always the case. It may be a painful and terrible hour for a newly-wedded pair: if they do not please the public, or if they have something to say against the match, or the persons themselves, they are then soon made to know what is thought of them. There is perhaps also heard some rude jest or another,

ancient copper coins found on him, bore witness that it was two hundred years since he had perished there.

accompanied by the laughter of the crowd. We were told, that even in Stockholm the same custom was observed among the lower classes until a few years ago ; so that a bridal pair, who, in order to avoid this exposure, wanted to drive off, were stopped by the crowd, the carriage-door was opened on each side, and the whole public marched through the carriage. They would see the bride and bridegroom — that was their right.

Here, in Fahlun, the exhibition was friendly ; the bridal pair smiled, the bridesmaids also, and the assembled crowd laughed and shouted hurra ! In the rest of the market-place and the streets around, there was dead silence and solitude.

The roseate hue of eve still shone : it passed, changed into that of morn — it was the Midsummer time.

XXIII.

WHAT THE STRAWS SAID.

ON the lake there glided a boat, and the party within it sang Swedish and Danish songs; but by the shore, under that tall, hanging birch, sat four young girls — so pretty — so sylph-like! and they each plucked up from the grass four long straws, and bound these straws two and two together, at the top and the bottom.

"We shall now see if they will come together in a square," said the girls: "if it be so, then that which I think of will be fulfilled," and they bound them, and they thought.

No one came to know the secret thought, the heart's silent wish of the others. But yet a little bird sings about it.

The thoughts of one flew over sea and land, over the high mountains, where the mule finds its way in the mists down to Mignon's beautiful land, where the old gods live in marble and painting. "Thither, thither! shall I ever get there?" That was the wish, that was the thought, and she opened her hand, looked at the bound straws, and they appeared only two and two bound together.

And where were the second one's thoughts? also in foreign lands, in the gunpowder's smoke, amongst the glitter of arms and cannons, with him the friend of her childhood, fighting for imperial power against the Hungarian people. Will he return joyful and unharmed — return to Sweden's peaceful, well-constituted, happy land? The straws showed no square: a tear dwelt in the girl's eye.

The third smiled: there was a sort of mischief in the smile. Will our aged bachelor and that old maiden-lady yonder, who now wander along so young, smile so young, and speak so youthfully to each other, not be a married couple before the cuckoo sings again next year? See — that is what I should like to know! and the smile played around the thinker's mouth, but she did not speak her thoughts. The straws were separated — consequently the bachelor and the old maid also. "It may, however, happen nevertheless," she certainly thought: it was apparent in the smile; it was obvious in the manner in which she threw the straws away.

"There is nothing I would know — nothing that I am curious to know!" said the fourth; but yet she bound the straws together; for within her also there was a wish alive; but no bird has sung about it; no one guesses it.

Rock thyself securely in the heart's lotus flower, thou shining humming-bird, thy name shall not be pronounced: and besides, the straws said as before — "Without hope!"

"Now you! now you!" cried the young girls to a stranger, far from the neighboring land, from the green isle, that Gylfe ploughed from Sweden. "What dear thing do you wish shall happen, or not happen! — tell us the wish!" — "If the oracle speaks well for me," said he, "then I will tell you the silent wish and prayer, with which I bind these knots on the grass straw; but if I have no better success than you have had, I will then be silent!" and he bound straw to straw, and as he bound, he repeated: "It signifies nothing!" He now opened his hand, his eyes shone brighter, his heart beat faster. The straws formed a square! "It will happen, it will happen!" cried the young girls. "What did you wish for?" — "That Denmark may soon gain an honorable peace!"

"It will happen! it will happen!" said the young girls; "and when it happens, we will remember that the straws have told it beforehand."

"I will keep these four straws, bound in a prophetic wreath for victory and peace!" said the stranger; "and if the oracle speaks truth, then I will draw the whole picture for you as we sit here under the hanging birch by the lake, and look on Säther's blue mountains, each of us binding straw to straw."

A red mark was made in the almanac; it was the 6th of July, 1849. The same day a red page was written in Denmark's history. The Danish soldier made a red, victorious mark with his blood, at the battle of Fredericia.

XXIV.

THE POET'S SYMBOL.

IF a man would seek for the symbol of the poet, he need not look farther than "The Arabian Nights' Entertainments." Scheherezade who interprets the stories for the Sultan — Scheherezade is the poet, and the Sultan is the public who is to be agreeably entertained, or else he will decapitate Scheherezade.

Powerful Sultan! Poor Scheherezade!

The Sultan-public sits in more than a thousand and one forms, and listens. Let us regard a few of these forms.

There sits a sallow, peevish scholar; the tree of his life bears leaves impressed with long and learned words: diligence and perseverance crawl like snails on the hog's leather bark: the moths have got into the inside — and that is bad, very bad! Pardon the rich fullness of the song, the inconsiderate enthusiasm, the fresh young intellect. Do not behead Scheherezade! But he beheads her out of hand, *sans* remorse.

There sits a dress-maker, a seamstress who has had some experience of the world. She comes from strange families, from a solitary chamber where she sat and gained a knowledge of mankind — she knows and loves the romantic. Pardon, Miss, if the story has not excitement enough for you, who have sat over the needle and the muslin, and having had so much of life's prose, gasp after romance.

"Behead her!" says the dress-maker.

There sits a figure in a dressing-gown — this oriental dress of the North, for the lordly minion, the petty prince, the brewer's son, etc., etc., etc. It is not to be learned from the dressing-gown, nor from that lordly look and the fine smile around the mouth, to what stem he belongs: his demands on Scheherezade are just the same as the dress-maker's; he must be excited, he must be brought to shudder all down the vertebræ, through the very spine: he must be crammed with mysteries, such as those which Spriez knew about.

Scheherezade is beheaded!

Wise, enlightened Sultan! Thou comest in the form of a school-boy; thou bearest the Romans and Greeks together in a satchel on thy back, as Atlas sustained the world. Do not cast an evil eye upon poor Scheherezade; do not judge her before thou hast learned thy lesson, and art a child again, — do not behead Scheherezade!

Young, full-dressed diplomatist, on whose breast we can count, by the badges of honor, how many courts thou hast visited with thy princely master, speak mildly of Scheherezade's name! speak of her in French, that she may be ennobled above her mother tongue! translate but one strophe of her song, as badly as thou canst, but carry it into the brilliant saloon, and her sentence of death is annulled in the sweet, absolving *charmant!*

Mighty annihilator and elevator! — the newspapers' Zeus — thou weekly, monthly, and daily journals' Jupiter, shake not thy locks in anger! Cast not thy lightnings forth, if Scheherezade sing otherwise than thou art accustomed to in thy family, or if she go without a *suite* of thine own clique. Do not behead her!

We will see one figure more — the most dangerous of them all; he with the praise on his lips, like that of the stormy river's swell — the blind enthusiast. The water in which Scheherezade dipped her fingers, is for him a fountain of Castalia; the throne he erects to her apotheosis becomes her scaffold.

This is the poet's symbol — paint it: —

    "THE SULTAN AND SCHEHEREZADE."

But why none of the worthier figures — the candid, the honest, and the beautiful? They come also, and on them Scheherezade fixes her eye. Encouraged by them, she boldly raises her proud head aloft toward the stars, and sings of the harmony there above, and here beneath in man's heart.

That will not clearly show the symbol: —

    "THE SULTAN AND SCHEHEREZADE."

The sword of death hangs over her head whilst she relates — and the Sultan-figure bids us expect that it will fall. Scheherezade is the victor: the poet is, like her, also a victor. He is rich, victorious — even in his poor chamber, in his most solitary hours. There, in that chamber, rose after rose shoots forth; bubble after bubble sparkles on the magic stream. The heavens shine with shooting-stars, as if a new firmament were created, and the old rolled away. The world does not know it, for it is the poet's own creation, richer than the king's costly illuminations. He is happy, as Scheherezade is; he is victorious, he is mighty. *Imagination* adorns his walls with tapestry, such as no land's ruler owns; *feeling* makes the beauteous chords sound to him from the human breast; *understanding* raises him, through the magnificence of creation, up to God, without his forgetting that he stands fast on the firm earth. He is mighty, he is happy, as few are. We will not place him in the stocks of misconstruction, for pity and lamentation; we merely paint his symbol, dip into the colors on the world's least attractive side, and obtain it most comprehensively from —

"THE SULTAN AND SCHEHEREZADE."

See — that is it! Do not behead Scheherezade!

XXV.

THE DAL-ELV.

BEFORE Homer sang there were heroes; but they are not known; no poet celebrated their fame. It is just so with the beauties of nature, they must be brought into notice by words and delineations, — be brought before the eyes of the multitude; get a sort of world's patent for what they are, and then they may be said first to exist. The elvs of the north have rushed and whirled along for thousands of years in unknown beauty. The world's great high-road does take this direction; no steam-packet conveys the traveller comfortably along the streams of the Dal-Elv; fall on fall makes sluices indispensable and invaluable. Schubert is as yet the only stranger who has written about the wild magnificence and southern beauty of Dalecarlia, and spoken of its greatness.

Clear as the waves of the sea does the mighty elv stream in endless windings through forest deserts and varying plains, sometimes extending its deep bed, sometimes confining it, reflecting the bending trees and the red-painted block-houses of solitary towns, and sometimes rushing like a cataract over immense blocks of rock.

Miles apart from one another, out of the ridge of mountains between Sweden and Norway, come the east and west Dal-Elvs, which first become confluent and have one bed above Bålstad. They have taken up rivers and lakes in their waters. Do but visit this place! here are pictorial riches to be found; the most picturesque landscapes, dizzyingly grand, smilingly pastoral — idyllic: one is drawn onward up to the very source of the elv, the bubbling well above Finman's hut: one feels a desire to follow every branch of the stream that the river takes in.

The first mighty fall, Njupeskœrs cataract, is seen by the Norwegian frontier at Sernasog. The mountain stream rushes perpendicularly from the rock to a depth of seventy fathoms.

We pause in the dark forest, where the elv seems to collect within itself nature's whole deep gravity. The stream rolls its clear waters over a porphyry soil, where the mill-wheel is driven, and the gigantic porphyry bowls and sarcophagi are polished.

We follow the stream through Lake Siljan, where superstition sees the water-sprite swim, like the sea-horse, with a mane of green sea-weed, and where the aërial images present visions of witchcraft in the warm summer days.

We sail on the stream from Lake Siljan, under the weeping-willows of the parsonage, where the swans assemble in flocks; we glide along slowly with horses and carriages on the great ferry-boat, away over the rapid current under Bålstad's picturesque shore. Here the elv widens and rolls its billows majestically in a woodland landscape, as large and extended as if it were in North America.

We see the rushing, rapid stream under Avesta's yellow clay declivities: the yellow water falls like fluid amber in picturesque cataracts before the copper-works, where rainbow-colored tongues of fire shoot themselves upward, and the hammer's blows on the copper plates resound to the monotonous, roaring rumble of the elv-fall.

And now, as a concluding passage of splendor in the life of the Dal-elvs, before they lose themselves in the waters of the Baltic, is the view of Elvkarleby Fall. Schubert compares it with the fall of Schaffhausen; but we must remember that the Rhine there has not such a mass of water as that which rushes down Elvkarleby.

Two and a half Swedish miles from Gefle, where the high-road to Upsala goes over the Dal-elv, we see from the walled bridge, which we pass over, the whole of that immense fall. Close up to the bridge, there is a house where the bridge toll is paid. There the stranger can pass the night, and from his little window look over the falling waters, — see them in the clear moonlight, when darkness has laid itself to rest within the thicket of oaks and firs, and all the effect of light is in those foaming, flowing waters; and see them when the morning sun stretches his rainbow in the trembling spray, like an airy bridge of colors, from the shore to the wood-grown rock in the centre of the cataract.

We came hither from Gefle, and saw at a great distance on the way the blue clouds from the broken, rising spray, ascend above the dark-green tops of the trees. The carriage stopped near the bridge; we stepped out, and close before us fell the whole redundant elv.

The painter cannot give us the true, living image of a water-fall on canvas — the movement is wanting: how can one describe it in words, delineate its majestic grandeur, brilliancy of color, and arrowy flight? One cannot do it; one may however attempt it; get together, by little and little, with words, an outline of that mirrored image which our eye gave us, and which even the strongest remembrance can only retain — if not vaguely, dubiously.

The Dal-elv divides itself into three branches above the fall: two of them inclose a wood-grown rocky island, and rush down round its smooth-worn stony wall. The one to the right of these two falls is the finer; the third branch makes a circuit, and comes again to the main stream, close outside the united fall; here it dashes out as if to meet or stop the others, and is now hurried along in boiling eddies with the arrowy stream, which rushes on foaming against the walled pillars that bear the bridge, as if it would tear them away along with it.

The landscape to the left was enlivened by a herd of goats, that were browsing amongst the hazel bushes. They ventured quite out to the very edge of the declivity, as they were bred here and accustomed to the hollow, thundering rumble of the water. To the right, a flock of screaming birds flew over the magnificent oaks. Cars, each with one horse, and with the driver standing upright in it, the reins in his hand, came on the broad forest road from Oens Brück.

Thither we will go in order to take leave of the Dal-elv at one of the most delightful of places, which vividly removes the stranger, as it were, into a far more southern land, into a far richer nature, than he supposed was to be found here. The road is so pretty — the oak grows here strong and vigorously, with mighty crowns of rich foliage.

Oens Brück lies in a delightfully pastoral situation. We came thither; here was life and bustle indeed! The mill-wheels went round; large beams were sawn through; the iron forged on the anvil; and all by water-power. The houses of the workmen form a whole town: it is a long street with red-painted wooden houses, under picturesque oaks, and birch-trees. The greensward was as soft as velvet to look at, and up at the manor-house, which rises in front of the garden like a little palace, there was, in the rooms and saloon, everything that the English call comfort.

We did not find the host at home; but hospitality is always the house-fairy here. We had everything good and homely. Fish and wild fowl were placed before us, steaming and fragrant, and almost as quickly as in beautiful enchanted palaces. The garden itself was a piece of enchantment. Here stood three transplanted beech-trees, and they throve well. The sharp north wind had rounded off the tops of the wild chestnut-trees of the avenue in a singular manner; they looked as if they had been under the gardener's shears. Golden-yellow oranges hung in the conservatory; the splendid southern exotics were to-day enjoying the windows half open, so that the artificial warmth met the fresh, warm, sunny air of the northern summer.

That branch of the Dal-elv which goes round the garden is strewn with small islands, where beautiful hanging birches and fir-trees grow in Scandinavian splendor. They are covered with green, silent groves; with rich grass, tall brackens, variegated bell-flowers, and cowslips: no Turkey carpet has fresher colors. The stream between these islands and holms is sometimes rapid, deep, and clear; sometimes like a broad rivulet with silky-green rushes, water-lilies, and brown-feathered reeds; sometimes it is a brook with a stony ground, and now it spreads itself out in a large, still mill-dam.

Here is a landscape in Midsummer for the games of the river-sprites, and the dancers of the elves and fairies! Here, in the lustre of the full moon, the dryads can tell their tales, the water-sprite seize the golden harp, and believe that one can be blessed, at least for one single night like this.

On the other side of Oens Brück is the main stream — the full Dal-elv. Do you hear the monotonous rumble? it is not from Elvkarleby Fall that it reaches hither; it is close by; it is from Laa-Foss, in which lies Ash Island: the elv streams and rushes over the leaping salmon.

Let us sit here, between the fragments of rock by the shore, in the red evening sunlight, which sheds a golden lustre on the waters of the Dal-elv.

Glorious river! But a few seconds' work hast thou to do in the mills yonder, and thou rushest foaming on over Elvkarleby's rocks, down into the deep bed of the river, which leads thee to the Baltic — thy eternity.

XXVI.

PICTURES AD INFINITUM.

YES, there is around us in the world an endless succession of pictures, a richness of beauty, and that even in minor things, — in that which disappears in a moment; in that which the multitude care nothing about.

The drop of water from the stagnant pool contains in itself a whole living world; but the daily drop of every-day life contains also in itself a world of images of beauty and poetry, if one will only open one's eyes to it.

The seer, the poet shall point to it, and with the clearness and precision of the microscope make it visible, and then it will also be seen by the multitude during its own wandering through life, and they will have the seer's joy, because life is thus become richer — richer in beauty. The stagnant home-life has its richness of pictures, and how much then must travelling life possess it! Even in what we call trivial, picture after picture moves before us to infinity, though each one may be little, very little, and lacking in great movements which we call events — landscapes, historic groups — the very flowers of the travelling garland; it is from these we will give a little of that leafy green, those scenes which melt into each other, which come and vanish, each a poem, each a picture, but still not important enough to be placed alone on the easel for exhibition.

We give a single hour of our journey, one of those hours in which we may say that nothing exactly happens; there was nothing to be seen worth telling about; there was —— straight through the wood to the high-road.

Nothing to tell and yet so much. Close by the road was a high bank, overgrown with juniper-bushes; in their fresh green they are like the cypress, but here they were all withered and had exactly the same color as Mephistopheles' hair; below there was a crowd of swine, both lean and fat, small and large; the swine-herd stood on the bank, ragged and barefooted, but with a book in his hand; he was so absorbed in his reading that he did not even look up when we passed by; perhaps he was a learned man of the future.

We drove by a farm, and just as we passed the open gate and looked at the house, whose roof was covered with grass turf, which a man was laying on and trimming, a little tree which had for a couple of years grown upon the roof was cut down; we passed just as the axe glittered in the sun and the little green tree fell.

The ground in the forest was overgrown with lilies of the valley, which bloomed and sent forth a fragrance which was almost stupefying. The sunbeams fell among some tall fir-trees, upon a spider's immense suspended web, where all the threads, which approached each other with mathematical exactitude, glittered like fine prisms; in the midst of his waving castle the spider was sitting fat and ugly. He is the witch of the wood, if we want him for a wonder story. We reached the inn: there was disorder both within and without, and nothing in its right place. The flies had manured the whitewashed walls in such a way that it might be taken for painting: the furniture was very shaky, and so thick with dust that it was as if well wrapped in coverings. The highway at the farm was a real dung-hill, and the daughter of the house was running over it; she was young and well formed, white and red, and with bare feet, but with large gold rings in her ears; the gold glittered in the sunshine toward her blooming red cheeks; her flax-colored hair was untied and hung down her beautiful shoulders. If she had been aware of her own beauty, she would certainly have washed herself!

We walked along the road and saw a white and hospitable looking house — quite in contrast to that of the farm. The door stood open, and a young mother sat and wept over her dying child; a small boy was standing by her side; the little one looked with cunning eyes at his mother, and opened the small hands in which he hid a little butterfly he had caught and brought with him; and the butterfly waved over the little corpse. The mother looked at it and smiled; she understood certainly the poetry of the accident.

The horses were put to the coach and we started; picture after picture came forth, in the wood, on the road, and in the mind — pictures *ad infinitum.*

XXVII.

DANNEMORA.

READER, do you know what giddiness is? Pray that she may not seize you, this mighty "Loreley" of the heights, this evil genius from the land of the sylphides; she whizzes around her prey, and whirls it into the abyss. She sits on the narrow rocky path, close by the steep declivity, where no tree, no branch is found, where the wanderer must creep close to the side of the rock, and look steadily forward. She sits on the church spire and nods to the plumber who works on his swaying scaffold; she glides into the illumined saloon, and up to the nervous, solitary one in the middle of the bright polished floor, and it sways under him — the walls vanish from him.

Her fingers touch one of the hairs of our head, and we feel as if the air had left us, and we were in a vacuum.

We met with her at Dannemora's immense gulf, whither we came on broad, smooth, excellent high-roads, through the fresh forest. She sat on the extreme edge of the rocky wall, above the abyss, and kicked at the tun with her thin, awl-like legs, as it hung in iron chains on large beams, from the tower-high corner of the bridge by the precipice.

The traveller raised his foot over the abyss, and set it on the tun, into which one of the workmen received him, and held him; and the chains rattled; the pulleys turned; the tun sank slowly, hovering through the air. But he felt the descent; he felt it through his bones and marrow, through all the nerves. Her icy breath blew in his neck, and down the spine, and the air itself became colder and colder. It seemed to him as if the rocks grew over his head, always higher and higher: the tun made a slight swinging, but he felt it, like a fall — a fall in sleep, that shock in the blood. Did it go quicker downward, or was it going up again? He could not distinguish by the sensation.

The tun touched the ground, or rather the snow — the dirty, trodden, eternal snow, down to which no sunbeam reaches, which no summer warmth from above ever melts. A hollow sound was heard from within the dark, yawning cavern, and a thick vapor rolled out into the cold air. The stranger entered the dark halls; there seemed to be a crashing above him: the fire burned; the furnaces roared; the beating of hammers sounded; the watery damps dripped down — and he again entered the tun, which was hoven up in the air. He sat with closed eyes, but giddiness breathed on his head and on his breast; his inwardly-turned eye measured the giddy depth through the tun: "It is appalling!" said he.

"Appalling!" echoed the brave and estimable stranger, whom we met at Dannemora's great gulf. He was a man from Scania, consequently from the same street as the Zealander — if the Sound be called a street (strait). "But, however, one can say one has been down there," said he, and he pointed to the gulf; "right down, and up again; but it is no pleasure at all."

"But why descend at all?" said I. "Why will men do these things?"

"One must, you know, when one comes here," said he. "The plague of travelling is, that one must see everything: one would not have it supposed otherwise. It is a shame to a man, when he gets home again, not to have seen everything that others ask him about."

"If you have no desire, then let it alone. See what pleases you on your travels. Go two paces nearer than where you stand, and become quite giddy: you will then have formed some conception of the passage downward. I will hold you fast, and describe the rest of it for you." And I did so, and the perspiration sprang from his forehead.

"Yes, so it is: I comprehend it all," said he: "I am clearly sensible of it."

I described the dirty gray snow covering, which the sun's warmth never thaws; the cold down there, and the caverns, and the fire, and the workmen, etc.

"Yes; one should be able to tell all about it," said he. "That *you* can, for you have seen it."

"No more than you," said I. "I came to the gulf; I saw the depth, the snow below, the smoke that rolled out of the caverns; but when it was time I should get into the tun — no, thank you. Giddiness tickled me with her long, awl-like legs, and so I stayed where I was. I have felt the descent, through the spine and the soles of the feet, and that as well as any one: the descent is the pinch. I have been in the Hartz, under Rammelsberg; glided, as on Russian mountains, at Hallein, through the mountain, from the top down to the salt-works; wandered about in the catacombs of Rome and Malta: and what does one see in the deep passages? Gloom — darkness! What does one feel? Cold, and a sense of oppression — a longing for air and light, which is by far the best; and that we have now."

"But, nevertheless, it is so very remarkable!" said the man; and he drew forth his "Handbook for Travellers in Sweden," from which he read: "Dannemora's iron-works are the oldest, largest, and richest in Sweden; the best in Europe. They have seventy-nine openings, of which seventeen only are being worked. The machine mine is ninety-three fathoms deep."

Just then the bells sounded from below: it was the signal that the time of labor for that day was ended. The hue of eve still shone on the tops of the trees above; but down in that deep, far-extended gulf, it was a perfect twilight. Thence and out of the dark caverns, the workmen swarmed forth. They looked like flies, quite small in the space below: they scrambled up the long ladders, which hung from the steep sides of the rocks, in separate landing-places: they climbed higher and higher — upward, upward — and at every step they became larger. The iron chains creaked in the scaffolding of beams, and three or four young fellows stood in their wooden shoes on the edge of the tun; chatted away right merrily, and kicked with their feet against the side of the rock, so that they swung from it: and it became darker and darker below; it was as if the deep abyss became still deeper!

"It is appalling!" said the man from Scania. "One ought,

however, to have gone down there, if it were only to swear that one *had* been. You, however, have certainly been down there," said he again to me.

"Believe what you will," I replied; and I say the same to the reader.

XXVIII.

THE SWINE.

THAT capital fellow, Charles Dickens, has told us about the swine, and since then it puts us into a good humor whenever we hear even the grunt of one. St. Anthony has taken them under his patronage, and if we think of the "prodigal son," we are at once in the midst of the sty, and it was just before such a one that our carriage stopped in Sweden. By the high-road, closely adjoining his house, the peasant had his sty, and that such a one as can scarcely be matched in the world. It was an old state-carriage; the seats were taken out of it, the wheels taken off, and thus it stood, without further ceremony, on its own bottom, and four swine were shut in there. If these were the first that had been in it one could not determine; but that it was once a state-carriage everything about it bore witness, even to the strip of morocco that hung from the roof inside, — all bore witness of better days. It is true, every word of it.

"Uff!" said the occupiers within, and the carriage creaked and complained — it was a sorrowful end it had come to.

"The beautiful is past!" so it sighed; so it said, or it might have said so.

We returned here in the autumn. The carriage, or rather the body of the carriage, stood in its old place, but the swine were gone: they were lords in the forests; rain and drizzle reigned there; the wind tore the leaves off all the trees, and allowed them neither rest nor quiet: the birds of passage were gone.

"The beautiful is past!" said the carriage, and the same sigh passed through the whole of nature, and from the human heart it sounded: "The beautiful is past! with the delightful green forest, with the warm sunshine, and the song of birds

—past! past!" So it said, and so it creaked in the trunks of the tall trees, and there was heard a sigh, so inwardly deep, a sigh direct from the heart of the wild rose bush, and he who sat there was the rose king. Do you know him! he is of a pure breed, the finest red-green breed: he is easily known. Go to the wild rose hedges, and in autumn, when all the flowers are gone, and the red hips alone remain, one often sees amongst these a large red-green moss-flower: that is the rose king. A little green leaf grows out of his head — that is his feather: he is the only male person of his kind on the rose bush, and he it was who sighed.

"Past! past! the beautiful is past! The roses are gone; the leaves of the trees fall off! — it is wet here, and it is cold and raw! The birds that sang here are now silent; the swine live on acorns; the swine are lords in the forest!"

They were cold nights, they were gloomy days; but the raven sat on the bough and croaked nevertheless: "Brah, brah!" The raven and the crow sat on the topmost bough: they have large families, and they all said: "Brah, brah! caw, caw!" and the majority is always right.

There was a great miry pool under the tall trees in the hollow, and here lay the whole herd of swine, great and small — they found the place so excellent. "Oui! oui!" said they, for they knew no more French, but that, however, was something. They were so wise, and so fat, and altogether lords in the forest.

The old ones lay still, for they thought: the young ones, on the contrary, were so brisk — busy, but apparently uneasy. One little pig had a curly tail — that curl was the mother's delight. She thought that they all looked at the curl, and thought only of the curl; but that they did not. They thought of themselves, and of what was useful, and of what the forest was for. They had always heard that the acorns they ate grew on the roots of the trees, and therefore they had always rooted there; but now there came a little one — for it is always the young ones that come with news — and he asserted that the acorns fell down from the branches; he himself had felt one fall right on his head, and that had given him the idea, so he had made observations, and now he was quite sure of what he asserted. The old ones laid their heads together. "Uff!" said the swine, "uff! the finery is past! the twittering of the birds is past! we will have fruit! whatever can be eaten is good, and we eat everything!"

"Oui! oui!" said they all together.

But the mother sow looked at her little pig with the curly tail.

"One must not, however, forget the beautiful!" said she.

"Caw! caw!" screamed the crow, and flew down, in order to be appointed nightingale; one there should be — and so the crow was directly appointed.

"Past! past!" sighed the rose king; "all the beautiful is past!"

It was wet; it was gloomy; there was cold and wind, and the rain pelted down over the fields, and through the forest, like long water jets. Where are the birds that sang? where are the flowers in the meadows, and the sweet berries in the wood? — past! past!

A light shone from the forester's house: it twinkled like a star, and shed its long rays out between the trees. A song was heard from within; pretty children played around their old grandfather, who sat with the Bible on his lap and read about God, and eternal life, and spoke of the spring that would come again; he spoke of the forest that would renew its green leaves, of the roses that would flower, of the nightingales that would sing, and of the beautiful that would again be paramount.

But the rose king did not hear it: he sat in the raw, cold weather, and sighed:

"Past! past!"

And the swine were lords in the forest, and the mother sow looked at her little pig, and his curly tail.

"There will always be some, who have a sense for the beautiful!" said the mother sow.

XXIX.

POETRY'S CALIFORNIA.

NATURE'S treasures are most often unveiled to us by accident. A dog's nose was dyed by the bruised purple fish, and the genuine purple dye was discovered; a pair of wild buffaloes were fighting on America's auriferous soil, and their horns tore up the greensward that covered the rich gold vein.

"In former days," as it is said by most, "everything came spontaneously. Our age has not such revelations; now one must slave and drudge if one would get anything; one must dig down into the deep shafts after the metals, which decrease more and more: when the earth suddenly stretches forth her golden finger from California's peninsula, and we there see Monte Cristo's foolishly invented riches realized; we see Aladdin's cave with its inestimable treasures. The world's treasury is so endlessly rich that we have, to speak plain and straightforward, scraped a little off the up-heaped measure; but the bushel is still full, the whole of the real measure is now refilled. In science also, such a world lies open for the discoveries of the human mind!

"But in poetry, the greatest and most glorious is already found, and gained!" says the poet. "Happy he who was born in former times; there was then many a land still undiscovered, on which poetry's rich gold lay like the ore that shines forth from the earth's surface."

Do not speak so! happy poet thou, who art born in our time! thou dost inherit all the glorious treasures which thy predecessors gave to the world; thou dost learn from them that truth only is eternal, — the true in nature and mankind.

Our time is the time of discoveries — poetry also has its new California.

"Where does it exist?" you ask.

The coast is so near, that you do not think that *there* is the new world. Like the bold Leander, swim with me across the stream: the black words on the white paper will waft you — every period is a heave of the waves.

. . . .

It was in the library's saloon. Book-shelves with many books, old and new, were ranged around for every one; manuscripts lay there in heaps; there were also maps and globes. There sat industrious men at little tables, and wrote out and wrote in, and that was no easy work. But suddenly, a great transformation took place: the shelves became terraces for the noblest trees, with flowers and fruit; heavy clusters of grapes hung amongst leafy vines, and there was life and movement all around.

The old folios and dusty manuscripts rose into flower-covered tumuli, and there sprang forth knights in mail, and kings with golden crowns on, and there was the clang of harp and shield; history acquired the life and fullness of poetry — for a poet had entered there. He saw the living visions; breathed the flowers' fragrance; crushed the grapes, and drank the sacred juice. But he himself knew not yet that he was a poet — the bearer of light for times and generations yet to come.

It was in the fresh, fragrant forest, in the last hour of leave-taking. Love's kiss, as the farewell, was the initiatory baptism for the future poetic life; and the fresh fragrance of the forest became sweeter, the chirping of the birds more melodious: there came sunlight and cooling breezes. Nature becomes doubly delightful where a poet walks.

And as there were two roads before Hercules, so there were before him two roads, shown by two figures, in order to serve him; the one an old crone, the other a youth, beautiful as the angel that led the young Tobias.

The old crone had on a mantle, on which were wrought flowers, animals, and human beings, entwined in an arabesque manner. She had large spectacles on, and beside her lantern she held a bag filled with old gilt cards — apparatus for witchcraft, and all the amulets of superstition: leaning on her crutch, wrinkled and shivering, she was, however, soaring, like the mist over the meadow.

"Come with me, and you shall see the world, so that a poet can have benefit from it," said she. "I will light my lantern; it is better than that which Diogenes bore; I shall lighten your path."

And the light shone; the old crone lifted her head, and stood there strong and tall, a powerful female figure. She was Superstition.

"I am the strongest in the region of romance," said she, — and she herself believed it.

And the lantern's light gave the lustre of the full moon over the whole earth; yes, the earth itself became transparent, as the still waters of the deep sea, or the glass mountains in the fairy tale.

"My kingdom is thine! sing what thou seest; sing as if no bard before thee had sung thereof."

And it was as if the scene continually changed. Splendid Gothic churches, with painted images in the panes, glided past, and the midnight bell struck, and the dead arose from the graves. There, under the bending elder-tree, sat the mother and swathed her newly born child; old, sunken knights' castles rose again from the marshy ground; the draw-bridge fell, and they saw into the empty halls. adorned with images, where, under the gloomy stairs of the gallery, the death-proclaiming white woman came with a rattling bunch of keys. The basilisk brooded in the deep cellar; the monster bred from a cock's egg, invulnerable by every weapon, but not from the sight of its own horrible form: at the sight of its own image, it bursts like the steel that one breaks with the blow of a stout staff. And to everything that appeared, from the golden chalice of the altar-table, once the drinking-cup of evil spirits, to the nodding head on the gallows-hill, the old crone hummed her songs; and the crickets chirped, and the raven croaked from the opposite neighbor's house, and the winding-sheet rolled from the candle. Through the whole spectral world sounded, "Death! death!"

"Go with me to life and truth," cried the second form, the youth who was beautiful as a cherub. A flame shone from his brow — a cherub's sword glittered in his hand. "I am *Knowledge*," said he: "my world is greater — its aim is truth."

And there was a brightness all around; the spectral images paled; it did not extend over the world they had seen. Superstition's lantern had only exhibited *magic-lantern* images on the old ruined wall, and the wind had driven wet misty vapors past in figures.

"I will give thee a rich recompense. Truth in the created — truth in God!"

And through the stagnant lake, where before the misty spectral figures rose, whilst the bells sounded from the sunken castle, the light fell down on a swaying vegetable world. One drop of the marsh water, raised against the rays of light, became a living world, with creatures in strange forms, fighting and reveling — a world in a drop of water. And the sharp sword of Knowledge cleft the deep vault, and shone therein, where the basilisk glared, and the animal's body was dissolved in a death-bringing vapor: its claw extended from the fermenting wine-cask; its eyes were air, that burnt when the fresh wind touched it.

And there resided a powerful force in the sword; *so* powerful, that a grain of gold was beaten to a flat surface, thin as the covering of mist that we breathe on the glass pane; and it shone at the sword's point, so that the thin threads of the cobweb seemed to swell to cables, for one saw the strong twistings of numberless small threads. And the voice of Knowledge seemed heard over the whole world, so that the age of miracles appeared to have returned. Thin iron ties were laid over the earth, and along these the heavily-laden wagons flew on the wings of steam, with the swallow's flight; mountains were compelled to open themselves to the inquiring spirit of the age; the plains were obliged to raise themselves; and then thought was borne in words, through metal wires, with the lightning's speed, to distant towns. "Life! life!" it sounded through the whole of nature. "It is our time! Poet, thou dost possess it! Sing of it in spirit and in truth!"

And the genius of Knowledge raised the shining sword; he raised it far out into space, and then — what a sight! It was as when the sunbeams shine through a crevice in the wall in a dark space, and appear to us a revolving column of myriads of grains of dust; but every grain of dust here was a world! The sight he saw was our starry firmament!

Thy earth is a grain of dust here, but a speck whose wonders astonish thee; only a grain of dust, and yet a star under stars. That long column of worlds thou callest thy starry firmament, revolves like myriads of grains of dust, visibly hovering in the sunbeam's revolving column from the crevice in the wall into that dark space. But still more distant stands the milky way's whitish mist, a new starry heaven, each column but a radius in the wheel! But how great is this itself! how many radii thus go out from the central point — God.

So far does thine eye reach, so clear is thine age's horizon! Son of time, choose, who shall be thy companion? Here is thy new career! with the greatest of thy time, fly thou before thy time's generation! Like twinkling Lucifer, shine thou in time's roseate morn.

. . . .

Yes, in knowledge lies Poetry's California! Every one who only looks backward, and not clearly forward, will, however high and honorably he stands, say that if such riches lie in knowledge, they would long since have been made available by great and immortal bards, who had a clear and sagacious eye for the discovery of truth. But let us remember that when Thespis spoke from his car, the world had also wise men. Homer had sung his immortal songs, and yet a new form of genius appeared, to which a Sophocles and Aristophanes gave birth; the Sagas and mythology of the North were as an unknown treasure to the stage, until Oehlenschläger showed what mighty forms from thence might be made to glide past us.

It is not our intention that the poet shall versify scientific discoveries. The didactic poem is and will be, in its best form, always but a piece of mechanism, or wooden figure, which has not the true life. The sunlight of science must penetrate the poet; he must perceive truth and harmony in the minute and in the immensely great with a clear eye: it must purify and enrich the understanding and imagination, and show him new forms which will supply to him more animated words. Even single discoveries will furnish a new flight. What fairy tales cannot the world unfold under the microscope, if we transfer our human world thereto? Electro-magnetism can present or suggest new plots in new comedies and romances; and how many humorous compositions will not spring forth, as we from our grain of dust, our little earth, with its little haughty beings, look out into that endless world's universe, from milky way to milky way? An instance of what we here mean is discoverable in that old noble lady's words: " If every star be a globe like our earth, and have its kingdoms and courts — what an endless number of courts — the contemplation is enough to make mankind giddy!"

We will not say, like that French authoress, " Now, then, let me die: the world has no more discoveries to make!" O, there is so endlessly much in the sea, in the air, and on the earth — wonders, which science will bring forth! — wonders, greater than the poet's philosophy can create! A bard will come, who, with a child's mind, like a new Aladdin, will enter the cavern of science, — with a child's mind, we say, or else the puissant spirits of natural strength would seize him, and make him their servant; whilst he, with the lamp of poetry, which is, and always will be, the human heart, stands as a ruler, and brings forth wonderful fruits from the gloomy passages, and has strength to build poetry's new palace, created in one night by attendant spirits.

In the world itself events repeat themselves; the human character was and will be the same during long ages and all ages; and as they were in the old writings, they must be in the new. But science always unfolds something new; light and truth are in everything that is created — beam out from hence with eternally divine clearness. Mighty image of God, do thou illumine and enlighten mankind; and when its intellectual eye is accustomed to the lustre, the new Aladdin will come, and thou, man, shalt with him, who concisely clear and richly sings the beauty of truth, wander through Poetry's California.

IN SWITZERLAND.

IN SWITZERLAND.

I.

RAGATZ.

BY rail and by steamboat we fly through Switzerland also, now, and gain thereby — time to linger about the most notable and most interesting places: one of these, most assuredly, is Ragatz, with Pfäffer's Baths. From Rorschach, by the Boden Lake, one reaches the place by rail in a few hours: a longer way, but one quite as convenient and with the entire variety of Swiss scenery, is open to the traveller who will take the course from Schaffhausen through Zurich to Ragatz, which the Rhine formerly followed before it forced its present channel into the Boden Lake.

Here, over the mighty fall of the Rhine, which showers us with its rain-dust, there is built a substantial bridge, and the train of cars flies across it and plunges into the pitch dark tunnel which undermines the castle of Lauf. At Olten, we travel through the solid ridge of the Jura Mountains. The minutes seem long drawn out that are passed in that uncanny, interminable vault, where so many ill-fated workmen met their death at the falling in of the tunnel. The shining lights of the train throw a gleam on the gray blocks of stone, which the oozing water drips over, warning us that the spirit of nature here steadily fights against the might of human will. The country about now rolls before us in luxurious fields, and the blue Alps, clad with snow and glaciers, rise before us as we approach Zurich. Villages and towns gleam out of the wealth of green that lies by the banks of the smiling, enticing lake. Steamboats glide back and forth, and on one of these we pass over the wide, outstretched sheet of water, and through the

Linth Canal come out at Wallen Lake, which is called the wildest, most weird, and exciting of the Swiss lakes. On its northern side there rise sheer from the lake black rocks with strange jagged peaks; when the storm coming over them hurls itself down on the lake, boat and sailing vessel are gulped down by the devouring waves, and only the steamboat can hold its own in such a storm.

Crossing the lake one soon comes to the eastern bank, where Sargans Valley opens, through which the Rhine by great freshets, especially that of 1618, has threatened to break away from its ancient course and take a new direction out into the Wallen and Zurich lakes. From Sargans, the railway takes us in a quarter of an hour to Ragatz. In St. Gall, by the broad, open Rhine Valley, close under the wood-covered heights, lies the little picturesque Swiss town. The houses, for the most part, are of timber, and have broad windows in front and wide-spreading balconies; white walls inclosing green vineyards. The road leads past the church-yard, above the low stones in which rises a monument; familiar features graven in marble welcome us, for here rests the thinker, the philosopher Schelling.

We arrived at sunset; the people sat in knots outside of their houses, and a ruddy sunlight illumined the mountains,—the nearest decked with their splendid covering of velvety green fields, embroidered with pine and leafy groves; the houses high up showing like Alpen roses in the green, while waterfalls gleamed like narrow ribbons of silver. Castle ruins stood out boldly, and the distant mountains were like clouds in the pale atmosphere, and the snowy tops shone as if afire. In amongst a row of water-mills the elder bushes hung picturesquely over the Tamina River, which tumbled milk-white over the black quartz stone blocks, hurrying on to mingle with the green waters of the Rhine.

A large, elegant-looking hotel stands like a showy crinoline-dressed lady in the midst of all this romantic scenery; one passes by it and comes to a still bigger one, which stretches out so as to take up a whole street. It is the most frequented and the best appointed hotel, as large as one of those which we hear of in America. In one wing there is built a chapel for the church-going English; and in the opposite corner there is a theatre opening upon the garden, where there is playing every other evening during the bathing season. While several days before, in Weber's great and frequented hotel at the Falls of the Rhine, there had been only three guests at the dinner table, here we found several hundred. The orchestra gave us music from the opposite poles of musical art, — from Wagner and Bellini, Beethoven and Strauss. In the café, as also in front of the hotel, and in the garden, there was a life, a bustle, a stirring; and then, not more than three hundred steps away, one stood again in the midst of great lonely nature, in face of the wild cleft where the Tamina has forced its way, and now, as it plunges into the open valley, makes a mighty waterfall almost the width of the entire ravine. A long wooden gallery nailed fast in the steep, rocky way, leads from the path to the waterfall, and by a light, slender bridge one crosses to the opposite side, where now a narrow path, forced through the rocks, takes one to Pfäffer's Baths.

The chronicle records that in the year 1038 there came here by the trackless heights, a hunter in quest of a raven's nest. As he climbed up he was aware of a thick steam which arose from the rocky fissure, while far below he heard the roaring of a stream, and from its springs of boiling water it was that the steam arose.

It was soon learned in the country about how much health-giving property there was in it. The rich flocked hither, and all the needy made their way down to the horrible abyss, where at that time there was no other shelter than that afforded by the rocks themselves; afterward a few wooden shanties were fashioned, hanging over the rushing stream. Here, where daylight gave only a dim glimmering, shut out from the world, the sick would stay for days and weeks, alone, shut up to themselves and the virtue of the water.

The monks in the convent upon the mountain built, two hundred years ago, a great solid building down in the ravine where the rocks meet. The path to it leads by the precipitous rocks, and many sick people were obliged to be lowered by ropes. It is only in our time that it has become easy and convenient of access. In the year 1839, they blasted a road from Ragatz to Pfäffer's Baths, so broad that a little wagon drawn by one horse can make the trip there in three quarters of an hour. During the bathing period the place is crowded with sick, lodging here, while still the greater part of the guests prefer to dwell in the lively large hotel at Ragatz. Two ways lead from that: one, most frequented, broad and commodious, goes by zigzag up the wooded hill-side, past the ruins of Wartenstein, where princely abbots and noble monks once led a very worldly life; by this way we come opposite the old monastery St. Pirminsberg, now an insane asylum. The other road leads, after a few steps from the garden of the hotel, to the fissure, where one goes by the hanging gallery and the little bridge at the waterfall till he comes to the path hewn out of the rocks.

As one reads in fairy tales that the mountain opens and offers a passage through, so one here sees it in reality. The mountain is rent and remains so, offering a bed for the brawling stream that twists and turns by the newly opened way. To the left rise precipitous rocks, far, far above; one almost falls over backward, as he looks up to the highest point fringed with pine-trees. Close by us, on the right, is a gentler and more varied scene, where one comes to fresh greensward and flowery field beneath beech and chestnut-trees, and anon to narrow passes between naked cliffs which the water drips over, or one goes through arches blasted out of the hard rock. At last one stands before the entrance to a monastic building, — it is Pfäffer's Baths, which looks as if it had been swallowed here by an earthquake and squeezed in between the perpendicular rocks, occupying the whole width of the cleft. We enter a long vaulted, low-studded hall. The kitchen, the eating room, and the cell-like chambers open upon it. The sun's rays penetrate here only in the middle of summer: in August, there is sunshine only from eleven o'clock in the morning until three in the afternoon.

Visitors procure tickets of admission to the springs at the entrance hall, and a guide conducts them thither. We met many sick people in the long close passages, from which we emerged into a more airy large hall, — the drinking hall, where the hot water is conducted from the spring that gushes out of the rock farther in: it is clear, without any disagreeable taste, and is spoken of as quite invigorating.

The oppressiveness one has felt all the long, winding way from Ragatz, at the ice-cold air which the sun has no power to warm, at the unceasing war of the stream, and at the thought of the possibility of the least stable rocks rolling down and crushing us, horse and wagon, seems at its height here in the heavy, close air of the building. One feels the need of getting at once out into the fresh air and drawing a long breath. The door of the drinking hall is opened, and we step out, feeling, if possible, still more oppressed, as we stand just before an abyss which yawns fearfully and is lost in pitchy darkness, as if it were the very entrance to the nether world. One stands upon a bridge, suspended over the rushing, seething flood; to the left, but only three or four steps, is solid ground; farther on, one has only a layer of beams spiked into the rocky way that leads into the yawning abyss. The mountain-high rocks meet and close, and our way continues still a quarter of an hour more before we reach the bubbling jets of the spring. The layer of beams is broad enough for two men to walk side by side, but hard by, above us, slope the wet blackened masses of rock; to the right, the rocky wall rises perpendicularly from the stream which rushes on in a wild, thundering chase. A single tree-trunk is nailed fast for a sort of bulwark, but below this, down to the wet, slippery beams on which we walk, there is nothing, should one fall, by which he could catch to prevent himself from being plunged below. The eyes, which at first look down for a foothold, find no resting place, nothing to stop at, — the flood rushes on as if shot out of a cannon: it seems to one as if the whole ground below was on a wild chase. Near the heavy rocks, high up the cleft, is an opening, looking to the eye like a mere scratch; there shines the blue sky; there waves the green that tells of life in the upper world: a footpath leads up there.

A quarter of the way, in the wet wooden gallery, is a long, uncomfortable time; the moving water rushes wilder and more noisily, and one is in twilight in the middle of a sunshiny day. The duskiness, the shut-in sensation, between these great rocks, the steaming flood beneath, here overpower the strongest. But we do not belong to that class, and already, when half through our course, perceived the singular dullness which takes hold of the giddy and nervous. But the will is a sturdy guide, and if one has, besides, a strong conductor to lean upon, one gets along very well, — so most think, and so thought we. But as the darkness increased, and the stream roared and boiled with deafening sound, nature's power quite overwhelmed us. Our feet trembled, drops of perspiration oozed from every pore. It helped, however, to stop for a moment, close our eyes, and cool the forehead with the icy water that dripped from the rocky wall. We undertook to go a few steps further, when the dizziness became greater and quite unendurable. All about seemed to swim and dance, and take on a misty shape and draw us down toward the abyss, a demoniac desire to plunge down was the momentary sensation, and only by a convulsive seizing hold of the guide, shutting the eyes, standing still, and forcibly extinguishing every thought, did we succeed in holding out.

Before one comes to the spring, the rocks have quite closed about one. It is almost night outside the so-called Magdalen's Grotto, — a great marble cave, which was once fixed upon by the Abbot Jacobus for a chapel of penance. One or two steps further and daylight again breaks through. One is at the outlet of the spring, where, from an opening like a well, the hot water, ninety degrees Fahr., sends out its hot vapor, which rises high into the air. One does not stand here altogether in safety. It is only a year or two since, as our guide told us, a company of people was here and a piece of rock became loose and crushed one of them on the spot, — a young girl from a Swiss town.

It was here that, hundreds of years ago, the wretched huts hung over the steaming water. Down here the sick were lowered, and had no other way back, no other exit than again to be hoisted up through the gaping fissure. Then, as now, the power of nature brewed the hot boiling water in the rock and poured it from the marble basin in abundance, — a great stream, Tamina.

II.

THE LION AT LUCERNE.

AS a symbol of bravery and faithfulness, they have placed a lion over the heroes' grave. One is soon to be placed also in the church-yard at Flensborg. The lion stands sculptured in the rocky wall at Lucerne — a memorial of Swiss valor.

Switzerland is not especially a land of monuments: it is itself a monument, by its mighty Alps, clad in everlasting snow, with forests of perpetual green, fresh pastures, and blue, deep lakes. Whatever men can erect in the midst of such scenery, always seems petty; it is only the thought in it that gives greatness, and such one finds in the Lion of Lucerne, that carries the memory of Swiss faithfulness. The people, in their union and bravery, have raised for themselves in history their own monument of grandeur, more glorious far than can be imitated in marble. The spirit of the people is incarnate in the heroic form of William Tell; his life and deeds are the flower of this land's history; his death, as tradition relates it, and as we find it given in the " Album de la Suisse pittoresque," and in the little narrative " Tell der Urner," is, on the other hand, less familiar to people. We will relate it as we steam past Rütli and Tell's chapel, in the steamboat, on our way to Lucerne, to visit the monument which our countryman, Thorwaldsen, modeled.

Schiller's drama of " William Tell " has become so popular in Switzerland, so impressed upon the peasantry, that this clan in the environs of Freiburg, last summer (1860), just outside the town, in an open field, before a great gathering of spectators, acted the drama, though not with the artistic ability which the neighboring people of the Bavarian Oberammergau display in their Passion-play, still with an intelligence and a life which gave each actor the highest interest. Some wooden seats formed the auditorium; the scenery consisted only of a pole with a hat, which intimated that the scene lay in Altorf.

Before Rütli, on one of the blocks of stone which rise out of the Lake of Lucerne, there was sculptured last year, upon Schiller's birthday, the name of the poet, and it was decked with flowers as the name of one who had again called into life William Tell. The drama does not give his death; that is told by tradition.

In the year 1354 there was a freshet in the little mountain stream Schäcken, which flows not far from Bürglen and Altorf, and falls at Reuss into the Lake of Lucerne. It was "God's weather,"[1] and the storm set the church bells ringing. The little stream rose more and more; in its violent passage it carried trees and houses along with it. There was seen, driving down the stream, a cradle with a little child in it. No one dared venture out to rescue it, when there came an old man of fourscore years, who went into the flood and laid hold of the cradle, but he was too weak to bring it to shore: he collected his last strength to reach a great tree which stood firmly in the rushing water; he placed the cradle in the boughs of the tree, where it was held fast: the child was saved, but he himself, exhausted and overpowered, was carried away, sank, was never again seen. The old man was William Tell.

The region about the Lake of Lucerne affords many historic memories of Tell's manhood and daring deeds, that shine again in the Swiss character. One can build on the Swiss fidelity. In Paris, when the Tuileries were stormed, August 10, 1792, the Swiss Guard there, officers and soldiers, were cut down — they would not give way. It is for these fallen braves that General Pfyffer has erected a monument in the rocky wall in his garden just outside Lucerne.

As one comes by steamboat from the places laden with memories of William Tell, and steps upon the landing at Lucerne, he has only a short way, out by the Wäggis Gate, to the little garden, where, in the sandstone itself, is carved a colossal dying lion pierced by a broken spear. In grief and pain he holds fast in his paws the lilies of France.

---

[1] An expression used in Denmark of any violent commotion in nature, as a thunder-storm, for example.

The artist, Aborn, from Constanz, chiseled it in the sandstone, after Thorwaldsen's model, which is preserved and exhibited near by in a little house; but upon the rock itself, in the name Thorwaldsen, the "l" has been left out, so that it stands engraved *Thorwadsen*, not Thorwaldsen, a blemish which has not yet been righted. Above the Lion, one reads in Latin a eulogistic record of the fidelity and courage of the Swiss Guard. Below are the names of the officers and the roll of the men who fell. Near by, in the chapel, — the altar-cloth of which was embroidered by the Duchess of Angoulême, — yearly masses are celebrated on the 10th of August.

The place itself, quite near the town, and by the public road, has a singular loneliness about it; it is as if the fallen heroes rested here under the shadow of the trees. An old soldier of the Swiss Guard keeps watch. He told us that when a little boy he served in the Guard as a drummer-boy; and he told us that the Danish sculptor who made the model was once here on his journey home to Denmark.

III.

THE CELEBRATION AT OBERAMMERGAU.

NEVER shall I forget the Passion-play at Oberammergau, so completely did it surpass all my expectation. I could not think of it beforehand without being scandalized at the idea of seeing Jesus acted on the stage; but as it here took place, in religious faith, full of fervor, and with a beauty quite unimagined, all offense was taken away, and one found himself taken possession of, — he came into sympathy with it and was quite borne along.

Edward Devrient, so well known as a skillful dramatic and theatrical critic, has written an interesting work on these representations,[1] which we especially recommend every one to read, — every one who thinks that sacred things are profaned by being brought upon the stage, — and "to come," in Devrient's words, "to see, and to learn." That is a wish which we echo, for, in truth, this whole religious play has a majesty, a simplicity, something so strangely absorbing, that even the most irreligious must needs be dumb and recognize that there is no sport in all this, but a veritable "means of revival." The story of the Passion, illustrated likewise by parallel passages from the Old Testament narratives, becomes a living reality to us, — the two Testaments are mingled in one harmonious whole. How every-day small and mean do not the usual theatrical pieces become when compared with this great tragedy of humanity!

Every tenth year this people's drama is reënacted, — the last remains, in our time, of the miracle-plays of the Middle Ages. From generation to generation, the play and its management are passed down as an inheritance, having been omitted for a short time only; but in the year 1633 an epidemic ravaged the whole district, when the people resolved, in remembrance

[1] Das Passions — Shauspiel im Dorfe Oberammergau in Ober favern, 1850.

of their delivery from this scourge, to repeat their religious play for edification and confirmation in faith and Christian life. It is now about fifty years since it acquired a new and higher character, when a monk from the neighboring monastery of Ettal worked over the old text and exscinded the burlesque passages, in which the devil appears. An intelligible, not ill-adapted music, was prepared for the words by a native organist.

"The people's play," says Devrient, "must, in course of time, develop itself after this pattern, and find a place in dramatic representation, where the people shall have a chance to see and become acquainted with the history of their country, with the conflict of races, and with progress, and not get at these things from books only."

The Passion-play at Oberammergau began this year [1] the 28th of May, and continued once nearly every week until the 16th of September. It is not an uncomfortable journey from Munich here: in an hour one comes by rail to Starnberg, where a steamboat, in the same space of time, takes one over the lake. We took this route to be present at the representation that was to occur on the 2d of July. Although we came two days before, the steamboat was full to overflowing, and, at the landing-place, Seeshaupt, a great rush and confusion took place in the desire to secure a place in one of the many diverse vehicles which are here to be found. We succeeded in obtaining a one-horse wagon, and immediately set off in a violent shower, followed by broiling sunshine, by way of Murnau, where many sought night-quarters, and so into the villages that lie by the monastery of Ettal. The way was crowded with people, riding and on foot, who came singing and begging; at last, after a good six hours' drive, we saw the church in Oberammergau shine before us. The bells rang and the cannon sounded till the hills echoed. There was a life and bustle here, within the houses and without; traders and peasants, ladies in crinoline and peasant girls in their national dress, moved about together.

As a favored guest, and not as a stranger, was each one who came received and harbored for a small price. The inhabitants live mainly by wood-carving, but at this time refrain from

[1] 1860.

their work. It was their ten-years' feast, when those who had been far away came back to take part in it. My friends in Munich had written and provided beforehand, so that I was most kindly cared for. The priest of the place, Daisenberger, who has written and published the history of Oberammergau, received me with great hospitality and gave me a large, light chamber; the passage outside was adorned with books and religious pictures. Here from the windows I could see almost the whole town, the houses of which were ornamented with sacred pictures painted in fresco. Notwithstanding that it again began to rain, the walks outside were quite lively. The street looked from above as if it had a movable pavement of outspread, variegated umbrellas. Omnibus followed omnibus, each more chock-full than the last. I met a number of acquaintances, and friends too, from Copenhagen, amongst others, Herr Eckardt and Herr Scharff, from the Royal Theatre; from Berlin, the distinguished actress Charlotte von Hagen, now Baroness von Ofen. The people of the town seemed to take great pleasure in hearing how some had come from a great distance to their festival; and when I mentioned my native land, Denmark, they were acquainted with it, for one of their own town children, a native Oberammergauer, had many years before gone to Copenhagen and was residing there; his name was Blankensteiner, and I recalled him and his shop on Kjöbmager Street.

The whole night long there was singing and music without, great excitement but no revelry. It rained in the morning, when Pastor Daisenberger took me to the theatre, which was built of beams and boards, upon a pretty, green meadow outside of the town. The signal gun was fired: the crowd was large; mothers carried their little children, who, in full array, with braided hair, would soon appear in the *tableaux vivants*, or act in the part of the youth of Jerusalem. I asked a little girl, dressed in white, with a garland in her hair, what part she played, and she replied, in her peasant dialect, *a genus* — an angel she was to be. The audience chamber will hold six thousand people; yet, for all that, it happens this summer that several thousands more were here than could be accommodated at once, and the representation had to be repeated on succeeding days.

It was half after seven when we came there; a half hour later and the Passion-play would begin, and with only an hour's interruption, would last until five o'clock in the afternoon. I had been warned to secure my seat the evening before, and I had thus one of the best, in the middle and front where, with some other visitors, I got a chair to sit on. It rained, but no one dared raise his umbrella, since this deprived those behind of a view; so there we sat in the rain, and were told that at the first representation this year it snowed so that the snowflakes fell upon the stage. The rain, meanwhile, held up, but the sky was heavy with clouds. The wind whistled over us, and birds flew in and out. We could see all the mountainous country, with its woods and pastures and towns about us. I was made to think of the old Indian dramas in the open air, where Sakuntala was given. In front of us, where the orchestra was, composed of native musicians, the stage reared itself; the foremost part of which, that extended across the entire width of the spectators' seats, was for the chorus and their leaders, who stepped up from each side and so arranged themselves that the tallest stood in the middle, and then the shorter, and so on. Song, recitative, and choral responses introduced and connected the larger action with an effect similar to that of the chorus in the Greek tragedy, of which the whole play strongly reminded us. There were sweet voices here, good delivery, and all was done with an astonishing precision.

In the centre of the stage was erected the theatre proper, with movable curtains, shifting scenes, — everything that belongs to representation on the stage. Upon the drop curtain was painted Faith, Hope, and Charity. The theatre itself was bounded on each side by a small building with a balcony, upon which various scenes and by-passages were acted. The structure on the right of the spectator stands for the High-priest's house; that on the left is Pilate's. From both houses a great arch springs, through which one sees the streets of Jerusalem. The spectators had thus, after a fashion, five distinct views before them, and in addition the larger open foreground where the chorus was displayed. All were employed, now individually, now in company, according as the play required.

The chorus-leader, a fine looking young man, stepped forward with noble gait and bearing. The choral song was likewise illustrated by *tableaux vivants* from the Old Testament. The persons, even from year-old children, stood here immovable and fixed longer than I ever had known actors to stand.

The entry into Jerusalem began with children shouting and swinging palm-branches, Christ, in a tunic and dark-red mantle, riding upon an ass; they came through the streets of Jerusalem where divers carpets were spread before him. His bearing was noble, a holy seriousness shone from his handsome face, which, with his hair and beard, reminded one of a picture by one of the old masters. It was plain that the actor was penetrated with faith and a deep earnestness. Through all his action there was displayed a repose and beauty that must needs impress every one. No actor, not the greatest, could surpass him. It was not comedy playing, it was a holy harmony, a real assumption of the Christ-man. We were told that the persons whom the community unanimously chose for the sacred *rôles* must be of spotless life, and that the one who acted Christ, always, before entering upon the Passion-play, received the sacrament for a consecration. This year it was the young sculptor, Schauer; they said that a spiritual and physical excitement so took hold of him that after the performance he could not eat or speak to a soul before he had recovered himself alone on the mountain.

When, after the entry into Jerusalem, Christ drove the traders out of the temple, the frightened doves flew over us, spectators, out into the open air, which strangely commingled here with the artistic scenery. In rich succession the incidents followed: the plot of the Sanhedrim, the farewell at Bethany, the institution of the Lord's Supper. Everything was arranged with artistic skill; the costumes were rich and appropriate. The larger groups consisted of several hundred persons, admirably placed, and with most picturesque effects. Especially to be noticed was the acting of the young Tobias, as he left his father's home, led by the angel; so, too, there was a fine *tableau* representing Job surrounded by his friends.

The dramatic action moved forward with quickness. The betrayal by Judas was introduced by the *tableau* of Joseph who was sold by his brethren. Judas himself was represented with striking truthfulness. It was masterly, — the manner in which, at the Sanhedrim, he received and counted out the pieces of silver. One trembled at his despair and death. There was no thought here of working upon the feelings of the audience, to make a showy appearance and gain applause; the actor himself passed through the experience which Judas had known. With a like truthfulness and dramatic power was Pilate given by the man who, ten years before, acted Christ.

The scenes where Jesus goes between Herod and Pilate might be shortened; there was too much repetition; while the replies, the Sanhedrim, the tumults of the people, were given with dramatic life; one could scarcely believe that it was peasants who were carrying on the play. I talked with one or two who were practiced in theatrical matters, artists from the most celebrated German theatres, and they confirmed the opinion which Devrient had pronounced, that the most skillful arranger of scenery could learn much by coming to Oberammergau and profiting by what he saw; how the masses of people here were arranged and grouped upon the stage in its fivefold division and great foreground. The dialogue at one time was from the open balconies, and again the players carried on the action far down the centre of the stage; then through the open streets, and forth into the foreground, the action by turns widened and closed. The cry, "Not this man but Barabbas!" sounded behind the stage; it resounded from the people in the streets and from the open square, and here Christ bore his cross; then with the robbers who were bound fast, he moved on to Golgotha; the crowd of people who followed was astonishingly great, and yet there were plainly to be seen the disciples, the mother of Jesus, and Mary Magdalene. The scenes where Christ was mocked and spit upon were given with a fine power, so that nothing served to interrupt the harmony; but painful, almost beyond endurance, was the nailing to the cross, — with too much of nature, even to the blood about the nails, was the representation given. For more than half an hour he hung fastened to the cross, and most pitiable was it to see when the soldiers brake the legs of the malefactors and thrust the spear into the side of Christ, so that the blood streamed forth. On the other hand, most exalting, and given with fervor and assurance, was the moment of death, when the Saviour bowed his head. It was perfectly still all about, and, notwithstanding the descent from the cross in its moving naturalness occupied a quarter of an hour, one heard only here and there the subdued grief.

During the entire representation we had had alternate rain and wind, all the while cloudy weather; but, by chance, just as Christ was lowered into the grave, the sun broke forth and illumined the stage, the spectators, the whole surrounding. Birds sang and flew here over us; it was a moment one never forgets.

While the Passion-scenes were going on the chorus wore black silk garments; at the resurrection they reappeared in bright robes and singing joyful songs. The entire play was like a going to church where the priest is not heard, but is seen as a living worker: each went away raised in spirit, filled with that soul of love that gave itself for unborn generations.

No loud merriment was heard as the people on foot went away in great crowds. Wagon followed wagon, it grew stiller and stiller in the village; it was like a holy festival evening. We had seen the great tragedy of humanity, we had seen the acting of a splendid popular play; new generations for a thousand years would, perhaps, in like manner but in greater fullness, see enacted the by-gone deeds of kingdoms and the world.

The mountain tops shone in the sunlight, an alpine horn sounded from the pastures; it was evening, it was still, starlit night.

A VISIT

AT

CHARLES DICKENS'S HOUSE.

A VISIT AT CHARLES DICKENS'S HOUSE.

ON the night of the 11th of May I went by steam from Calais to Dover. The sea rolled, and there was a strong wind. At daybreak I was on English ground, where I had not been for ten years. When I left the coast at that time, Charles Dickens was the last to wave me a good-by; my visit now was at his instance. He had invited me to come this summer and spend some time with him and his family.

"We are not in London itself," he wrote; "we go out in the beginning of June to a little country place I own, seventeen to twenty miles from London; it lies in one of the prettiest districts of Kent, near a railway station, and one can thus be in London in half an hour."

It was a happy fortune that allowed me to call Dickens's house my home, to spend a season there, and come close to him and his family circle. Since my former visit in England we had kept up an interchange of letters. He was a sympathizing friend to me: I was indeed singularly fortunate.

The steamer lay at ebb-tide, and it was stagnant all about. The Customs took up some time, and it was almost too late for us to take the first morning train to London. It rushed through tunnel after tunnel, and soon the great Crystal Palace was gleaming in the sunshine, and London, wrapped in coal smoke, stole forth from the horizon. At London Bridge the signal had already been given on the other side of the station for the train to start on the North Kent Railway, that goes by Higham Station, near Dickens's place. I hurried to take a seat, and then we sped past village and country-seat, always near the Thames that flowed on our left, filled with vessels and steamboats.

Dickens had offered to come and meet me at London, or at

whatever station I should choose; but I had replied that I could easily get to him from Higham, where I could learn of one of the men at the station whereabout his house was; it would be easy to get a conveyance in such a place; but Higham is a village lying about an English mile distant from the station, which is only a solitary house. I got off here; the train set off for Rochester, and I stood quite forsaken.

"Are you the foreigner who is to go to Mr. Dickens's?" asked the station-keeper, who heard that I was to come. No conveyance was to be had at Higham. The man advised me therefore to stay here till he had sent to Dickens for one, or else to go afoot with him. It was, he said, two English miles to Gadshill, where Dickens lived. I determined to go; so the station-master took my valise on his back, my bag and hat-box over his shoulder, and our journey began, steadily up hill, between blooming gardens with sweet-brier and wild roses. Every cottage, however little, looked as if meant for a country place of some well-to-do tradesman, very much as several of the houses on the Strand at Copenhagen; but here in England it is the countryman who lives thus snugly and cheerfully. A little mat was laid before the open door, flowers stood on the table, or in the window; every one of the country people whom I met seemed to be dressed in his Sunday clothes.

After a pretty tiresome walk we came to the high road between Rochester and Gravesend; before us lay Gadshill Place, Dickens's country-seat. Gadshill has been made famous by Shakespeare. In the first part of Henry IV. Poins says:—
"To-morrow morning by four o'clock early at Gadshill, there are pilgrims going to Canterbury with rich offerings, and traders riding to London with fat purses. I have vizards for you all; you have horses for yourselves."

Gadshill lies on the old high road between Dover and London, about half-way. Here, where pilgrims and travellers formerly went anxiously, expecting to be waylaid, there is now a charming home, with the fragrance of wild roses, flowering elder, and great fields of clover, all quite otherwise than when Shakespeare looked on it and made Falstaff say of the dangerous place:— There were "a hundred upon poor four of us . . . . as the devil would have it, three misbegotten knaves in

Kendal green came at my back and let drive at me; for it was so dark, Hal, that thou couldst not see thy hand."

I stood at Gadshill Place, and before me by the broad highway was Dickens's house, the tower of which, with its gilded weathercock, I had already caught sight of amongst the trees some way off. It was a pretty, new house, with red walls, four balcony windows, and a porch resting upon pillars; in the upper story was a great window; a thick hedge of *laurus cerasus* was close by the house, from which one looked out over a pretty lawn to the road, upon the opposite side of which rose two great cedars of Lebanon, whose crooked branches stretched their shade over a great grass plat which was encircled by ivy and grape-vines — so close, so dark was this hedge, that not a ray of sunlight could pierce it.

As I stepped into the house, Dickens came out to meet me, happy, and with a cordial greeting. He looked a little older now than he did ten years ago when we bade each other good-by, but the difference in age was chiefly in the beard which he had grown. His eyes shone as before, the same smile was on his lips, his voice was as hearty, if possible still more cordial than before. Dickens was now in the prime of life, his forty-fifth year, youthful, full of life, talkative, and rich in humor, that broke forth from the warmth of his heart. I know no words more expressive than those I used in my first letter home: "Take the best out of all of Dickens's writings, make from them the picture of a man, and you have Charles Dickens." And just as he stood before me the first time, so was he without change all the weeks that I spent with him. always in the best of spirits, and of unfailing kindness.

One would fain look for and find in a writer's nearest surroundings originals of the sketches which are to be found in his works. I had before heard several say that Agnes, in the novel "David Copperfield," was the picture of Dickens's wife, and although she probably never flitted before him as such, I know no one in his books who, for beauty and lovableness, can come nearer to her than Agnes. I found a quiet, a womanliness, and a reserve in Mrs. Dickens; yet when she talked, her gentle eyes would flash, and her mouth take on a smile of good nature, while there was in her voice something so attractive that I could only think of Agnes.

The apartment where we gathered with most of the household was a snug one that seemed to have a holiday air; around the great windows there hung outside in rich clusters blooming roses; one could look out over the garden to green fields and the hills behind Rochester. A good portrait of Cromwell hung over the chimney, and amongst the other paintings on the wall that attracted my attention, there was one in particular which represented a carriage in which sat two young ladies, deep in the reading of a book, upon the back of which could be read the title, "Bleak House;" the little groom behind them leaned way forward so as also to read the book. Some birds in a cage sang joyously — the more people talked at the table, the more they sang.

At dinner Dickens took the place of the head of the family at the end of the table, and after the English fashion, always began the meal with a short and silent prayer; my place was at his side during all my visit.

In a letter to me in Denmark, Dickens had written: "I have finished 'Little Dorrit,' and I am a free man. Now we can have a holiday, and play cricket on the green meadow." But the holiday was put off, for the very day before I came the humorist and playwright Douglas Jerrold had died, and on his death-bed he had said to his weeping wife, "Dickens will take care of you, should I die;" and in truth Dickens did take most excellent care of the poor widow. It was his project that, when carried out, resulted in the collection of one or two thousand pounds, the income of which secured her a comfortable living. Dickens had gotten together a committee with names of eminence like his own, — Bulwer, Thackeray, and Macready, — and a programme was made out with a brilliant array of talent. It is quite well known that Dickens has a real genius for acting; in his own house he has fitted up a little theatre, where, with individuals from his family and friends, he gives dramatic entertainments to a select circle; one or two of these plays he now proposed to bring out in fine style. Besides, Dickens and Thackeray agreed to give some readings, in which Dickens, for his share, had chosen one of his own Christmas stories.

To accomplish all this at once took a deal of time and hard

work. There were days at home when I saw him write and send off over a score of letters, but he did everything with a lightsomeness and mirth as if it were all a fine joke. Yet I had to lament that our companionship was so shortened and limited, since he was obliged, in his labor for this object, to go up to London and spend entire days there much more frequently than was his wont. When I arrived, he and his family had only been a fortnight at their new country-seat. The country about and all the walks were new to them. I soon found for myself the prettiest points, and to one of these, overlooking Gadshill, I carried Dickens and his family. The road lay by the highway, and not far from the house was an inn with a sign quite washed out by the rain, denoting that this place had been made famous by Shakespeare; upon one side was painted Falstaff and Prince Henry, upon the other the Merry Wives of Windsor putting Falstaff into the basket of dirty linen. From the inn a lane led up between gardens to a cluster of cottages, all two stories high, their walls clad with grape-vines; long clean white curtains hung at the windows; the house at the top of the group was guarded by an old blind dog; cows and sheep grazed in the meadow, and at the highest point there had been erected an obelisk from which the plastering had peeled off; the monument had great cracks in it, and looked as if it would fall at the first storm. The inscription on it was not wholly legible, but we could make out so much as to know that it had been erected long since in honor probably of the former owner of the place. I knew about the monument, and since I was the one who had first brought Dickens to this pretty spot, he has always called the place since, "Hans Christian Andersen's Monument."

From this point there was a most charming view. North Kent is rightly called the Garden of England; it is Danish country, but richer and more highly cultivated. The eye roams over green meadows, yellow cornfields, woods, and mossy banks; if the weather is clear, one can see the North Sea. The landscape offers no inland lake; but a mile away one has the Thames, that winds with a broad and shining stream through the green meadow. Some traces can be made out of old Roman fortifications, and many an evening we wandered up here and lay on the grass and saw the sun go down; its rays were reflected in the windings of the Thames, like gold, and the ships appeared like black silhouettes, while round about from the houses rose the blue chimney-smoke. The grasshopper chirped, and there was a peace brooding over all that was heightened by the sound of evening bells. A great bowl of claret, decked with a garland of wild flowers, passed round the circle; the moon rose, round, red, and big, till it shone in clear splendor, and made me think that it was all a charming midsummer night dream in Shakespeare's land; and it was more than this, for it was a reality. I sat with Dickens, and heard him joyous and merry drink in the lovely evening, that surely as it sported in his soul would some day shine back upon us in some new, picturesque, and immortal work.

Without any practice before in talking English or hearing it spoken, I understood from the very first nearly all that Dickens said to me. If anything was said that I could not understand, he would repeat it in a new form. No one was so quick to understand me as he. Danish and English are so much alike, that we both of us often wondered at the similarity; and so whenever a word bothered me, Dickens would tell me to say it in Danish, and often it happened that it was quite of the same sound as in English.

"Der er en Græshoppe i den Höstak," I wanted to say one day, and when I gave it in Danish, Dickens translated it, "A grasshopper in the hay-stack." I saw a number of green plants growing on the roof of a cottage. I asked what they were called here, saying that with us the name was *huus lög*, and the woman in the cottage whom we asked about it said "house leek;" and so on in numberless instances. We met on the road a little girl; she courtesied low to us, and I said that with us we said that was "at stöbe lys" (to dip candles), and Dickens told me that here they called it "at dyppe" (dipping), with just the same notion of candle-making.

In France, Italy, and Spain, the Dane feels himself amongst strangers, but this is not the case in England; here he sees that they are blood of our blood, branches from the same root. The shore at the mouth of the Thames, and Rochester, once watched fearfully for the adventurous Danes who came, effected a landing, and wrought many deeds of violence. One can still perceive in the people and their speech ties of kinship from the time when the Danish king Knud (Canute) reigned over England and the three northern kingdoms; but England was the chief land, the king's residence. Worsaae has, in his interesting work on England, shown us clearly many Danish memorials to be found in the names of places, and also in speech and song. When the wind sighs with a melancholy air in the evening over the heath, the countryman says, "It is the Danish boys' song." It rang through my heart with the thought of what my fatherland, the oldest kingdom in Europe, once signified; now it is only in art and science, song and sculpture, that the music of its name sounds from that rich land which the sea has cut off from West Jutland.

It is by understanding the language of a land that one first becomes at home there; one can soon make himself understood, but it takes longer to understand others; he can find words to express his thoughts — words which he has appropriated; but the connection in which they are used makes their meaning to vary. The whole language, in all its wealth, and with all its turns, is in the possession of the people that speak it, and one is constantly hearing new and strange expressions.

I soon understood when a person addressed himself especially to me; when the whole company carried on a lively conversation, the words flew back and forth, and I sat like one deaf amongst the talkers. But the ear accustoms itself by degrees to strange sounds and tones; little by little, as one in a fog can make out one mountain top after another, and then the separate parts of the landscape, so my ear got hold of words and sentences, and the ordinary conversation became intelligible to me by bits, and then in its completeness.

As I grew more familiar in expressing myself, I felt the need of talking about something else than the most plain matters. I wanted to give of my own personality, and find in the strange tongue, expressions that would be as natural to me as in my mother tongue. I felt myself more and more at home; even the smallest children in the house began to understand me; yes, even the littlest of all, who, the first time I asked him if he liked me, answered honestly, "I will put you out of the window!" assured me with laughing face that now he would "put me in of the window." Dickens has no fewer than nine children: two grown daughters, Mary and Kate; and seven sons, Charles, Walter Lander, Francis Jeffrey, Alfred Tennyson, Sidney Smith, Henry Fielding, and Edward Lytton Bulwer. The two eldest and the two youngest were at home; the three between came for a visit from France, where they were at a boarding-school in Boulogne. It was now vacation, and I saw them clambering up among the branches in the great cedar-trees, or with their other brothers and Dickens himself in shirt sleeves, playing cricket upon the great green field near the garden. The ladies sat in the high grass under the trees, the country children peeped into the garden, and the dog Turk that was kept chained all night, was now let loose and reveled in his liberty, while his long iron chain and kennel were presided over by an old great raven, that carried himself like the raven in "Barnaby Rudge," which was still to be seen, but stuffed and set up in the dwelling-house.

We took several short excursions; one of the most enjoyable in the neighborhood was by Lord Darnley's park. The impression I received in driving by, did not make me wish to live there. The sun shone brightly over the green meadows, and in among the great boughs of the moss-laden trees; one could find wildness here to his heart's desire, but I saw no living person. The whole park did not give the picture of wooded solitude, with its winning, refreshing rest; but on the contrary, the picture was of a landscape asleep: it stretched before me as if a castle and park in one summer night in Queen Elizabeth's time had been sunk in the earth, and now had suddenly risen again in the clear sunshine, and lay here lighted but not warmed and awakened. I would like to have looked at the blooming garden, but I did not care to enter. The road home lay through the citified Gravesend; we followed the highway, which was crowded with full omnibuses, heavy draught wagons, and soldiers on the march. One evening at sundown, I saw near Gadshill a great company — I dare not say how many — of gypsies, that in their wandering had encamped on the road side, built a fire, and were cooking their meal in a great kettle; a horse stood fastened to a heavy laden wagon, children were running about, and the whole formed a capital subject for a picture.

Higham was the nearest railway station to us, but Dickens most frequently took the train for London from Rochester, and I sometimes accompanied him. We talked with freshness and life in the bright morning hours; the dewy cobwebs lay like veils flung out over the fields and ditches; the foot passengers had scratched their names in the clay banks by the way, — a transient immortality in earthly mould, yet that is quite all that earthly immortality ever is. Very often, as we came, the greatest part of the town lay stretched before us sleeping in the morning mist; then the mist would rise, and disclose the picturesque old castle ruin, with its ivy clad walls and the grand Cathedral. We drew near the new bridge, and the ruins of the old were close by; sometimes it was ebb-tide, then the ships lay upon their sides like dead fishes upon the muddy ground. I wandered about Rochester; it was the scene of several sketches of the Pickwick Club. I heard the Scotch bagpipe here one day; an old Scotsman clad in plaid, that did not cover his naked knees, played on the instrument; two small boys, dressed like the old fellow, walked on their hands, and did other tricks, while their little sister danced on the flagging, swung her plaid about, and sang. It looked melancholy enough. I wanted to weep at the sound of the bagpipe; and ever since, when Rochester comes up to my thoughts with its long narrow streets, I seem to see these children and their old sire from Burns' mountain country, the "land of the brown heath."

From Strood, the nearest place to Rochester, one can go by the quickest train in half an hour to London; I used to take this train, either alone or with Dickens and his family, and stay at their city house, which was filled with paintings and other works of art, just like their country home. Tavistock House is in Tavistock Square: a grated door separates the yard and little garden from the noisy street; a larger garden with a grass plat and high trees spreads out behind the house, and gives the whole a country look in the midst of this coal and gas stricken London. In the hall that runs from the street to the garden there hang paintings and engravings; here stood Dickens's bust, very like himself, young and handsome, and over the doors to the bed-chamber and dining-hall were Thorwaldsen's bas-reliefs, "Night and Day." On the first floor was a fine library with fire-place and working table; and leading from this to the garden was the place where Dickens with his family and friends, in the winter time, played comedies for their mutual enjoyment. In the cellar is the kitchen, and higher up in the house are the sleeping apartments. I had a snug room looking out on the garden, where I could see over the trees the Tower of London, sharp or blurred, according as it was clear or misty. It was a long way from here to the very busy streets; in one of them, just opposite the Lyceum Theatre, is the office of "Household Words," Dickens's literary counting-house, if I may so call it, from which this story-telling, widely-circulated weekly issues to the number of not less than fifty thousand copies.

Here I was, again, in the crowded London, with its waves of humanity. It seemed as if but yesterday since I was here, and that no years had rolled by. I seemed to be looking upon the same great flood of men, the same throng of omnibuses, cabs, and carriages; men with signs on their backs and on poles, moved along among the high houses; the Thames rolled along with the same crowd of sail and steamships, yachts and boats, that crossed and recrossed; there was the same rush and life as ten years before.

This time I was in company with Dickens, to see and observe many notable things in the art world. One of these was the Handel festival at the Crystal Palace, the chorus and orchestra numbering no less than two thousand persons. One can reach Sydenham Park in fifteen minutes by the railway, and be carried directly into the palace; but it was more the "fashion" to go out with horse and carriage. The whole route thither was filled therefore with equipages, one right behind the other; the sun burned down, the dust rose, and we could not go faster than a walk.

It is the Crystal Palace which first stood in London, and has been moved out here, receiving, I believe, a new minaret-like tower. It is like a great town under roof, as if all the glass-roofed *passages* of great towns were collected here, and crossed and recrossed by galleries and hanging balconies. It is just as if one saw here a fairy enchanted castle, with richly endowed halls that grew by caprice; here are Pompeian rooms, French galleries, fantastically towering into one another in arabesque fashion around a mighty, lofty hall, where in a marble basin grow blue and white lotus flowers, and upon the pillars climb fresh leafy vines; fine statues stand among flowering trees; one is in a garden and yet under roof, where even the giant tree lifts its great branches surrounded by forms that represent groups of wild men and beasts. The sun shone upon the enormous building, a huge canvas was extended inside under the roof, to keep out the glare of the sun, and the galleries and passages were filled with crowds of people passing hither and thither. In company with Dickens's family, I had a excellent place just opposite the Queen and her retinue. In the middle of the hall, from the floor, and high up, there rose an amphitheatre containing the two thousand singers and players. Handel's statue, decked with flowers, stood forward, — a little point, a golden key, that held together the great human fan. Now the organ burst forth, the musicians fell in, and the chorus broke into the hymn, "God save the Queen!" it was as if a roaring sea of music rolled forth. The music and all the accompanying spectacle filled full the ear and eye, and during the pauses in the music, one could hear the strong wind without rush in by the roof of the palace, as if it would join in the sound. The solos sounded feeble in the immense hall, and even Clara Novello's full voice had not strength enough here, where the room was suitable only for a great choir. The price of admission was two guineas; but for all that, there were over twenty-four thousand hearers; and when these came to go away, all the fountains, more than two thousand, began to play outside in the bright sunshine; the drops of falling water shining like diamonds, were carried by the wind, looking like floating veils colored with the rainbow, all over the green sward. The wind bore the water-dust from fountain to fountain; it was a sight such as one imagines at the bottom of the ocean, in the garden of the water-sprites, where swinging kiosks, domes, temples, even trees themselves are built of the living water; and charming indeed it looked when a gust of wind suddenly swept over the groups of people looking on; they scampered away over the wet grass, and many a little crinoline heap was swelled by the gust, like an open umbrella, looking as if just setting out for London by balloon post.

One of my wishes was to be gratified at the Lyceum Theatre, for there I was to see the famous queen of tragedy, Ristori. Rachel, that woman of genius, had been set aside for her by the Parisians. Often had I heard of Signora Ristori's wonderful performances, that even made beautiful the unlovely chief part in Alfieri's "Myrrha." I had especially heard of her representation of *Marie Stuart*, which was spoken of as a great result of study and genius. She must then surpass in this *rôle* Rachel, whom I had seen in it great and satisfying; others had in quite the opposite manner expressed themselves respecting Ristori; one highly cultivated lady had given me a characteristic sketch of her, that Ristori always reminded her of the epileptic in Raphael's "Transfiguration," eternally and always in ecstasy. I was now to see for myself the tragic muse of our day. Unfortunately it was not permitted me to see her in *Marie Stuart*, because this evening "Camma" was given, a tragedy by a new Italian author, Montanelli; it was a sort of Norma-Medea, written, it was said, for Ristori, and quite in Alfieri's manner. Ristori stood upon the stage when I entered my box; the house was only half full; the flocking after Ristori this year was rather on the decline, and the tragedy of "Camma" not a favorite one.

Amongst the audience on the floor I was made aware of a young, good-looking lady, with shining black hair. It was the actor Kemble's sister, granddaughter of Mrs. Siddons, England's Ristori. Several authors of repute, dramatic artists, such as the singer Clara Novello, sat here, and the audience seemed made up of friends of Ristori. We know that she is the daughter of poor Italian strolling players. It is related that as a little child she lay in a basket behind the scenes while her mother played. She herself began to play at a very early age, and it was in Turin that her extraordinary talent was first observed. Afterward she married an Italian nobleman, whose family, it was said, was angry at getting a daughter-in-law from the theatre; but her personal attractions soon won them all; and when at a later period financial reasons led her to resume her place in the theatre, where she won great renown, her husband accompanied her to Paris, and there her greatness was recognized. She held the tragic sceptre alone, and Rachel went to America. Ristori's name soon became famous in neighboring lands, and England and Germany followed the example of France in enthusiasm over her.

Signora Ristori has an excellent appearance on the stage, a noble bearing, speaking eyes, and a pantomimic power, which in my opinion is too strong, and only suited to the ballet, where mimicry has to express its meaning without the aid of words. Her transitions were so rapid that they could only be warranted on the ground of the truthfulness of genius. At first I could not quite accustom myself to them. I had to think of a story that is told, the point of which lies in the narrator's change of face, while the words are only those of an old woman who always used to frighten children by her angry face, and who one day took great pains to look kind and smiling at her neighbor's children who had come to her, and to say with a laugh and with beaming eyes, beginning in the softest tones, "Wouldn't the little children like to go down into the garden and get some apples, pears, and cherries?" but the good-will, with the smile and friendly countenance, always underwent a change in the middle of the sentence, so that "apples and pears" took on an amount of gruffness that culminated in the last word — "cherries." The short sentence that began like a mild breeze ended as in a hurricane. I was reminded of this story by seeing and hearing Ristori. Her whole surroundings seemed only a feeble echo of her. She did not excite me, and yet every word was in exactly the right tone, every movement true to the Italian fiery nature; but the whole was underscored, and raised to a pitch which I believed uncalled for by reality. Still I must confess that I came from the great concert in the Crystal Palace, tired out and filled intellectually, rather desiring now simple nature, and looking for it in this famous actress. But in the closing scene of the piece, where the heroine has given the poison to her treacherous bridegroom, and now her self drains the chalice, and dying prays the priests to sound their harps while her soul and thought, as if borne on these tones, are lifted into the company of spirits, so that she there thinks she sees her mother, her husband, and her children, there was in this a power displayed which laid strong hold of me, and made me bow in admiration of the might of this actress.

Far more interesting and of great artistic excellence seemed to me her acting of *Lady Macbeth*, which I afterward saw once or twice. Shakespeare's tragedy has been translated into Italian, and seemed expressly written for Signora Ristori; Macbeth's part was given not without talent, but with all the wild passion which I think belongs to the Moors, and not to a Scottish clan. The piece itself was in many respects well mounted. During the table scene, where Banquo's murderers bring the intelligence to Macbeth that they have accomplished the murder, they stepped forward, dressed like the other servants of the castle, and while they stood in the foreground and pour out the king's wine, they tell him of the horrid deed. The witches appeared without music and song, but their melodramatic delivery and action were very effective. Signora Ristori as *Lady Macbeth*, was the principal character in the piece; there was in all her acting a profound psychologic truth, fearful, and yet within the limits of the beautiful; the great scene was the sleep-walking one; it is impossible that at any time before or since, a more true and moving picture could have been given of this woman so troubled in soul and body; never can I forget the terribly dry, deep voice, with which the words came forth; it was not speech, but thoughts, deep from within, that uttered themselves in the painful sighs which broke from her, which were not strong, but so full of sorrow, so heart-rending, as to go through every one's nerves. It was not to be forgotten! One sees the terrible woman, as Macbeth in fright says to her, "Bear me no daughters but sons." It was as if the final remnant of human nature within her turned pale at the horrid drop of blood; involuntarily one held his breath; a despairing human soul falling into perdition went by us; its body was only a holster. Something like this, having the same characteristic of truth and genius, was recalled by me — I mean Jenny Lind's pure, mournful somnambulism in the opera "La Sonnambula."

For the rest, as regards the setting of the piece on the stage, — and I must here acknowledge the carrying of this too far, — one gets in London a conception of what can be done, by the splendid display with which the director Kean brings Shakespeare's plays upon the stage. Kean is a son of the eminent actor, but in this act there is nothing whatever of the father's distinction; on the contrary, there is the great difference, that he by his historical studies and true genius has put Shakespeare's plays on the stage in a manner never seen by the poet himself, and as no one before Kean had ever seen them. He has had a regard to truthfulness never before known. Thus before no one had ever hesitated in "King Lear" to leave out the fool, who is one of the most important characters in the tragic group. The actor Macready, Dickens told me, had been the first to restore this notable character. After most lavish expenditure had been made, and many rehearsals, Shakespeare's "Tempest" was ready to be given; and I saw it on its first presentation, when the house was crowded with spectators. The theatre itself is not large, so that it is incredible what the will and genius of one man could here effect. The scene-painter and costumer had given their aid to produce the most striking effects. Really it was placed on the stage with all the fancy of a Shakespeare. During the overture, a storm was heard muttering, the thunder rolled, cries and screams were heard from behind the stage; the entire prelude was thus given while the curtain was still down; and when it rolled up, great waves seemed to be rolling toward the footlights, the whole stage was a furious sea, a great ship was tossed back and forth; this occupied all the next scene; seamen and passengers tumbled about, there was a death shriek, the masts fell, and then the ship was swallowed up by the sea. Then it turned out, as Dickens told me, that the whole ship was made of air-tight linen, which had been puffed out, and from which they now all at once let out the air; the great hulk shrunk together into a piece of cloth, and was hidden by the waves which rose to half the height of the stage.

Ariel's first appearance was highly poetical; when Prospero summons him, a shooting-star falls from heaven and touches the grass; it burns with blue and green flames, and then one suddenly sees Ariel's beautiful angelic form; he stood clad in white, with wings from his shoulder reaching to the ground; he appeared to have come with the shooting-star. Every revelation of Ariel was different, and always beautiful. He would appear suddenly, hanging by the hand, in a garland of vine leaves; then he would float over the stage by means of a mechanism which it was not possible to discover; there was no string or iron bar to be seen, and yet there was some such thing below that sustained him in his flying position. In one of the acts there was seen a desert, wintry place, that, as the sun's rays became more and more strong, was transformed little by little to the most luxuriant nature. Trees shot up, flowered, and bore fruit; springs bubbled up and down by a great waterfall; nymphs were dancing, lightly as swan's down upon the water. In a succeeding act, Olympus shone with all its forms of beauty; the whole background was an airy place, filled with floating gods and goddesses. Juno drove by in her chariot drawn by peacocks whose tails glittered in the sunshine. The signs of the zodiac were displayed: the whole was a fantastic kaleidoscope. The splendor and excitement of a single act was enough to have drawn a full house for the most insignificant piece, and here it was lavished on all the acts of one of Shakespeare's works — it was really quite too much; aye, one sailed with the lovers in the gliding boat, and saw their thoughts at work! The entire background was in motion; landscape followed landscape, a moving panorama.

The closing scene in the "Tempest" was undeniably the one which produced the greatest effect. The entire stage represented a broad sea that was stirred by the wind. Prospero, who leaves his island, stood in the stern of the ship that came sailing down from the background to the footlights; the sails swelled, and after the final epilogue had been spoken, the ship glided down one of the side scenes, and now floating over the water appeared Ariel nodding farewell. The whole light fell upon him with the effect that he seemed under the electric light to be the one that, as a meteor, gave the whole stage its brilliancy; a pretty rainbow was seen over the water, the moon became only a faint ball of fire against the sunlight and the rainbow glory which Ariel caused to stream forth at the moment of his departure.

It was surpassingly fine. The public was enthusiastic through the long acts and the representation, which stretched out indefinitely. The first evening people sat from seven in the evening till half past twelve. Everything was done which machinery and mounting of the piece could give, and yet after one had seen the whole, one felt worn out, tired, and dull. Shakespeare himself was changed. His work was petrified in illustrations; the living word evaporated, there was nothing of the spiritual nature left, all was forgotten for the gold dish that was carried out.

None of the players appeared to me of any consequence as dramatic artists, except the one who had Caliban's part. Ariel, who was played by a girl, had a pretty form; and when I have named these two I have named all who had any special character. Kean himself preached constantly, and has not at all an agreeable voice. A work of Shakespeare's artistically brought out among three screens only, is for me a greater pleasure than this which was suffocated in beauty.

However impressive such an evening with Director Kean may have been, one can be quite as much overwhelmed in other places in London the next day. I mention the British Museum — to go through which, relate, and explain all its wonders, belongs only to those who wish to write volumes. I know no comparison more significant than with a scholar's brain, where everything in literature, art, and science, is disposed in the best order, and one is going through the veins and fibres like an animalcule. The British Museum is also a treasury of all the wonders of the world for the last two thousand years. The great building containing it extends along several streets, and incloses mighty halls of learning. One enters and stands suddenly among the curiosities of Nineveh, which seem just as new as if carved and polished in one day; we see what Nimrod and Semiramis saw in murky antiquity. We step in among the sacred mysteries of Egypt; hideous statues of gods of brightly polished stone stand in rows. We see mummies, which are shown all the way from the one in the unopened coffin to that which has been freed from each swathing, a dried, blackened body; the long black hair still hangs down from the crown of the head; here is a foot, here a hand, fallen from one or another mighty man or woman from the land of the Nile. We wander through the art of Greece, forms of beauty from the time of Phidias and Praxiteles. Here we find the Parthenon bas-reliefs, the groups from the temple of Ægina — wonder after wonder.

Not only can we follow here the imprint of man's nature and skill through two thousand dead years; representations of all the animals of the earth before man appeared stand before us; we see shapes of animals that have become extinct; the strata of the earth have preserved them for us, as a herbarium keeps plants. In one of the larger halls there is a row of gigantic skeletons of mammoths and other antique creatures.

A contrast to these is in the beauty of the birds here. Lovely white flamingoes we see, humming-birds that display colored fire-works, and possess a beauty that makes the most beautiful butterfly a dowdy thing. The British Museum is a veritable old curiosity shop that awaits its poetical writer. It is a treasure, a great pearl, which only the Queen of the Sea, mighty England, could possess.

One place more in London I must mention; it lies in one of the narrow, dirty streets, down by the Thames, in the very heart of the grimy part of the city. There we must go, for there grows the *nymphæa alba* of newspapers, the queen-flower, with more than fifty thousand leaves; twice a day it puts out its flowers and leaves, and scatters them all over the world from Lapland to Hindostan. I saw this flower opening, heard its leaves unroll themselves each minute; it was so overpowering, so exciting, that I seemed to be standing in the midst of a rushing waterfall. I was in the "Times" printing-office. I saw a series of cellars, halls, rooms, and chambers that constituted a remarkably united whole under almost military discipline; not only the different columns in the paper, but the various articles had their divisions, their leaders. One followed the journal in all its stages, from white paper till it stood compact in the printed columns. Man's intellect here shares the empire with the might of steam. Master Bloodless stretches his iron fingers and moves his muscles of cord and leather. The great heavy bundles of paper are stored away and dragged on railways through the rooms. The commands of the master spirit fly by the electric wire from one part of the building to another. In a sort of rotunda, where I took my place upon a gallery running round the wall, the pulse of the whole was beating. The room was nearly filled with an enormous wheel at which the workmen sat, separated from each other, while everything was whirling and rushing. The sheets were lifted, moistened, turned on a machine, and came out with the printed words on one side, turned themselves, and the other side then appeared with the columns printed; then they were passed over heated cylinders, spread out, laid together, came, and vanished. I saw that the great white sheets moved with a flash, took up the print, and fell from hand to hand. It sounded as if a great brawling stream were pouring forth. The gallery on which I stood shook with the motion of the machinery; a shudder ran through my nerves; I did reverence to Master Bloodless and his lord, Human Thought.

If I have given any conception with my words of this roaring, whirling maelstrom which London displays, one will understand how welcome is the sensation to one of escaping to some home snuggery, aye, to one of choicest surroundings.

Miss Burdett Coutts is called the richest lady in England. Dickens has dedicated "Martin Chuzzlewit" to her; her fortune is said to be unbounded, but what is most to her honor is, that she is one of the noblest and most beneficent women in the land. It is not merely that she has built many churches, but she cares in the most Christian manner for the poor, the sick and distressed; her house in London is sought by the richest and most highly esteemed. I found at Dickens's house at Gadshill the first day I was there, an old, poorly dressed lady, and one somewhat younger; they were there several days, and were most amiable, straightforward, and hearty. We strolled together to the monument. I drove with them to Rochester; and when they left us the youngest said that I was to come and stay in her house when, one of these days, I went to London. I heard from Dickens that it was Miss Coutts; he spoke of her with profound respect, and of the beautiful Christian use which she made of her immense fortune; I should find with her, he said, an English house in its most wealthy condition. I went; and it was not the rich paintings, the liveried servants, the entire impression as of a great castle, which together formed the splendor of the place, but it was the noble, womanly, most amiable Miss Coutts herself. She stood in her good-hearted, simple nature, quite in contrast to the show of servants. She had noticed in the country that I found it cold the first day I was there. It was not yet quite warm, and so a cheerful fire was burning in the grate. It was very cozy here; there were books, comfortable arm-chairs, sofas, and rococo furniture, and from the windows a view out over a little garden to Picadilly and the great park.

Just outside London lies Miss Coutts's country house and garden. Here there are great avenues of rhododendrons, that strewed their red flowers over the carriage in which I rode; immense cedar-trees, and rare plants; and in the hot-house grew palms, grapes, bananas, and fragrant fruits, in such abundance as I never before had seen. From all this splendor the proprietor carried me to a little kitchen garden with pease and beans; she seemed to like this place best; it was as if these plants, which grew to so much use, especially satisfied her. Before us lay London, half concealed in smoke; the railway train came and went with screaming pipe and rushing cloud of vapor.

One other home that I found in London I must name, — a home where the greatest sympathy and attention were shown me both by elders and children. It was at my publisher's, the well-known and honored Richard Bentley. He has been Dickens's publisher, and since that Marryatt's. "The Improvisatore" and most of my other writings have appeared in English with his imprint. The house where he transacts his business is in town, but he lives with his family in one of the outskirts of London, almost in the country. Here I saw kind faces, heard music, and felt myself understood, and was happy. Here and at Gadshill I was with friends; Gadshill was at a distance from London, quite in the open country, and it was refreshing to go there from the heated, dusty, noisy city of the world. Upon the back of the steam-dragon I delighted to go there, while the setting sun shone on the Crystal Palace, and upon the great waves which would roll in the Thames when the wind blew. From Higham I walked in the quiet evening up to the friendly home where the light shone and music greeted me. Miss Mary and her aunt played pieces from Beethoven, Mozart, and Mendelssohn. How sociable it was in that little room at the piano, where Dickens with his wife and guests sat in company; afterward in the starlit evening, and in the moonlight, we went out on the grass free from dew. There was a peace brooding over all, the sky hung over us high and clear; how often I thought not of this, and thereby grew moody; after the lapse of days this time will become like a vanished dream, dead as music which but recently was sung; the music can be enjoyed again, perhaps if in the same mood as when I heard it I can hear it again, but this time spent at this place can never come to me again. One evening when I was feeling thus, Dickens suddenly seized my hand, and with unutterable kindness, as if he could see into my very thoughts, he bade me stay with them still longer, and see the dramatic entertainment in which he and several of his family were to take part; he told me how glad he was at having me with him; he took me in his arms; I felt that he understood me, that I was welcome there, for it shone from his eyes and sounded full in his hearty voice. This was a happy time, days full of joy, and yet there came a moment of heaviness, not from within but from without; this time it was a criticism on my last book which put me in ill-humor, as it ought not. I mention it here only to tell the impression which Dickens's inexpressible kindness made upon me. He came from London, where he had been for a day or two. I had been going about, gloomy and reserved, tormenting myself. Dickens found out what was the matter with me, and at once let off a whole piece of fire-works of jest and quips; and when still this did not make its way into the dark crooks of my ill-humor, a seriousness followed, which was full of heartfelt care for me, such warm appreciation, that I felt myself raised up, strengthened, and filled with pleasure, and a strong desire to merit his regard. I looked into my friend's bright, gentle eyes, and I dared thank a severe critic for bringing me one of the most enjoyable moments of my life. The dark sea of grief had cast up the rich amber of sympathy for me. On this occasion Dickens told me the judgment, now so amusing to us, passed upon Shakespeare's "Macbeth" by one of the great poet's clever contemporaries. The opinion ran somewhat thus: "Mr. Shakespeare has written a new tragedy, "Macbeth," but a greater piece of nonsense was never before committed to paper." I was soon in good humor again; I saw the world in sunshine, and one cannot help that who lives with Dickens; his sparkling conversation warms and lights one; the glance of his soul in his eye wins your confidence — it recognizes and appreciates every one who comes within its range.

The old countryman whose cows and sheep grazed up by the monument, near Gadshill, knew that I was staying with Dickens, and told me that he brought us fresh bread every day. "They are splendid people!" said he; "you can see that at once of both of them." They had both talked so frankly and kindly with him. "Aye," he went on, "and some years ago there also lived close by here a lady who was called the Swedish Nightingale," — it was Jenny Lind who lived here; "she was also just such a person, just as kind and honest as Mr. Dickens."

I went to find the place where Jenny Lind had stayed; the windows were plastered over, the door fastened up, no one lived there; the cage was empty, the nightingale had flown away. Many thoughts and old memories were awakened in me, and I never went by the place that there did not come over me a peculiar sadness.

The time soon came for me to leave Gadshill and Dickens; but first I was to discover how great an actor there was in him. The rehearsals for the dramatic entertainment for the benefit of Douglas Jerrold's widow called us for a week to London. Dickens was to read his "Christmas Carol" in St. Martin's Hall. The Adelphi Theatre contributed its portion by bringing out Jerrold's two best known pieces, "The Rent Day," and "Black Eyed Susan." The chief attraction, however, was the representation, in which Dickens and some of his family and friends took part, of a new romantic drama, "The Frozen Deep," by Wilkie Collins; the author was to act the part of one of the lovers, Dickens that of the other.

It had long been the Queen's wish to see one of the entertainments which Dickens gave. Her majesty and court were to be present at one of these, an evening or two before the regular time, at the little theatre, The Gallery of Illustration. The Queen, Prince Albert, the royal children, as well also as the young Prince and Princess of Prussia, and his majesty the King of Belgium, were present. Besides this high society, there was a select audience admitted, almost exclusively family friends of the players. From Dickens's house went his wife, his mother-in-law, and myself.

Had we gone to London Sunday evening by the last train, and not, as we accidentally did Monday morning, the whole affair might have had a most sorrowful ending. I saw the evening train leave Gadshill, and two stations from London occurred the most frightful collision, an account of which we read the next morning at the place itself, while we were on the train for London. The train was in readiness the evening before; all were in their places ready to start, when another train came behind; the conductor made no signal that the train in advance was still at the station, and it came upon it with great violence; the rear carriages filled with people were crushed, thirteen persons were instantly killed, and twenty-four had arms or legs broken.

It had been a fearful sight. I talked with a gentleman whose house was quite near the station where the accident occurred; he had been just on the point of going to bed, when he heard the collision, the cry of despair, and the piercing shrieks of the wounded and spectators. He flew to the spot; carriages and people lay in a hideous ruin, wet with blood. It was a peculiar feeling which one had who passed over the place in the train that came next after. A strong attempt was made to discover the one to blame, and the railway company was compelled to pay not less than seventy thousand pounds sterling to the heirs of those who were killed.

In the Gallery of Illustration the hall was beautifully decked with flowers and green leaves, in honor of the Queen's presence. A separate buffet was spread with refreshments for the royal guests, and another for us who had been invited to be present at the entertainment, which was given several evenings before the public one, which I also attended.

The story of the play is briefly this: A young naval officer, Richard Wardour, and Clara Burnham have grown up from childhood, and are attached to one another; but with Richard the feeling is one of love, and when he learns that Clara is betrothed to another naval officer, Frank Aldersby, he believes that the betrothal is an arrangement of her family, and that she does not love her betrothed, but on the contrary loves him. Both the lovers go on an expedition to the North Pole, but in different ships; the young girl, who loves her betrothed and not Richard Wardour, spends most unhappy days in the fear that the rivals will meet.

In the second act the scene is at the North Pole, where both ships lie frozen in. The action is in the cabin of one of the vessels. The snow is falling outside; Frank Aldersby lives happy in his love, and sees in the smoke of the fire the picture of his love. Now enters Richard Wardour, and by the drawing of lots it falls out that these two are to set out together from the ship to find land and people. One is certain that the ball with which Richard Wardour loads his rifle will enter the happy lover's heart; but out on the frozen deep, in the snow, fog, and storm, strayed away and lost, in dire necessity and deadly peril, the nobler nature awakes in Richard. He believes that Frank not only loves, but is loved in turn by Clara, and now in his affection for her it becomes Richard's whole aim to save and guard him for her. At the close of the piece, when Clara, with the wife of another of the naval officers, journeys to Newfoundland to get some tidings, if possible, of the lost ships, Richard, feeble, and shaking in body and soul, brings his young friend to Clara, and dies after the exertion, sinking down before her.

Dickens acted Richard's part with remarkable truthfulness and great dramatic power. He gave it with a repose, a fidelity to nature, which was quite different from the usual manner in which tragedy is played in England and France. With us at home, if one did not know he was a great writer, he would at once be recognized and appreciated as an actor. He was in many respects like Michael Wiehe. Besides Dickens there also appeared in the same piece his two daughters, his eldest son, both his sisters-in-law, and his brother Alfred. Collins himself played the part of Frank Aldersby.

The entertainment given for her majesty the Queen closed with "Two o'Clock in the Morning," a farce which we have under the name of "A Night Visitor." It was acted with exceeding liveliness and sparkling humor by Charles Dickens and the editor of "Punch," Mr. Mark Lemon. The two also gave at the regular evening afterward, the two principal characters in the farce "Uncle John." Dickens was quite as remarkable in comedy as in tragedy, and unquestionably belongs among the first actors of the day.

After the first evening all the players and attendants gathered late at night in the office of "Household Words" for a lively night of it. There was fun and happiness and sparkling humor. The gathering was renewed later, in the country at Albert Smith's, the climber of Mont Blanc, of whose capital account of the ascent we at home here can read in "Bille's Sketches from England."

The happy days at Dickens's house fled all too quickly for me. I must leave the celebrated writer, and yet, before I reached Denmark, see the apotheosis of Germany's poetic greatness. I was invited to the festival in Weimar at the unveiling of Goethe's, Schiller's, and Wieland's statues. From the land of Shakespeare, Dickens's home, I went now to the Minnesinger's land, to the poet-town Weimar.

Dickens had his little carriage brought round, and taking the driver's seat carried me to Maidstone, where I took rail to Folkestone, where the steamer lay. We had the pleasure thus of an hour or two together, and that in the most charming part of Kent; we rolled by rich fields and lovely woodland. Dickens was full of fun and good nature, but I could not arouse myself from the dismal mood into which I had entered at the prospect of departure. At the railway station we embraced each other; I looked into his honest, affectionate eyes; I looked at him whom I admire as a writer and love as a man. A pressure of the hand, and he drove away. I was hurried off by the train. "Gone, gone, and that is the way with all stories."

www.ingramcontent.com/pod-product-compliance
Lightning Source LLC
Chambersburg PA
CBHW032042230426
43672CB00009B/1432